KETO DIET

#For Two Cookbook

500 Keto Recipes

Simple Low-Carb and High-Fat Recipes for Beginners with 28-Day Meal Plan

Michael Newman

Warning-Disclaimer

The purpose of this book is to educate and entertain. The author or publisher does not guarantee that anyone following the techniques, suggestions, tInstant Pots, ideas, or strategies will become successful. The author and publisher shall have neither liability or responsibility to anyone with respect to any loss or damage caused, or alleged to be caused, directly or indirectly by the information contained in this book.

CONTENTS

LUNCH & DINNER 53

VEGAN & VEGETABLES 69

MEAT RECIPES 95

POULTRY 128

FISH & SEAFOOD.. 164

SNACKS & SIDE DISHES 173

DESSERTS & DRINKS... 195

28-DAY MEAL PLAN 218

INTRODUCTION

By now you've certainly heard of the keto diet and the many people who have had success losing weight and keeping it off. But just what is a ketogenic diet and how does it work so you can reach your weight loss goal.

The keto diet is a food plan that is high in fat and low in carbs. The human body uses carbohydrates as its main fuel source, however when carbs are replaced by fats, the body enters a metabolic state known as "ketosis". During ketosis, because of the lack of carbs, the body will start to burn stored fat as fuel which can help you lose weight.

Not only can the keto diet promote weight loss, but it also comes with numerous health benefits:

- Management of diabetes
- Lower cholesterol
- Improved mental clarity
- Reduces the risk and symptoms of polycystic ovary syndrome (POS)
- Lower risk of some cancers
- Lower risk of cardiovascular disease

The keto diet requires a change in your eating habits. It's easier to make these changes when you have the active support of your partner or other family members. As a couple, you'll be able to encourage each other on those days that are more difficult than others for sticking to your food plan.

Keto Basics

The basics of the keto diet are simple – foods that are high in carbs are limited if not restricted altogether on the food plan.

Foods allowed on the keto diet

Plan your meals and snacks around the following foods:

- Eggs
- Meats, including beef, pork, chicken, and veal
- Fish, including fish high in fat such as mackerel, trout, and salmon
- Cheeses
- Nuts and seeds, including nut and seed butter
- Cream and butter
- Avocadoes
- Healthy oils, such as olive, avocado, and coconut oils
- Low-carb vegetables, such as peppers, onions, tomatoes, and green vegetables
- Herbs and spices, including salt and pepper

To be sure you're getting enough of the right nutrients, eat a wide variety of the meats, vegetables, seeds, and nuts on the allowed food list.

Foods restricted on the keto diet

These are the foods that are restricted on a ketogenic food plan:

- Grains and starches, such as bread, pasta, cereal, and rice
- Carrots, potatoes, yams, sweet potatoes, and parsnips
- Beans and legumes, including chickpeas, lentils, and peas
- Fruit, except for small quantities of berries
- Sugar in any form, including foods that contain fructose
- Processed diet foods
- Condiments that contain sugar
- Unhealthy fats, such as processed vegetable oils and mayonnaise
- Alcohol

Getting Started With Your Keto Diet

Before starting the keto diet, take some time to research the foods that are on the allowed list and those foods that are restricted. Plan your meals ahead of time and shop accordingly, filling your kitchen with keto-friendly foods.

Healthy snacks

To make it easier to stick to the keto diet, it's important to have healthy snacks available. If you're on the keto diet with your partner, have keto-approved snacks on hand that you both enjoy. Approved snacks include:

- Hard-boiled eggs
- Cheese and olives
- A handful of nuts and seeds
- Celery and red pepper sticks with guacamole and salsa
- No-sugar plain yogurt mixed with berries

Intermittent Fasting and the Keto Diet

Intermittent fasting is all about restricting the number of calories you consume within a period of time, so that you put your body into a "fasted" state. When this happens, insulin levels in the body will start to lower which increases the fat burning process.

The benefits of intermittent fasting include:

- **Weight loss**
- **Improved mental clarity**
- **Management and reducing the risk of type 2 diabetes**
- **Lower risk of cardiovascular disease**
- **Lower risk of some cancers**

The most common method of fasting is to fast each day for 14 to 16 hours, restricting the time you eat to a "window" of 8 to 10 hours. During the eating window, you should be eating at least 2 to 3 healthy, keto meals. An excellent way to approach intermittent fasting is eating your last meal by 8 pm on any day and not eating your first meal until 12 pm the next day.

Another method of intermittent fasting includes the 5:2 rule where you only eat 500 to 600 calories per day on two days of the week, eating a healthy keto diet for the other five days. Still, another fasting method is the eat-stop-eat plan, where you fast for 24 hours twice a week.

Both intermittent fasting and the keto diet put the body into a state of ketosis so that it uses up stored fat for energy. When you combine intermittent fasting with the keto diet, you may be able to put your body into ketosis faster than by dieting alone. This can lead to faster and more efficient weight loss.

What To Expect

When starting the keto diet, some people may notice some minor side effects. During the first few days, you may experience an increase in hunger, lack of energy, and problems sleeping. Some people may also experience nausea and digestive problems. These flu-like symptoms are known as the "keto flu." To alleviate these symptoms, consider doing a low-carb diet for two weeks, slowly transitioning into the full keto diet.

During the first month, always eat until you feel full without focusing on restricting calories. Ease into the food plan, so you're less likely to stop eating a ketogenic diet.

The keto diet changes the mineral and water balance of your body. Make sure that you're drinking more water each day. As well, taking a mineral supplement and adding a bit of extra salt to your diet can keep help maintain a healthy balance of minerals and water, helping to relieve any of the flu-like symptoms. For a mineral supplement take 300 mg of magnesium and 1,000 mg of potassium.

Should You Try the Keto Diet?

The keto diet can help you lose weight and keep it off. When you're eating nutritiously, exercising, and following a ketogenic food plan, you'll be joining the many other people around the world who have successfully lost weight.

Whether you're starting the keto diet on your own or as a couple, start with the basics of the keto food plan so you can become familiar with the foods you can and can't eat. As you start to lose weight and learn how to customize your meals, the keto diet plan will become a natural part of your lifestyle, allowing you to maintain your health and weight loss.

SMOOTHIES & BREAKFAST

Breakfast Blueberry Coconut Smoothie

Prep + Cook Time: 5 minutes | Serves: 2

Ingredients

1 avocado, pitted and sliced
2 cups blueberries
1 cup coconut milk

6 tbsp coconut cream
2 tsp erythritol
2 tbsp coconut flakes

Directions

Combine the avocado slices, blueberries, coconut milk, coconut cream, erythritol, and ice cubes in a smoothie maker and blend until smooth. Pour the smoothie into drinking glasses, and serve sprinkled with coconut flakes.

Nutritional info per serving: Calories 492, Fat 36.3g, Net Carbs 8.6g, Protein 9.6g

Vegan Chocolate Smoothie

Prep + Cook Time: 10 minutes | Serves: 2

Ingredients

¼ cup pumpkin seeds
¾ cup coconut milk
¼ cup water
1 ½ cups watercress

2 tsp vegan protein powder
1 tbsp chia seeds
1 tbsp unsweetened cocoa powder

Directions

In a blender, add all ingredients except for the chia seeds and process until creamy and uniform. Place into two glasses, dust with chia seeds and chill before serving.

Nutritional info per serving: Calories 335; Fat: 29.7g Net Carbs: 5.7g, Protein: 6.5g

Power Green Smoothie

Prep + Cook Time: 5 minutes | Serves: 2

Ingredients

1 cup collard greens, chopped
3 stalks celery, chopped
1 ripe avocado, skinned, pitted, sliced
1 cup ice cubes

2 cups spinach, chopped
1 large cucumber, peeled and chopped
Chia seeds to garnish

Directions

Add the collard greens, celery, avocado, and ice cubes in a blender, and blend for 50 seconds. Add the spinach and cucumber, and process for another 40 seconds until smooth. Transfer the smoothie into glasses, garnish with chia seeds and serve right away.

Nutritional info per serving: Calories 187, Fat 12g, Net Carbs 7.6g, Protein 3.2g

Kiwi Coconut Smoothie

Prep + Cook Time: 3 minutes | Serves: 2

Ingredients

2 kiwis, pulp scooped
1 tbsp xylitol
4 ice cubes

2 cups unsweetened coconut milk
1 cup coconut yogurt
Mint leaves to garnish

Directions

Process the kiwis, xylitol, coconut milk, yogurt, and ice cubes in a blender, until smooth, for about 3 minutes. Transfer to serving glasses, garnish with mint leaves, and serve.

Nutritional info per serving: Calories 423, Fat 35.7g, Net Carbs 9.2g, Protein 14g

Mixed Nuts & Smoothie Breakfast

Prep + Cook Time: 5 minutes | Serves: 2

Ingredients

3 cups buttermilk
2 tbsp peanut butter
1 tbsp unsweetened cocoa powder

2 tsp erythritol
1 cup mixed nuts, chopped for topping

Directions

Combine the buttermilk, peanut butter, cocoa powder, and erythritol in a smoothie maker; puree until smooth and well mixed.

Share the smoothie into breakfast bowls, top with mixed nuts, and serve.

Nutritional info per serving: Calories 654, Fat 55.2g, Net Carbs 4.2g, Protein 16g

Superfood Red Smoothie

Prep + Cook Time: 6 minutes | Serves: 2

Ingredients

1 Granny Smith apple, peeled and chopped
1 cup strawberries + extra for garnishing
1 cup blueberries
2 small beets, peeled and chopped

2/3 cup ice cubes
½ lemon, juiced
2 cups almond milk

Directions

For the strawberries for garnishing, make a single deep cut on their sides, and set aside. In a smoothie maker, add the apples, strawberries, blueberries, beets, almond milk, and ice and blend the ingredients at high speed until nice and smooth, for about 75 seconds.

Add the lemon juice, and puree further for 30 seconds. Pour the drink into tall smoothie glasses, fix the reserved strawberries on each glass rim and serve with a straw.

Nutritional info per serving: Calories 233, Fat 4.3g, Net Carbs 11.3g, Protein 5g

Coconut Shake with Avocado

Prep + Cook Time: 4 minutes | Serves: 2

Ingredients

3 cups coconut milk, chilled
1 avocado, pitted, peeled, sliced

2 tbsp erythritol
Coconut cream for topping

Directions

Combine the coconut milk, avocado, and erythritol, into the smoothie maker, and blend for 1 minute to smooth.

Pour the drink into serving glasses, lightly add some coconut cream on top of them, and garnish with mint leaves. Serve immediately.

Nutritional info per serving: Calories 395, Fat: 27g, Net Carbs: 3.4g, Protein: 13.7g

Creamy Vanilla Keto Cappuccino

Prep + Cook Time: 6 minutes | Serves: 2

Ingredients

2 cups unsweetened vanilla almond milk, chilled
1 tsp swerve sugar
½ tbsp powdered coffee
1 cup cottage cheese, cold

½ tsp vanilla bean paste
¼ tsp xanthan gum
Unsweetened chocolate shavings to garnish

Directions

In a blender, combine the almond milk, swerve sugar, cottage cheese, coffee, vanilla bean paste, and xanthan gum and process on high speed for 1 minute until smooth. Pour into tall shake glasses, sprinkle with chocolate shavings, and serve immediately.

Nutritional info per serving: Calories 253, Fat 17.7g, Net Carbs 6.2g, Protein 12.8g

Golden Turmeric Latte with Nutmeg

Prep + Cook Time: 7 minutes | Serves: 2

Ingredients

2 cups almond milk
1/3 tsp cinnamon powder
½ cup brewed coffee

¼ tsp turmeric powder
1 tsp xylitol
Nutmeg powder to garnish

Directions

Add the almond milk, cinnamon powder, coffee, turmeric, and xylitol in the blender. Blend the ingredients at medium speed for 50 seconds and pour the mixture into a saucepan.

Over low heat, set the pan and heat through for 6 minutes, without boiling. Keep swirling the pan to prevent from boiling. Turn the heat off, and serve in latte cups, topped with nutmeg powder.

Nutritional info per serving: Calories 153, Fat 13.2g, Net Carbs 0.9g, Protein 3.9g

Almond Breakfast Smoothie

Prep + Cook Time: 4 minutes | Serves: 2

Ingredients

2 cups almond milk
2 tbsp almond butter
½ cup Greek yogurt
1 tsp almond extract

1 tsp cinnamon
4 tbsp flax meal
30 drops of stevia
A handful of ice cubes

Directions

Put the yogurt, almond milk, almond butter, flax meal, almond extract, collagen peptides, and stevia to the bowl of a blender. Blend until uniform and smooth, for about 30 seconds.

Pour in smoothie glasses, add the ice cubes and sprinkle with cinnamon.

Nutritional info per serving: Calories 412, Fat: 31g, Net Carbs: 5.6g, Protein: 21g

Quick Raspberry Vanilla Shake

Prep + Cook Time: 2 minutes | Serves: 2

Ingredients

2 cups raspberries
2 tbsp erythritol
6 raspberries to garnish

½ cup cold unsweetened almond milk
2/3 tsp vanilla extract
½ cup heavy whipping cream

Directions

In a large blender, process the raspberries, milk, vanilla extract, whipping cream, and erythritol for 2 minutes; work in two batches if needed. The shake should be frosty.

Pour into glasses, stick in straws, garnish with raspberries and serve.

Nutritional info per serving: Calories 213, Fat 13.4g, Net Carbs 7.7g, Protein 4.5g

Strawberry Chia Seed Pudding in Glass Jars

Prep + Cook Time: 10 minutes + chilling time | Serves: 2

Ingredients

1 tsp vanilla extract
1 cup water
2 tbsp chia seeds
2 tbsp flax seed meal
4 tbsp almond meal

½ tsp granulated stevia
2 tbsp walnuts, chopped
4 mint leaves, chopped
½ cup strawberries, mashed

Directions

Place chia seeds, flaxseed meal, almond meal, strawberries, and granulated stevia in a bowl and pour over the water. Stir in vanilla. Refrigerate for at least 2 hours or overnight.

When the pudding is ready, spoon into glass jars, sprinkle with walnuts and mint serve warm.

Nutritional info per serving: Calories 275, Fat: 19g, Net Carbs: 4.5g Protein: 14g

Yummy Blue Cheese & Mushroom Omelet

Prep + Cook Time: 15 minutes | Serves: 2

Ingredients

4 eggs, beaten
4 button mushrooms, sliced
Salt, to taste
1 tbsp olive oil

½ cup blue cheese, crumbled
1 tomato, thinly sliced
1 tbsp parsley, chopped

Directions

Set a pan over medium heat and warm the oil. Sauté the mushrooms for 5 minutes until tender; season with salt. Add in the eggs and cook as you swirl them around the pan using a spatula.

Cook eggs until partially set. Top with cheese; fold the omelet in half to enclose filling. Decorate with tomato and parsley and serve warm.

Nutritional info per serving: Calories 310; Fat: 25g, Net Carbs: 1.5g, Protein: 18.5g

Chorizo Sausage Egg Cakes

Prep + Cook Time: 15 minutes | Serves: 2

Ingredients

1 tsp butter, melted
4 eggs, beaten
Salt and black pepper, to taste

1 cup mozzarella cheese, grated
2 chorizo sausages, cooked and chopped
1 tbsp parsley, chopped

Directions

In a bowl, stir the eggs, sausages and cheese; season with salt and pepper. Add into greased with butter muffin cups, and bake in the oven for 8-10 minutes at 400 F. Sprinkle with parsley to serve.

Nutritional info per serving: Calories 512; Fat: 35.5g, Net Carbs: 5.4g, Protein: 41g

Morning Herbed Eggs

Prep + Cook Time: 15 minutes | Serves: 2

Ingredients

1 spring onion, finely chopped
2 tbsp butter
1 tsp fresh thyme
4 eggs
½ tsp sesame seeds

2 garlic cloves, minced
½ cup parsley, chopped
½ cup sage, chopped
¼ tsp cayenne pepper
Salt and black pepper, to taste

Directions

Melt butter in a non-stick skillet over medium heat. Add garlic, parsley, sage and thyme and cook for 30 seconds. Carefully crack the eggs into the skillet. Lower the heat and cook for 4-6 minutes.

Adjust the seasoning. When the eggs are just set, turn the heat off and transfer to a serving plate. Drizzle the cayenne pepper and sesame seeds on top of the egg. Top with spring onions and serve.

Nutritional info per serving: Calories 283, Fat: 22.3g, Net Carbs: 5.3g, Protein: 13.3g

Ham & Cheese Keto Sandwiches

Prep + Cook Time: 15 minutes | Serves: 2

Ingredients

4 eggs
½ tsp baking powder
5 tbsp butter, at room temperature
4 tbsp almond flour

2 tbsp psyllium husk powder
2 slices mozzarella cheese
2 slices smoked ham

Directions

To make the buns, whisk together almond flour, baking powder, 4 tbsp of butter, husk powder, and eggs in a bowl; mix until a dough forms. Place the batter in two oven-proof mugs, and microwave for 2 minutes or until firm. Remove, flip the buns over and cut in half.

Place a slice of mozzarella cheese and a slice of ham on one bun half and top with the other. Warm the remaining butter in a skillet. Add the sandwiches and grill until the cheese is melted and the buns are crispy.

Nutritional info per serving: Calories 516, Fat: 45.2g, Net Carbs: 2.3g, Protein: 23.5g

Rolled Smoked Salmon with Avocado & Cheese

Prep + Cook Time: 10 minutes + time refrigeration | Serves: 2

Ingredients

2 tbsp cream cheese, softened
1 lime, zested and juiced
½ avocado

1 tbsp mint, chopped
Salt to taste
2 slices smoked salmon

Directions

Mash the avocado with a fork in a bowl. Add in the cream cheese, lime juice, zest, mint, and salt and mix to combine.

Lay each salmon slice on a plastic wrap, spread with cream cheese mixture. Roll up the salmon and secure both ends by twisting. Refrigerate for 2 hours, remove plastic, cut off both ends of each wrap, and cut wraps into half-inch wheels.

Nutritional info per serving: Calories 410, Fat 26g, Net Carbs 2.7g, Protein 38g

Pesto Mug Sandwiches with Bacon & Ricotta

Prep + Cook Time: 8 minutes | Serves: 2

Ingredients

2 eggs
¼ cup flax meal
2 tbsp buttermilk

2 tbsp pesto
¼ cup almond flour
Salt and black pepper, to taste

Filling:

2 tbsp ricotta cheese
2 oz bacon, sliced

1 avocado, sliced

Directions

Whisk eggs, buttermilk and pesto in a bowl. Season with salt and pepper. Gently add in flax meal and almond flour and divide the mixture between two greased ramekins.

Place in the microwave and cook for 1-2 minutes. Leave to cool slightly before filling.

In a nonstick skillet over medium heat, cook the bacon until crispy, for about 5 minutes; set aside. Invert the cups onto a plate and cut in half, crosswise.

Assemble the sandwiches by spreading ricotta cheese and topping with bacon and avocado slices.

Nutritional info per serving: Calories 488, Fat: 37g, Net Carbs: 3.9g, Protein: 17g

Jalapeno & Cheese Waffles with Bacon & Avocado

Prep + Cook Time: 20 minutes | Serves: 2

Ingredients

2 tbsp butter, melted
¼ cup almond milk
2 tbsp almond flour
Salt and black pepper, to taste
½ tsp parsley, chopped

½ jalapeño pepper, minced
4 eggs
½ cup cheddar cheese, crumbled
4 slices bacon, chopped
1 avocado, sliced

Directions

In a skillet over medium heat, fry bacon until crispy, about 5 minutes. Remove to a plate and cover to keep warm.

In a mixing bowl, combine the remaining ingredients, except for the avocado. Preheat a waffle iron and spray with a cooking spray. Pour in the batter and close the lid.

Cook for 5 minutes or until golden-brown, do the same with the rest of the batter. Decorate with avocado and reserved bacon and serve while warm.

Nutritional info per serving: Calories 771; Fat: 67.3g, Net Carbs: 6.9g, Protein: 27.4g

Chia Seed Pudding with Strawberries

Prep + Cook Time: 5 minutes | Serves: 2

Ingredients

10 strawberries
2 cups unsweetened almond milk
¼ tsp vanilla extract
4 oz heavy cream

2 tbsp chia seeds
4 tsp liquid stevia
Chopped walnuts for topping
4 Mint leaves for topping

Directions

Mash 8 strawberries with a fork until pureed, in a medium bowl. Pour in the almond milk, heavy cream, chia seeds, and liquid stevia. Mix and refrigerate the pudding overnight. Slice 2 strawberries.

Spoon the pudding into serving glasses, top with strawberry slices, walnuts, and mint leaves to serve.

Nutritional info per serving: Calories 532, Fat 42g, Net Carbs 5.3g, Protein 14g

Quesadillas with Bacon & Mushrooms

Prep + Cook Time: 30 minutes | Serves: 2

Ingredients

1 cup mushrooms, sliced
4 low carb tortilla shells
3 eggs, hard-boiled and chopped
2 tbsp butter

½ cup cheddar cheese, grated
1 cup Swiss cheese, grated
3 oz bacon
1 shallot, sliced

Directions

Fry the bacon in a skillet over medium heat for 4 minutes until the bacon is crispy. Remove, chop and set aside. Sauté the shallot and mushrooms in the same grease for 5 minutes. Set aside.

Melt 1 tablespoon of butter in a separate skillet over medium heat. Lay one tortilla in a skillet; sprinkle with some Swiss cheese. Add some chopped eggs and bacon over the cheese, top with shallot, mushrooms, and sprinkle with cheddar cheese. Cover with another tortilla shell.

Cook for 45 seconds, then carefully flip the quesadilla, and cook the other side too for 45 seconds. Remove to a plate and repeat the cooking process using the remaining tortilla shells.

Nutritional info per serving: Calories 434, Fat 42.7g, Net Carbs 6.1g, Protein 27g

Broccoli, Egg & Pancetta Gratin

Prep + Cook Time: 25 minutes | Serves: 2

Ingredients

1 head broccoli, cut into small florets
1 red bell pepper, seeded and chopped
4 slices pancetta, chopped
2 tsp olive oil

1 tsp dried oregano
Salt and black pepper to taste
4 fresh eggs
4 tbsp Parmesan cheese

Directions

Line a baking sheet with parchment paper and preheat the oven to 420 F. Warm the olive oil in a frying pan over medium heat; cook the pancetta, stirring frequently, for about 3 minutes.

Arrange the broccoli, bell pepper, and pancetta on the baking sheet in a single layer, toss to combine; season with salt, oregano, and black pepper. Bake for 10 minutes until the vegetables have softened.

Remove, create four indentations with a spoon, and crack an egg into each one. Sprinkle with Parmesan cheese. Return to the oven and bake for 5-7 minutes until the egg whites are firm and cheese melts.

Nutritional info per serving: Calories 464, Fat 38g, Net Carbs 4.2g, Protein 24g

Spinach Nests with Egg and Cheese

Prep + Cook Time: 35 minutes | Serves: 2

Ingredients

1 tbsp olive oil
1 tbsp dried dill
½ lb spinach, chopped
1 tbsp pine nuts

Salt and black pepper to taste
¼ cup feta cheese, crumbled
2 eggs

Directions

Sauté spinach in the olive oil over medium heat, to wilt for about 5 minutes, and season with salt and black pepper. Allow cooling.

Grease a baking sheet with cooking spray, mold 2 (firm and separate) spinach nests on the sheet, and crack an egg into each nest. Top with feta cheese and scatter the dried dill over.

Bake for 15 minutes at 350 F just until the egg whites have set and the yolks are still runny. Plate the nests and serve right away sprinkled with pine nuts.

Nutritional info per serving: Calories 218, Fat 16.5g, Net Carbs 4.4g, Protein 12.3g

Roasted Stuffed Avocados

Prep + Cook Time: 13 minutes | Serves: 2

Ingredients

2 large avocados, halved and pitted
4 eggs
1 tbsp Parmesan cheese, grated

Salt and black pepper to season
1 tbsp parsley, chopped to garnish

Directions

Grease a baking dish with cooking spray. Crack each egg into each avocado half, season with salt and black pepper, and place them on the baking sheet. Top with Parmesan cheese.

Bake the filled avocados in the oven for 8 or 10 minutes at 380 F or until eggs are cooked and cheese is melted. Garnish with parsley.

Nutritional info per serving: Calories 468, Fat 39.1g, Net Carbs 6.2g, Protein 17.2g

Asparagus & Goat Cheese Frittata

Prep + Cook Time: 20 minutes | Serves: 2

Ingredients

1 tbsp olive oil
½ onion, chopped
1 cup asparagus, chopped
4 eggs, beaten
½ tsp habanero pepper, minced

Salt and red pepper, to taste
¾ cup goat cheese, cut into chunks
½ tbsp basil pesto
1 tbsp parsley, to serve

Directions

Preheat oven to 370 F.

Sauté onion in warm olive oil over medium heat until caramelized. Place in the asparagus and cook until tender, about 5 minutes.

Add in habanero pepper and eggs; season with red pepper and salt. Cook until the eggs are set.

Scatter goat cheese over the frittata. Transfer to the oven and cook for approximately 12 minutes, until the frittata is set in the middle. Slice into wedges and decorate with parsley before serving.

Nutritional info per serving: Calories 345; Fat: 27g, Net Carbs: 5.2g, Protein: 21.6g

Coconut Crepes with Vanilla Cream

Prep + Cook Time: 35 minutes | Serves: 2

Ingredients

2 tbsp coconut flour
2 tbsp unsweetened cocoa powder
2 eggs

Vanilla cream:

¼ cup butter
2 tbsp erythritol

½ cup flax milk
1 tbsp coconut oil, melted

½ tsp vanilla extract
½ cup coconut cream

Directions

Beat the eggs with a whisk in a bowl. Add in the coconut flour, cocoa powder, baking powder, flax milk, and the coconut oil and mix until combined.

Set a skillet over medium heat, grease with cooking spray, and pour in a ladleful of the batter. Swirl the pan quickly to spread the dough all around the skillet and cook the crepe for 2-3 minutes.

Slide the crepe into a flat plate. Continue cooking until the remaining batter has finished.

Put the butter and erythritol in a saucepan and melt the butter over medium heat while stirring continually. Stir in the coconut cream, reduce the heat to low, and let the sauce simmer for 6-8 minutes while stirring continually. Turn the heat off and stir in the vanilla extract. Once the crepes are ready, drizzle the sauce over them, and serve.

Nutritional info per serving: Calories 326, Fat 22.3g, Net Carbs 5.1g, Protein 10g

Mini Pancakes with Mascarpone & Raspberries

Prep + Cook Time: 40 minutes | Serves: 2

Ingredients

½ cup almond flour
2 tsp stevia
1 tsp baking powder
½ cup almond milk
1 tsp vanilla extract

1 large egg
¼ cup olive oil
Whole raspberries to garnish
1 cup mascarpone cheese, at room temperature
1 tsp mint, chopped

Directions

Beat the egg with a whisk in a bowl, add in the almond milk, vanilla extract, and half of the stevia and stir to combine. In another bowl, whisk the almond flour and baking powder together. Then, pour the egg mixture into the almond flour mixture and continue whisking until smooth.

Heat the oil in a pan over medium heat and pour in 1 soup spoon of batter. Cook on one side for 2 minutes, flip the pancake, and cook the other side for 2 minutes.

Transfer the pancake to a plate and repeat the cooking process until the batter is exhausted.

Mix the mascarpone with the remaining stevia in a small bowl. Spread each mini pancake with mascarpone and scatter raspberry over to serve.

Nutritional info per serving: Calories 687, Fat 61g, Net Carbs 5.2g, Protein 23g

Lemon-Ginger Pancakes

Prep + Cook Time: 15 minutes | Serves: 2

Ingredients

1 cup almond flour
1 tsp cinnamon powder
2 tbsp swerve brown sugar
¼ tsp baking soda

1 tsp ginger powder
1 egg
1 cup almond milk
2 tbsp olive oil

Lemon sauce:

¼ cup stevia
½ tsp arrowroot starch
1 cup water

½ lemon, juiced and zested
2 tbsp butter

Directions

Combine together the almond flour, cinnamon powder, swerve brown sugar, baking soda, ginger powder, egg, almond milk, and olive oil in a mixing bowl.

Heat oil in a skillet over medium heat and spoon 2-3 tablespoons of the mixture into the skillet. Cook the batter for 1 minute, flip it and cook the other side for another minute.

Remove the pancake onto a plate and repeat the cooking process until the batter is exhausted.

Mix the stevia and arrowroot starch in a medium saucepan. Set the pan over medium heat and gradually stir the water until it thickens, about 1 minute.

Turn the heat off and add the butter, lemon juice, and lemon zest. Stir the mixture until the butter melts. Drizzle the sauce on the pancakes immediately and serve them warm.

Nutritional info per serving: Calories 343, Fat 25g, Net Carbs 6.1g, Protein 8g

Sausage Cakes with Poached Eggs

Prep + Cook Time: 20 minutes | Serves: 2

Ingredients

½ pound sausage patties
1 tbsp olive oil
2 tbsp guacamole
½ tsp vinegar

Salt and black pepper to taste
2 eggs
1 tbsp cilantro, chopped

Directions

Fry the sausage patties in warm oil over medium heat until lightly browned, about 6-8 minutes. Remove the patties to a plate. Spread the guacamole on the sausages.

Boil the vinegar with 2 cups of water in a pot over high heat, and reduce to simmer, without boiling.

Crack each egg into a small bowl and gently put the egg into the simmering water; poach for 2 to 3 minutes. Use a perforated spoon to remove from the water on a paper towel to dry. Repeat with the other egg.

Top each stack with a poached egg, sprinkle with cilantro, salt, and black pepper to serve.

Nutritional info per serving: Calories 523, Fat 43g, Net Carbs 2.5g, Protein 28g

Spinach & Feta Cheese Pancakes

Prep + Cook Time: 10 minutes | Serves: 2

Ingredients

½ cup almond flour
½ tsp baking powder
½ cup feta cheese, crumbled

½ cup spinach, chopped
2 tbsp coconut milk
1 egg

Directions

Beat the egg with a fork in a medium bowl. Add in the almond flour, baking powder, feta cheese, coconut milk, and spinach; and whisk to combine.

Set a skillet over medium heat and let it heat for a minute. Fetch a soup spoonful of mixture into the skillet and cook for 1 minute. Flip the pancake and cook further for 1 minute. Remove onto a plate and repeat the cooking process until the batter is exhausted.

Nutritional info per serving: Calories 412, Fat 32g, Net Carbs 5.9g, Protein 12g

Lettuce Cups Filled Mushrooms & Cheese

Prep + Cook Time: 20 minutes | Serves: 2

Ingredients

1 tbsp olive oil
½ onion, chopped
Salt and black pepper, to taste
½ cup mushrooms, chopped

¼ tsp cayenne pepper
2 fresh lettuce leaves
2 slices gruyere cheese
1 tomato, sliced

Directions

Warm the olive oil in a pan over medium-high heat. Sauté the onion for 3 minutes, until soft. Stir in the mushrooms and cayenne and cook for 4-5 minutes until tender. Season with salt and pepper. Spoon the mushroom mixture into the lettuce leaves, top with tomato and cheese slices to serve.

Nutritional info per serving: Calories 481; Fat: 42g, Net Carbs: 5.7g, Protein: 20g

Chili Avocado Boats

Prep + Cook Time: 20 minutes | Serves: 2

Ingredients

1 tbsp olive oil
2 avocados, halved and pitted, skin on
½ cup cheddar cheese, grated
2 eggs, beaten

A pinch of chili powder
Salt and black pepper, to taste
1 tbsp fresh basil, chopped

Directions

In a mixing dish, mix cheese, chili powder, eggs, pepper, and salt. Split the mixture equally into the avocado halves. Bake in the oven for 15 to 17 minutes at 360 F. Decorate with basil before serving.

Nutritional info per serving: Calories 355; Fat: 29g, Net Carbs: 6.9g, Protein: 12g

Breakfast Serrano Ham Frittata with Fresh Salad

Prep + Cook Time: 22 minutes | Serves: 2

Ingredients

2 tbsp extra virgin olive oil
3 slices serrano ham, chopped
1 tomato, cut into 1-inch chunks
1 cucumber, sliced
1 small red onion, sliced

1 tbsp balsamic vinegar
4 eggs
1 cup Swiss chard, chopped
Salt and black pepper to taste
1 green onion, sliced

Directions

Whisk the vinegar, 1 tbsp of olive oil, salt, and pepper to make the dressing; set aside. Combine the tomato, red onion, and cucumber in a salad bowl, drizzle with the dressing and toss the veggies.

Sprinkle with the serrano ham and set aside. Crack the eggs into a bowl and whisk together with salt and pepper; set aside.

Heat the remaining olive oil in the cast iron pan over medium heat.

Sauté the onion for 3 minutes. Add the Swiss chard to the skillet, season with salt and pepper, and cook for 2 minutes.

Pour the egg mixture all over the Swiss chard, reduce the heat to medium-low, cover, and cook for 4 minutes. Transfer the pan to the oven. Bake to brown on top for 5 minutes at 390 F.

Cut the frittata into wedges and serve with the prepared salad.

Nutritional info per serving: Calories 364, Fat 26.3g, Net Carbs 4.7g, Protein 20.2g

Belgium Waffles with Lemon Cheese Spread

Prep + Cook Time: 25 minutes | Serves: 2

Ingredients

½ cup cream cheese, at room temperature
1 lemon, zested and juiced
2 tbsp stevia
2 tbsp olive oil

½ cup unsweetened almond milk
3 eggs
½ cup almond flour

Directions

In a bowl, combine the cream cheese, lemon juice and zest and stevia. In a separate bowl, whisk the olive oil, almond milk, and eggs. Stir in the almond flour and combine until no lumps exist.

Let the batter sit for 5 minutes to thicken. Spritz a waffle iron with a non-stick cooking spray.

Ladle a ¼ cup of the batter into the waffle iron and cook until golden, about 5 minutes. Repeat with the remaining batter.

Slice the waffles into quarters; apply the lemon spread in between each of two waffles and snap and serve.

Nutritional info per serving: Calories 322, Fat 26g, Net Carbs 7.7g, Protein 11g

Microwave Bacon Mug Eggs

Prep + Cook Time: 5 minutes | Serves: 2

Ingredients

4 eggs
4 tbsp coconut milk
½ cup bacon, cubed

½ tsp oregano
Salt and black pepper, to taste
1 spring onion, sliced

Directions

In a bowl, crack the eggs and beat until combined; season with salt and black pepper. Add coconut milk, bacon, spring onion, and oregano. Pour the mixture into two microwave-safe cups. Transfer to the microwave and cook for 1 minute. Serve warm.

Nutritional info per serving: Calories: 370; Fat 17.5g, Net Carbs 1.9g, Protein 23.7g

Savory Waffles with Cheese & Tomato

Prep + Cook Time: 20 minutes | Serves: 2

Ingredients

2 eggs, beaten
2 tbsp sour cream
¼ tsp allspice

Salt and black pepper, to taste
1/3 cup Gouda cheese, shredded
1 tomato, sliced

Directions

Mix the eggs, allspice, black pepper, salt, and sour cream in a shallow bowl. Add in shredded cheese.

Spritz a waffle iron with a cooking spray. Pour in half of the batter. Cook for 5 minutes until golden. Repeat with the remaining batter. Serve with tomato slices.

Nutritional info per serving: Calories 254; Fat: 18g, Net Carbs: 1.7g, Protein: 17.2g

Peanut Butter & Pastrami Gofres

Prep + Cook Time: 20 minutes | Serves: 2

Ingredients

4 eggs
½ tsp baking soda
2 tbsp peanut butter, melted
4 tbsp coconut flour

¼ tsp salt
½ tsp dried rosemary
3 tbsp tomato puree
4 ounces pastrami, chopped

Directions

Preheat closed waffle iron to high. In a mixing bowl, whisk eggs with rosemary and salt. Stir in coconut flour, baking soda, and peanut butter.

To the waffle iron, add in a third of the batter and cook for 3 minutes until golden. Repeat with the remaining batter. To serve, spread the tomato puree over each gofre and top with chopped pastrami.

Nutritional info per serving: Calories 411, Fat: 27g, Net Carbs: 4.2g, Protein: 25.6g

Vanilla Lemon Crepes

Prep + Cook Time: 25 minutes | Serves: 2

Ingredients

2 ounces almond milk, softened
2 eggs
½ tbsp granulated swerve
2 ounces almond flour

¼ cup water
1 tbsp lemon juice
½ tbsp butter
¾ cup swerve, powdered

Directions

In a bowl, mix almond milk, eggs, granulated swerve, and almond flour until well incorporated.

Grease a frying pan with cooking spray and set over medium heat; cook the crepes until the edges start to brown, about 2 minutes. Flip and cook the other side for a further 2 minutes; repeat the process with the remaining batter. Put the crepes on a plate.

In the same pan, mix powdered swerve, butter and water; simmer for 6 minutes as you stir. Add in lemon juice and allow to sit until the syrup is thick. Pour the syrup over the crepes to serve.

Nutritional info per serving: Calories 251, Fat: 20g, Net Carbs: 5.3g, Protein: 7g

Turkey Bacon & Spinach Crepes

Prep + Cook Time: 40 minutes | Serves: 2-4

Ingredients

3 eggs
½ cup cottage cheese
1 tbsp coconut flour
1/3 cup Parmesan cheese, grated
A pinch of xanthan gum
1 cup spinach
4 oz turkey bacon, cubed

4 oz mozzarella cheese, shredded
1 garlic clove, minced
½ onion, chopped
2 tbsp butter
½ cup heavy cream
Fresh parsley, chopped
Salt and black pepper, to taste

Directions

In a bowl, combine cottage cheese, eggs, coconut flour, xanthan, and Parmesan cheese to obtain a crepe batter.

Grease a pan with cooking spray over medium heat, pour some of the batter, spread well into the pan, cook for 2 minutes, flip to the other side, and cook for 40 seconds more or until golden.

Do the same with the rest of the batter, greasing the pan with cooking spray between each one. Stack all the crepes on a serving plate.

In the same pan, melt the butter and stir in the onion and garlic; sauté for 3 minutes, until tender. Stir in the spinach and cook for 5 minutes.

Add in the turkey bacon, heavy cream, mozzarella cheese, black pepper, and stir. Cook for 2-3 minutes. Fill each crepe with this mixture, roll up each one, and arrange on a serving plate.

Garnish with parsley to serve.

Nutritional info per serving: Calories 321, Fat 21g, Net Carbs 5.2g, Protein 26.5g

Arugula Pesto Egg Scramble

Prep + Cook Time: 15 minutes | Serves: 2

Ingredients

1 tbsp butter
4 eggs

1 tbsp almond milk
Salt and black pepper, to taste

Arugula pesto

1 cup arugula
1 cup Parmesan cheese, grated
1 tbsp pine nuts

1 garlic clove, minced
¼ cup olive oil
1 tbsp lime juice

Directions

Beat the eggs in a bowl with almond milk, salt, and black pepper. Set a skillet over medium heat and warm butter. Pour in the egg mixture and cook while stirring gently, until eggs are set but still tender and moist.

In a blender, place all the ingredients for the pesto, excluding the olive oil. Pulse until smooth. While the machine is still running, slowly add in the olive oil until the desired consistency is obtained. Serve alongside warm scrambled eggs.

Nutritional info per serving: Calories 512; Fat: 44g, Net Carbs: 6.7g, Protein: 20.5g

Sour Cream Crabmeat Frittata with Onion

Prep + Cook Time: 25 minutes | Serves: 2

Ingredients

1 tbsp olive oil
½ onion, chopped
Salt and black pepper to taste
½ tsp cilantro

3 ounces crabmeat, chopped
1 tsp cajun seasoning
4 large eggs, slightly beaten
½ cup sour cream

Directions

Put a large skillet over medium heat and warm the oil. Add in onion and sauté until soft; place in crabmeat and cook for 2 more minutes. Season with salt and black pepper.

Distribute the ingredients at the bottom of the skillet. Whisk the eggs with yogurt. Transfer to the skillet. Set the skillet in the oven and bake for about 18 minutes at 350 F or until eggs are cooked through. Slice into wedges and serve warm.

Nutritional info per serving: Calories 265; Fat: 16g, Net Carbs: 6.5g, Protein: 23g

Asparagus & Goat Cheese Omelet

Prep + Cook Time: 10 minutes | Serves: 2

Ingredients

1 tbsp olive oil
½ bunch asparagus, chopped
1 green onion, chopped
4 eggs, beaten

1 tsp rosemary, chopped
1 tsp parsley, chopped
Sea salt and black pepper
½ cup goat cheese, crumbled

Directions

In a frying pan, cook the asparagus and green onion for 4-5 minutes in olive oil. Add in eggs, parsley, black pepper, salt, and rosemary.

Scatter the cheese over half of the omelet; using a spatula fold in the other half over the filling. Cook for a minute or until cooked through, and serve immediately.

Nutritional info per serving: Calories 410; Fat: 28.1g, Net Carbs: 2.5g, Protein: 24.3g

Chili Omelet with Avocado

Prep + Cook Time: 15 minutes | Serves: 2

Ingredients

2 tsp olive oil
1 ripe avocado, chopped
2 spring onions, chopped
2 spring garlic, chopped
4 eggs

1 cup buttermilk
2 tomatoes, sliced
1 green chili pepper, minced
2 tbsp fresh cilantro, chopped
Salt and black pepper, to taste

Directions

Crack the eggs into a bowl and whisk buttermilk, salt, and black pepper. Set a pan over high heat and warm the olive oil. Sauté garlic and onions until tender and translucent.

Pour into the pan and use a spatula to smooth the surface; cook until eggs become puffy and brown to bottom. Add cilantro, chili pepper, avocado and tomatoes, to one side of the omelet.

Fold the omelet in half and slice into wedges.

Nutritional info per serving: Calories 392; Fat: 28.5g, Net Carbs: 3.6g, Protein: 18.9g

Vegetable Keto Bread

Prep + Cook Time: 70 minutes | Serves: 2-4

Ingredients

1 cup pumpkin, shredded
1 cup zucchini, shredded and squeezed
1/3 cup coconut flour
6 eggs
1 tbsp olive oil

¾ tsp baking soda
1 tbsp cinnamon powder
½ tsp salt
½ cup buttermilk
1 tsp apple cider vinegar

Directions

Mix the pumpkin, zucchini, coconut flour, eggs, olive oil, baking soda, cinnamon powder, salt, buttermilk, and vinegar. Pour the batter into a greased loaf pan and bake for 55 minutes at 360 F.

Let cool for 5 minutes, slice and serve.

Nutritional info per serving: Calories 283, Fat 17g, Net Carbs 3.5g, Protein 13g

Thyme Eggs with Parma Ham

Prep + Cook Time: 15 minutes | Serves: 2

Ingredients

2 tbsp butter
1 shallot, chopped
½ tsp dill
Salt and black pepper to taste

2 slices Parma ham, chopped
4 eggs
1 thyme sprig, chopped
½ cup olives, pitted and sliced

Directions

Beat the eggs lightly with a fork. Over medium heat, set a skillet and warm butter. Add in shallot and sauté for 4 minutes until tender. Stir in ham, black pepper, and salt; cook for 5-6 more minutes.

Add in eggs and sprinkle with thyme; cook for 4 minutes. Garnish with sliced olives before serving.

Nutritional info per serving: Calories 321; Fat: 26.6g, Net Carbs: 3.1g, Protein: 15.9g

Lazy Eggs with Feta Cheese

Prep + Cook Time: 5 minutes | Serves: 2

Ingredients

4 eggs
¼ cup coconut milk
¼ cup feta cheese, grated

1 garlic clove, minced
¼ tsp dried dill
Sea salt and red pepper flakes, to taste

Directions

Beat the eggs lightly with a fork in a bowl. Mix in the feta cheese, red pepper flakes, garlic, coconut milk, and salt. Divide the mixture between greased microwave-safe mugs. Microwave the mugs for 40 seconds. Stir well and continue microwaving for 70 seconds. Sprinkle with dried dill and serve.

Nutritional info per serving: Calories 234; Fat: 16.8g, Net Carbs: 2.7g, Protein: 15.7g

Power Cinnamon Porridge

Prep + Cook Time: 25 minutes | Serves: 2

Ingredients

2 eggs
4 tbsp xylitol
½ cup heavy cream

2 oz coconut oil
½ tsp ginger paste
¼ cup walnuts, chopped

Directions

Crack the eggs into a mixing bowl, and lightly beat with a fork. Stir in xylitol and heavy cream.

Set a pot over medium heat and warm coconut oil. Add in egg/cream mixture and simmer until cooked through. Remove from heat and let sit for 5 minutes. Split the porridge into individual bowls, spread chopped walnuts on top, and serve.

Nutritional info per serving: Calories 423, Fat: 37g, Net Carbs: 5.8g, Protein: 10.5g

Hard-Boiled Eggs with Tuna & Chili Mayo

Prep + Cook Time: 20 minutes | Serves: 2-4

Ingredients

4 eggs
14 ounces tuna in brine, drained
½ small head lettuce, torn into pieces
2 spring onions, chopped
¼ cup ricotta cheese, crumbled
2 tbsp sour cream
½ tbsp mustard powder
½ cup mayonnaise
½ tbsp lemon juice
½ tbsp chili powder
2 dill pickles, sliced
Salt and black pepper, to taste

Directions

Boil the eggs in salted water over medium heat for 10 minutes. Place in an ice bath, cool and chop into small pieces. Transfer to a bowl.

Place in tuna, onion, mustard powder, ricotta cheese, lettuce, and sour cream. In a separate bowl, mix in mayonnaise, lemon juice, and chili powder. Add in pepper and salt. Add in the tuna mixture and stir to combine well. Serve in a serving platter, topped with dill pickle slices.

Nutritional info per serving: Calories: 311; Fat 19.5g, Net Carbs 1.5g, Protein 31g

Tofu Scrambled with Tomatoes & Mushrooms

Prep + Cook Time: 20 minutes | Serves: 2-4

Ingredients

5 fresh eggs
1 tbsp butter
1 cup mushrooms, sliced
2 cloves garlic, minced
16 oz firm tofu, pressed and crumbled
Salt and black pepper to taste
1 tomato, chopped
2 tbsp sesame seeds

Directions

Melt the butter in a skillet over medium heat, and sauté the mushrooms for 5 minutes until tender. Add the garlic and cook for 1 minute. Crumble the tofu into the skillet, season with salt and pepper.

Cook for 6 minutes, continuous stirring. Add the tomato and cook to soften for about 5 minutes.

Whisk the eggs in a bowl and pour all over the tomato. Use a spatula to immediately stir the eggs while cooking until scrambled and no more runny, about 5 minutes.

Adjust the taste with salt and pepper, sprinkle with sesame seeds, and serve.

Nutritional info per serving: Calories 315, Fat 22g, Net Carbs 4.5g, Protein 25.5g

Almond & Raspberries Cakes

Prep + Cook Time: 30 minutes | Serves: 2-4

Ingredients

2 cups almond flour
2 tsp baking soda
1 tsp vanilla extract
2 tbsp almond flakes
½ tsp salt
2 tbsp stevia

8 oz cream cheese, softened
¼ cup butter, melted
1 egg
10 raspberries
1 cup unsweetened almond milk

Directions

Mash the raspberries with a fork and set aside. Mix the almond flour, baking soda and salt in a large bowl. In a separate bowl, beat the cream cheese, stevia, and butter. Whisk in egg and almond milk.

Fold in the flour, and mashed raspberries and spoon the batter into greased muffin cups two-thirds way up. Bake for 20 minutes at 400 F until golden brown, remove to a wire rack to cool slightly for 5 minutes before serving.

Nutritional info per serving: Calories 353, Fat 32.6g, Net Carbs 8.6g, Protein 9.4g

Sesame & Poppy Seed Bagels

Prep + Cook Time: 25 minutes | Serves: 2-4

Ingredients

½ cup coconut flour
6 eggs
½ cup water
½ cup flax seed meal
½ tsp onion powder

½ tsp garlic powder
1 tsp dried oregano
1 tsp sesame seeds
1 tsp poppy seeds

Directions

Mix the coconut flour, eggs, water, flax seed meal, onion powder, garlic powder, and oregano. Spoon the mixture into a greased donut tray. Sprinkle with poppy seeds and sesame seeds. Bake the bagels for 20 minutes at 360 F. Let cool on a wire rack for 5 minutes before serving.

Nutritional info per serving: Calories 431, Fat 20g, Net Carbs 1.3g, Protein 29g

Eggplant Sausage Pie

Prep + Cook Time: 55 minutes | Serves: 2-4

Ingredients

3 eggs
6 oz raw sausage roll
2 tomatoes, chopped
1 tbsp sour cream
1 tbsp Parmesan cheese

¼ tsp salt
A pinch of black pepper
2 tbsp oregano, chopped
1 eggplant, sliced

Directions

Preheat your oven to 390 F. Press the sausage roll at the bottom of a greased pie dish. Arrange the eggplant slices on top of the sausage. Top with tomatoes.

Whisk the eggs along with the sour cream, salt, Parmesan cheese, and black pepper. Spoon the mixture over the sausage. Bake for about 40 minutes until browned around the edges. Serve warm sprinkled with oregano.

Nutritional info per serving: Calories 343, Fat: 27g, Net Carbs: 4.3g, Protein: 16.5g

Chocolate Cupcakes

Prep + Cook Time: 45 minutes | Serves: 2-4

Ingredients

1 cup almond flour
2 tbsp stevia
2 tbsp unsweetened cocoa powder
1 tsp baking powder

1 egg
½ cup plain yogurt
2 tbsp butter, melted
3 oz unsweetened dark chocolate chips

Directions

Preheat the oven to 350 F. Line muffin cups with parchment paper and set aside. In a medium bowl, whisk the almond flour, stevia, cocoa powder, and baking powder together.

In a separate bowl, whisk the egg, yogurt, and butter, and pour the mixture gradually into the flour mixture while mixing with a spatula just until well incorporated. Try not to over-mix.

Fold in some chocolate chips and fill the muffin cups with the batter - ¾ way up. Top with the remaining chocolate chips, place them on a baking tray, and bake for 20 to 25 minutes. Let the muffins to cool for 15 minutes before serving.

Nutritional info per serving: Calories 210, Fat 13g, Net Carbs 3.2g, Protein 3.9g

Salty Muffins with Bacon & Blue Cheese

Prep + Cook Time: 30 minutes | Serves: 2-4

Ingredients

2 tbsp olive oil
6 eggs
2 tbsp coconut milk
Salt and black pepper to taste

½ cup blue cheese, crumbled
4 oz bacon, chopped
2 tbsp chives, chopped
1 serrano pepper, seeded and minced

Directions

Preheat oven to 390 F. Beat the eggs a bowl and whisk in coconut milk until combined. Season with salt and pepper; add in the blue cheese.

Grease muffin cups with olive oil and spread the bottom of each one with chopped bacon. Fill each with the egg mixture two-thirds way up. Top with the serrano pepper and bake in the oven for 18 to 20 minutes or until golden. Remove and allow cooling for a few minutes before serving, sprinkled with chives.

Nutritional info per serving: Calories 354, Fat 28.7g, Net Carbs 1.5g, Protein 24g

STARTERS (SOUPS, SALADS)

Feta & Sun-Dried Tomato Salad with Bacon

Prep + Cook Time: 10 minutes | Serves: 2

Ingredients

3 oz bacon slices, chopped
5 sun-dried tomatoes in oil, sliced
4 basil leaves
1 cup feta cheese, crumbled

2 tsp extra virgin olive oil
1 tsp balsamic vinegar
Salt to taste

Directions

Fry the bacon in a pan over medium heat, until golden and crisp, for about 5 minutes. Remove with a perforated spoon and set aside. Arrange the sun-dried tomatoes on a serving plate.

Scatter feta cheese over and top with basil leaves. Add the crispy bacon on top, drizzle with olive oil and sprinkle with vinegar and salt.

Nutritional info per serving: Calories 411, Fat: 36g, Net Carbs: 2.5g, Protein: 16.2g

Minty Green Chicken Salad

Prep + Cook Time: 25 minutes | Serves: 2

Ingredients

1 chicken breast, cubed
1 tbsp avocado oil
2 eggs
2 cups green beans, steamed
1 avocado, sliced
4 cups mixed salad greens

2 tbsp olive oil
2 tbsp lemon juice
1 tsp Dijon mustard
1 tbsp mint, chopped
Salt and black pepper, to taste

Directions

Boil the eggs in salted water over medium heat for 10 minutes. Remove to an ice bath to cool, peel and slice. Warm the oil in a pan over medium heat. Add the chicken and cook for about 4 minutes.

Divide the green beans between two salad bowls. Top with chicken, eggs, and avocado slices. In another bowl, whisk together the lemon juice, olive oil, mustard, salt, and pepper, and drizzle over the salad. Top with mint and serve.

Nutritional info per serving: Calories 612, Fat: 47.9g, Net Carbs: 6.9g, Protein: 27.3g

Spinach Salad with Goat Cheese & Pine Nuts

Prep + Cook Time: 20 minutes | Serves: 2

Ingredients

2 cups spinach
½ cup pine nuts
1 ½ cups hard goat cheese, grated

2 tbsp white wine vinegar
2 tbsp extra virgin olive oil
Salt and black pepper, to taste

Directions

Preheat oven to 390 F. Place the grated goat cheese in two circles on two pieces of parchment paper. Place in the oven and bake for 10 minutes.

Find two same bowls, place them upside down, and carefully put the parchment paper on top to give the cheese a bowl-like shape. Let cool that way for 15 minutes. Divide spinach among the bowls sprinkle with salt and pepper and drizzle with vinegar and olive oil. Top with pine nuts to serve.

Nutritional info per serving: Calories 410, Fat: 31.2g, Net Carbs: 3.4g, Protein: 27g

Chicken Salad with Parmesan

Prep + Cook Time: 30 minutes + chilling time | Serves: 2

Ingredients

½ pound boneless, skinless chicken thighs
¼ cup lemon juice
2 garlic cloves, minced
2 tbsp olive oil

Dressing:

2 tbsp extra virgin olive oil
1 tbsp lemon juice

1 head romaine lettuce, shredded
3 Parmesan crisps
Parmesan cheese, grated for garnishing

Salt and black pepper to taste

Directions

In a Ziploc bag, put the chicken, lemon juice, olive oil, and garlic. Seal the bag, shake to combine, and refrigerate for 1 hour.

Preheat the grill to medium heat and grill the chicken for about 4 minutes per side.

Combine the dressing ingredients in a small bowl and mix well.

On a serving platter, arrange the lettuce and Parmesan crisps. Scatter the dressing over and toss to coat. Top with the chicken and grated Parmesan cheese to serve.

Nutritional info per serving: Calories 529, Fat: 36.5g, Net Carbs: 4.3g, Protein: 34g

Salmon Salad with Lettuce & Avocado

Prep + Cook Time: 5 minutes | Serves: 2

Ingredients

2 slices smoked salmon, chopped
1 tsp onion flakes
3 tbsp mayonnaise
1 cup romaine lettuce, shredded

1 tbsp lime juice
1 tbsp extra virgin olive oil
Sea salt to taste
½ avocado, sliced

Directions

Combine the salmon, mayonnaise, lime juice, olive oil, and salt in a small bowl; mix to combine well.

In a salad platter, arrange the shredded lettuce and onion flakes. Spread the salmon mixture over; top with avocado slices and serve.

Nutritional info per serving: Calories 231, Fat: 20g, Net Carbs: 2.2g, Protein: 8.5g

Classic Greek Salad

Prep + Cook Time: 10 minutes | Serves: 2

Ingredients

3 tbsp extra virgin olive oil
½ lemon, juiced
3 tomatoes, sliced
1 cucumber, sliced
1 red bell pepper, sliced

1 small red onion, chopped
10 kalamata olives, chopped
4 oz feta cheese, cubed
1 tsp parsley, chopped
Salt to taste

Directions

Mix the olive oil with lemon juice and salt, in a small bowl. In a salad plate, combine the tomatoes, cucumber, bell pepper and parsley; toss with the dressing. Top with the feta and olives, and serve.

Nutritional info per serving: Calories 288, Fat: 25.8g, Net Carbs: 6.8g, Protein: 10.3g

Pesto Caprese Salad with Tuna

Prep + Cook Time: 10 minutes | Serves: 2

Ingredients

1 tomato, sliced
4 oz canned tuna chunks in water, drained
1 ball fresh mozzarella cheese, sliced
4 basil leaves

½ cup pine nuts
½ cup Parmesan cheese, grated
½ cup extra virgin olive oil
½ lemon, juiced

Directions

Put in a food processor the basil leaves, pine nuts, Parmesan cheese and extra virgin olive oil, and blend until smooth. Add in the lemon juice. Arrange the cheese and tomato slices in a serving plate. Scatter the tuna chunks and pesto over the top and serve.

Nutritional info per serving: Calories 364, Fat 31g, Net Carbs 1g, Protein 21g

Kale & Broccoli Slaw Salad with Bacon & Parmesan

Prep + Cook Time: 10 minutes | Serves: 2

Ingredients

2 tbsp olive oil
1 cup broccoli slaw
1 cup kale slaw
2 slices bacon, chopped

2 tbsp Parmesan cheese, grated
1 tsp celery seeds
1 ½ tbsp apple cider vinegar
Salt and black pepper, to taste

Directions

Fry the bacon in a skillet over medium heat until crispy, about 5 minutes. Set aside to cool.

Place broccoli, kale slaw and celery seeds in a large salad bowl. Pour the olive oil and vinegar over. Season with salt and black pepper, and mix with your hands to combine well. Sprinkle with the cooled bacon and Parmesan cheese, and serve.

Nutritional info per serving: Calories 305, Fat: 26.9g, Net Carbs: 3.2g, Protein: 7.3g

Seared Rump Steak Salad

Prep + Cook Time: 40 minutes | Serves: 2

Ingredients

½ cup water
½ lb rump steak
3 green onions, sliced
3 tomatoes, sliced
1 cup green beans, steamed and sliced
1 avocado, sliced

2 cups mixed salad greens
2 tsp yellow mustard
Salt and black pepper to taste
3 tbsp extra virgin olive oil
1 tbsp balsamic vinegar

Directions

In a bowl, mix the mustard, salt, black pepper, balsamic vinegar, and extra virgin olive oil. Set aside.

Preheat a grill pan over high heat while you season the meat with salt and pepper.

Place the steak in the pan and brown on both sides for 4 minutes each. Remove to rest on a chopping board for 4 more minutes before slicing thinly.

In a shallow salad bowl, add the green onions, tomatoes, green beans, salad greens, and steak slices. Drizzle the dressing over and toss with two spoons. Top with avocado slices to serve.

Nutritional info per serving: Calories 611, Fat 45.7g, Net Carbs 6.4g, Protein 32.8g

Arugula & Watercress Turkey Salad with Walnuts

Prep + Cook Time: 25 minutes | Serves: 2-4

Ingredients

1 tbsp xylitol
1 red onion, chopped
2 tbsp lime juice
3 tbsp olive oil
¼ cup water
1 ¾ cups raspberries
1 tbsp Dijon mustard

Salt and black pepper, to taste
1 cup arugula
1 cup watercress
1 pound turkey breasts, boneless
4 ounces goat cheese, crumbled
½ cup walnut halves

Directions

Start with the dressing: in a blender, combine xylitol, lime juice, 1 cup raspberries, pepper, mustard, water, onion, oil, and salt, and pulse until smooth. Strain this into a bowl, and set aside.

Heat a pan over medium heat and grease lightly with cooking spray. Coat the turkey with salt and black pepper and cut in half. Place skin side down into the pan.

Cook for 8 minutes flipping to the other side and cooking for 5 minutes.

Place the arugula and watercress in a salad platter, scatter with the remaining raspberries, walnut halves, and goat cheese.

Slice the turkey breasts, put over the salad and top with raspberries dressing to serve.

Nutritional info per serving: Calories 511, Fat 35.5g, Net Carbs 7.5g, Protein 37g

Spinach Salad with Bacon & Mustard Vinaigrette

Prep + Cook Time: 20 minutes | Serves: 2

Ingredients

1 cup spinach
1 large avocado, sliced
1 spring onion, sliced

2 bacon slices
½ lettuce head, shredded
1 hard-boiled egg, chopped

Vinaigrette:

Salt to taste
¼ tsp garlic powder
3 tbsp olive oil

1 tsp Dijon mustard
1 tbsp white wine vinegar

Directions

Chop the bacon and fry in a skillet over medium heat for 5 minutes until crispy. Set aside to cool.

Mix the spinach, lettuce, egg, and spring onion, in a bowl. Whisk together the vinaigrette ingredients in another bowl. Pour the dressing over, toss to combine and top with avocado and bacon.

Nutritional info per serving: Calories 547, Fat: 51g, Net Carbs: 4.7g, Protein: 11.7g

Mackerel Lettuce Cups

Prep + Cook Time: 20 minutes | Serves: 2

Ingredients

2 mackerel fillets, cut into pieces
1 tbsp olive oil
Salt and black pepper to taste
2 eggs

1 ½ cups water
1 tomato, seeded, chopped
2 tbsp mayonnaise
½ head green lettuce, firm leaves removed for cups

Directions

Preheat a grill pan over medium heat. Drizzle the mackerel fillets with olive oil, and sprinkle with salt and black pepper. Add the fish to the preheated grill pan and cook on both sides for 6-8 minutes.

Bring the eggs to boil in salted water in a pot over medium heat for 10 minutes. Then, run the eggs in cold water, peel, and chop into small pieces. Transfer to a salad bowl.

Remove the mackerel fillets to the salad bowl. Include the tomatoes and mayonnaise; mix evenly with a spoon. Layer two lettuce leaves each as cups and fill with two tablespoons of egg salad each.

Nutritional info per serving: Calories 445, Fat 31.5g, Net Carbs 3.4g, Protein 31g

Salad of Prawns and Mixed Lettuce Greens

Prep + Cook Time: 15 minutes | Serves: 2

Ingredients

2 cups mixed lettuce greens
¼ cup aioli
1 tbsp olive oil
½ pound tiger prawns, peeled and deveined

½ tsp Dijon mustard
Salt and chili pepper to season
1 tbsp lemon juice

Directions

Season the prawns with salt and chili pepper. Fry in warm olive oil over medium heat for 3 minutes on each side until prawns are pink. Set aside. Add the aioli, lemon juice and mustard in a small bowl. Mix until smooth and creamy.

Place the mixed lettuce greens in a bowl and pour half of the dressing on the salad. Toss with 2 spoons until mixed, and add the remaining dressing. Divide salad aming plates and serve with prawns.

Nutritional info per serving: Calories 223, Fat 21g, Net Carbs 1,9g, Protein 6.8g

Classic Egg Salad with Olives

Prep + Cook Time: 15 minutes | Serves: 2

Ingredients

4 eggs
¼ cup mayonnaise
½ tsp sriracha sauce
½ tbsp mustard
¼ cup scallions

¼ stalk celery, minced
Salt and black pepper, to taste
1 head romaine lettuce, torn into pieces
¼ tsp fresh lime juice
10 black olives

Directions

Boil the eggs in salted water over medium heat for 10 minutes. When cooled, peel and chop them into bite-size pieces. Place in a salad bowl.

Stir in the remaining ingredients, except for the scallions, until everything is well combined. Scatter the scallions all over and decorate with olives to serve.

Nutritional info per serving: Calories 312; Fat 21.5g, Net Carbs 6.3g, Protein 17.4g

Spinach & Brussels Sprouts Salad with Hazelnuts

Prep + Cook Time: 35 minutes | Serves: 2

Ingredients

1 lb Brussels sprouts, halved
2 tbsp olive oil
Salt and black pepper to taste
1 tbsp balsamic vinegar

2 tbsp extra virgin olive oil
1 cup baby spinach
1 tbsp Dijon mustard
½ cup hazelnuts

Directions

Preheat oven to 400 F. Drizzle the Brussels sprouts with olive oil, a little salt and black pepper, in a bowl, and spread on a baking sheet. Bake until tender for about 20 minutes.

In a dry pan over medium heat, toast the hazelnuts for 2-3 minutes, cool and then chop into small pieces.

Transfer the Brussels sprouts to a salad bowl and add the baby spinach, Dijon mustard and hazelnuts. Mix until well combined.

In a small bowl combine the vinegar with the olive oil. Scatter the dressing over the salad to serve.

Nutritional info per serving: Calories 511, Fat 42.3g, Net Carbs 9.6g, Protein 14.5g

Watercress & Shrimp Salad with Lemon Dressing

Prep + Cook Time: 1 hour 10 minutes | Serves: 2

Ingredients

1 cup watercress leaves
2 tbsp capers

Dressing:

¼ cup mayonnaise
½ tsp apple cider vinegar
¼ tsp sesame seeds

½ pound shrimp, cooked
1 tbsp dill, chopped

Salt and black pepper to taste
1 tbsp lemon juice
2 tsp stevia

Directions

Combine the watercress leaves, shrimp, and dill in a large bowl. Whisk together the mayonnaise, vinegar, sesame seeds, black pepper, stevia, and lemon juice in another bowl. Season with salt.

Pour the dressing over and gently toss to combine; refrigerate for 1 hour. Top with capers to serve.

Nutritional info per serving: Calories 232, Fat: 12.5g, Net Carbs: 2.2g, Protein: 27g

Mediterranean Artichoke & Red Onion Salad

Prep + Cook Time: 30 minutes | Serves: 2

Ingredients

6 baby artichoke hearts, halved
½ lemon, juiced
½ red onion, sliced
¼ cup cherry peppers, halved
¼ cup pitted olives, sliced
¼ cup olive oil

¼ tsp lemon zest
2 tsp balsamic vinegar, sugar-free
1 tbsp chopped dill
Salt and black pepper to taste
1 tbsp capers

Directions

Bring a pot of salted water to a boil. Add the artichokes to the pot. Lower the heat, and let simmer for 20 minutes until tender. Drain and place the artichokes in a bowl.

Add in the rest of the ingredients, except for the olives; toss to combine well. Transfer to a serving platter and top with the olives.

Nutritional info per serving: Calories 464, Fat: 31.2g, Net Carbs: 9.5g, Protein: 13.4g

Tomato & Pesto Sausage Salad

Ready in about: 10 minutes | Serves: 2

Ingredients

½ pound pork sausage links, sliced
½ cup mixed cherry tomatoes, cut in half
1 cups mixed lettuce greens
¼ cup radicchio, sliced
1 tbsp olive oil
¼ pound feta cheese, cubed

½ tbsp lemon juice
½ cup basil pesto
¼ cup black olives, pitted and halved
Salt and black pepper, to taste
1 tbsp Parmesan shavings

Directions

Cook the sausages in warm olive oil over medium heat for 4 minutes per side.

In a salad bowl, combine the mixed lettuce greens, radicchio, feta cheese, pesto, cherry tomatoes, black olives, and lemon juice, and toss well to coat.

Season with salt and black pepper and add the sausage pieces. Finish with Parmesan shavings and serve.

Nutritional info per serving: Calories 611, Fat 48g, Net Carbs 7.5g, Protein 31.2g

Pickled Pepper & Cheese Salad with Grilled Steak

Prep + Cook Time: 15 minutes | Serves: 2

Ingredients

½ cup feta cheese, crumbled
1 lb skirt steak, sliced
Salt and black pepper to season
1 tsp olive oil

1 cup watercress
1 cup arugula
3 pickled peppers, chopped
2 tbsp red wine vinegar

Directions

Preheat grill to high heat. Season the steak slices with salt and black pepper and drizzle with olive oil. Grill the steaks on each side to the desired doneness, for about 5-6 minutes. Remove to a bowl, cover and leave to rest while you make the salad.

Mix the watercress and arugula, pickled peppers, and vinegar in a salad bowl. Add the beef and sprinkle with feta cheese.

Nutritional info per serving: Calories 633, Fat 34.6g, Net Carbs 4.7g, Protein 71.8g

Arugula Chicken Salad with Gorgonzola Cheese

Prep + Cook Time: 15 minutes | Serves: 2

Ingredients

1 chicken breast, boneless, skinless, flattened
Salt and black pepper to taste
1 tbsp garlic powder
2 tsp olive oil

1 cup arugula
1 tbsp red wine vinegar
½ cup gorgonzola cheese, crumbled

Directions

Rub the chicken with salt, black pepper, and garlic powder. Heat half of the olive oil in a pan over high heat and fry the chicken for 4 minutes on both sides until golden brown.

Remove chicken to a cutting board and let cool before slicing.

Toss arugula with red wine vinegar and the remaining olive oil; share the salads into plates.

Divide chicken slices on top and sprinkle with gorgonzola cheese.

Nutritional info per serving: Calories 291, Fat 24g, Net Carbs 3.5g, Protein 13.2g

Modern Greek Salad with Avocado

Prep + Cook Time: 10 minutes | Serves: 2

Ingredients

2 tomatoes, sliced
1 avocado, sliced
6 kalamata olives
¼ lb feta cheese, sliced

1 red bell pepper, roasted and sliced
1 tbsp vinegar
1 tbsp olive oil
1 tbsp parsley, chopped

Directions

Put the tomato slices on a serving platter and place the avocado slices in the middle. Arrange the olives and bell pepper slices around the avocado slices and drop pieces of feta on the platter. Drizzle with olive oil and vinegar and sprinkle with parsley to serve.

Nutritional info per serving: Calories 411, Fat: 35g, Net Carbs: 5.2g, Protein: 12.9g

Cheesy Beef Salad

Prep + Cook Time: 15 minutes | Serves: 2-4

Ingredients

1 tsp cumin
3 tbsp olive oil
½ pound beef rump steak, cut into strips
Salt and ground black pepper, to taste
1 tbsp thyme
1 garlic clove, minced

½ cup ricotta cheese, crumbled
½ cup pecans, toasted
2 cups watercress
1½ tbsp lemon juice
¼ cup fresh mint, chopped

Directions

Preheat grill to medium-high heat. Rub the beef with salt, 1 tbsp of olive oil, garlic, thyme, black pepper, and cumin. Place on the preheated grill and cook for 10 minutes, flip once.

Sprinkle the pecans on a dry pan over medium heat and cook for 2-3 minutes, shaking constantly. Remove the grilled beef to a cutting board, leave to cool, and slice into strips.

In a salad bowl, combine the watercress with mint, remaining olive oil, salt, lemon juice, ricotta cheese, and pecans, and toss well to coat. Top with the beef slices to serve.

Nutritional info per serving: Calories 437, Fat 41.5g, Net Carbs 4.2g, Protein 15.6g

Smoked Salmon, Bacon & Poached Egg Salad

Prep + Cook Time: 15 minutes | Serves: 2-4

Ingredients

6 eggs
1 head romaine lettuce, torn
½ cup smoked salmon, chopped

6 slices bacon
Salt and black pepper to taste

Dressing:

½ cup mayonnaise
½ tsp garlic puree

1 tbsp lemon juice
1 tsp tabasco sauce

Directions

In a bowl, mix well the dressing ingredients and set aside. Bring a pot of salted water to a boil. Crack each egg into a small bowl and gently slide into the water. Poach for 2 to 3 minutes, remove with a perforated spoon, transfer to a paper towel to dry, and plate. Poach the remaining eggs.

Put the bacon in a skillet and fry over medium heat until browned and crispy, about 6 minutes, turning once. Remove, allow cooling, and chop in small pieces.

Toss the lettuce, smoked salmon, bacon, and dressing in a salad bowl. Divide the salad onto plates, top with the eggs each, and serve immediately or chilled.

Nutritional info per serving: Calories 452, Fat 36.9g, Net Carbs 4.4g, Protein 26.7g

Seafood Salad with Avocado & Tomato

Prep + Cook Time: 30 minutes | Serves: 2-4

Ingredients

2 tomatoes, chopped
½ pound medium shrimp
3 tbsp olive oil
1 avocado, chopped

1 tbsp cilantro, chopped
1 lime, zested and juiced
Salt and black pepper to taste

Directions

Heat a skillet over medium heat, add in 1 tbsp olive oil and cook the shrimp until opaque, about 8-10 minutes. Place the shrimp, tomatoes, and avocado in a large bowl.

Whisk together the remaining olive oil, lime zest, juice, salt and black pepper, in another bowl. Pour the dressing over, toss to combine and serve topped with cilantro.

Nutritional info per serving: Calories 229, Fat: 18.3g, Net Carbs: 4.2g, Protein: 10g

Cheddar & Turkey Meatball Salad

Prep + Cook Time: 25 minutes | Serves: 2-4

Ingredients

3 tbsp olive oil
1 tbsp lemon juice or vinegar
1 lb ground turkey
Salt and black pepper to season

1 head romaine lettuce, torn into pieces
2 tomatoes, sliced
¼ red onion, sliced
3 oz yellow cheddar cheese, shredded

Directions

Mix the ground turkey with salt and black pepper and shape into meatballs. Refrigerate for 10 minutes. Heat half of the olive oil in a frying pan over medium heat and fry the meatballs on both sides for 10 minutes until browned and cooked within. Transfer to a wire rack to drain oil.

Mix the lettuce, tomatoes, and red onion in a salad bowl, season with the remaining olive oil, salt, lemon juice, and black pepper. Toss and add the meatballs on top.

Melt the cheese in the microwave for about 90 seconds. Drizzle the cheese over the salad and serve.

Nutritional info per serving: Calories 312, Fat 22.6g, Net Carbs 1.9g, Protein 19.5g

Warm Cauliflower Salad

Prep + Cook Time: 15 minutes + chilling time | Serves: 2-4

Ingredients

1 head cauliflower, cut into florets
1 red onion, sliced
1 cup roasted bell peppers, chopped
¼ cup extra-virgin olive oil
1 tbsp wine vinegar

1 tsp yellow mustard
Salt and black pepper, to taste
½ cup black olives, pitted and chopped
½ cup cashew nuts
Celery leaves, chopped for garnish

Directions

Steam cauliflower in salted water in a pot over medium heat for 5 minutes; drain and transfer to a salad bowl. Add in roasted peppers, olives and red onion.

In a small dish, combine salt, olive oil, mustard, black pepper, and vinegar. Sprinkle the mixture over the veggies. Top with cashew nuts and celery and serve.

Nutritional info per serving: Calories 213; Fat: 16.6g, Net Carbs: 7.4g, Protein: 5.2g

Celery & Cauliflower Soup with Bacon Croutons

Prep + Cook Time: 25 minutes | Serves: 2-4

Ingredients

2 tbsp olive oil
1 onion, chopped
¼ celery root, grated
1 head cauliflower, cut into florets
3 cups water

Salt and black pepper to taste
1 cup almond milk
1 cup white cheddar cheese, shredded
2 oz bacon, cut into strips

Directions

Sauté the onion in warm olive oil over medium heat for 3 minutes until fragrant. Include the cauli florets and celery root, sauté for 3 minutes to slightly soften, add the water, and season with salt and black pepper. Bring to a boil, and then reduce the heat to low. Cover and cook for 10 minutes.

Puree the soup with an immersion blender until the ingredients are evenly combined and stir in the almond milk and cheese until the cheese melts. Adjust taste with salt and black pepper.

In a non-stick skillet over high heat, fry the bacon, until crispy. Divide soup between serving bowls, top with crispy bacon, and serve hot.

Nutritional info per serving: Calories 323, Fat 27g, Net Carbs 7.6g, Protein 22.8g

Iceberg Lettuce Salad with Gorgonzola & Bacon

Prep + Cook Time: 15 minutes | Serves: 2-4

Ingredients

1 head lettuce, separated into leaves
4 oz bacon
1 ½ cups gorgonzola cheese, crumbled
1 tbsp white wine vinegar

3 tbsp extra virgin olive oil
Salt and black pepper to taste
2 tbsp pumpkin seeds

Directions

Chop the bacon into small pieces and fry in a skillet over medium heat for 6 minutes, until browned and crispy. In a small bowl, whisk the white wine vinegar, olive oil, salt, and black pepper until dressing is well combined.

To assemble the salad, arrange the lettuce on a serving platter, top with the bacon and gorgonzola cheese. Drizzle the dressing over the salad, lightly toss, and top with pumpkin seeds to serve.

Nutritional info per serving: Calories 339, Fat 31.2g, Net Carbs 2.9g, Protein 16.3g

Beef Salad with Yogurt Dressing

Prep + Cook Time: 20 minutes | Serves: 2-4

Ingredients

2 tbsp almond milk
1 pound ground beef
1 onion, grated
¼ cup pork rinds, crushed
1 egg, whisked
1 tbsp fresh parsley, chopped
Salt and black pepper, to taste
1 garlic clove, minced

1 tbsp fresh mint, chopped
½ tsp dried oregano
2 tbsp olive oil
1 cup cherry tomatoes, halved
1 cucumber, sliced
1 cup arugula
1½ tbsp lemon juice
1 cup Greek yogurt

Directions

In a bowl, mix the beef, salt, onion, parsley, black pepper, egg, pork rinds oregano, and garlic. Form balls out of this mixture and place on a working surface.

Set a pan over medium heat and warm half of the oil; fry the meatballs for 8-10 minutes. Set aside.

In a salad plate, combine the arugula with the cherry tomatoes and cucumber. Mix in the remaining oil, lemon juice, black pepper, and salt. Whisk the yogurt with mint and spread it over the salad; top with meatballs to serve.

Nutritional info per serving: Calories 488, Fat 31.4g, Net Carbs 8.3g, Protein 42g

Parma Ham & Egg Salad

Prep + Cook Time: 20 minutes | Serves: 2-4

Ingredients

8 eggs
1/3 cup mayonnaise
1 tbsp minced onion
½ tsp mustard

1 ½ tsp lime juice
Salt and black pepper, to taste
10 lettuce leaves
4 Parma ham slices

Directions

Boil the eggs for 10 minutes in a pot filled with salted water. Remove and run under cold water. Then peel and chop. Transfer to a mixing bowl together with the mayonnaise, mustard, black pepper, lime juice, onion, and salt. Top with fresh lettuce leaves and ham slices to serve.

Nutritional info per serving: Calories: 723; Fat 52.3g, Net Carbs 5.6g, Protein 46.7g

Vegan Cream Soup with Avocado & Zucchini

Prep + Cook Time: 35 minutes | Serves: 2

Ingredients

3 tsp vegetable oil
1 leek, chopped
1 rutabaga, sliced
3 cups zucchinis, chopped

1 avocado, chopped
Salt and black pepper to taste
4 cups vegetable broth
2 tbsp fresh mint, chopped

Directions

In a pot, sauté leek, zucchini, and rutabaga in warm oil for about 7-10 minutes. Season with black pepper and salt. Pour in broth and bring to a boil. Lower the heat and simmer for 20 minutes.

Lift from the heat. In batches, add the soup and avocado to a blender. Blend until creamy and smooth. Serve in bowls topped with fresh mint.

Nutritional info per serving: Calories 378 Fat: 24.5g, Net Carbs: 9.3g, Protein: 8.2g

Chinese Tofu Soup

Prep + Cook Time: 15 minutes | Serves: 2

Ingredients

2 cups chicken stock
1 tbsp soy sauce, sugar-free
2 spring onions, sliced
1 tsp sesame oil, softened
2 eggs, beaten

1-inch piece ginger, grated
Salt and black ground, to taste
½ pound extra-firm tofu, cubed
A handful of fresh cilantro, chopped

Directions

Boil in a pan over medium heat, soy sauce, chicken stock and sesame oil. Place in eggs as you whisk to incorporate completely. Change heat to low and add salt, spring onions, black pepper and ginger; cook for 5 minutes. Place in tofu and simmer for 1 to 2 minutes.

Divide into soup bowls and serve sprinkled with fresh cilantro.

Nutritional info per serving: Calories 163; Fat: 10g, Net Carbs: 2.4g, Protein: 14.5g

Awesome Chicken Enchilada Soup

Prep + Cook Time: 30 minutes | Serves: 2-4

Ingredients

2 tbsp coconut oil
1 lb boneless, skinless chicken thighs
¾ cup red enchilada sauce, sugar-free
¼ cup water
¼ cup onion, chopped
3 oz canned diced green chilis

1 avocado, sliced
1 cup cheddar cheese, shredded
¼ cup pickled jalapeños, chopped
½ cup sour cream
1 tomato, diced

Directions

Put a large pan over medium heat. Add coconut oil and warm. Place in the chicken and cook until browned on the outside. Stir in onion, chillis, water, and enchilada sauce, then close with a lid.

Allow simmering for 20 minutes until the chicken is cooked through.

Spoon the soup on a serving bowl and top with the sauce, cheese, sour cream, tomato, and avocado.

Nutritional info per serving: Calories: 643, Fat: 44.2g, Net Carbs: 9.7g, Protein: 45.8g

Curried Shrimp & Green Bean Soup

Prep + Cook Time: 20 minutes | Serves: 2-4

Ingredients

1 onion, chopped
2 tbsp red curry paste
2 tbsp butter
1 pound jumbo shrimp, peeled and deveined
2 tsp ginger-garlic puree

1 cup coconut milk
Salt and chili pepper to taste
1 bunch green beans, halved
1 tbsp cilantro, chopped

Directions

Add the shrimp to melted butter in a saucepan over medium heat, season with salt and pepper, and cook until they are opaque, 2 to 3 minutes. Remove to a plate. Add in the ginger-garlic puree, onion, and red curry paste and sauté for 2 minutes until fragrant.

Stir in the coconut milk; add the shrimp, salt, chili pepper, and green beans. Cook for 4 minutes. Reduce the heat to a simmer and cook an additional 3 minutes, occasionally stirring. Adjust taste with salt, fetch soup into serving bowls, and serve sprinkled with cilantro.

Nutritional info per serving: Calories 351, Fat 32.4g, Net Carbs 3.2g, Protein 7.7g

Spinach & Basil Chicken Soup

Prep + Cook Time: 15 minutes | Serves: 2-4

Ingredients

1 cup spinach
2 cups cooked and shredded chicken
4 cups chicken broth
1 cup cheddar cheese, shredded
4 ounces cream cheese

½ tsp chili powder
½ tsp ground cumin
½ tsp fresh parsley, chopped
Salt and black pepper, to taste

Directions

In a pot, add the chicken broth and spinach, bring to a boil and cook for 5-8 minutes. Transfer to a food processor, add in the cream cheese and pulse until smooth. Return the mixture to a pot and place over medium heat. Cook until hot, but do not bring to a boil.

Add chicken, chili powder, and cumin and cook for about 3-5 minutes, or until it is heated through.

Stir in cheddar cheese and season with salt and pepper. Serve hot in bowls sprinkled with parsley.

Nutritional info per serving: Calories 351, Fat: 22.4g, Net Carbs: 4.3g, Protein: 21.6g

Sausage & Turnip Soup

Prep + Cook Time: 40 minutes | Serves: 2-4

Ingredients

3 turnips, chopped
2 celery sticks, chopped
2 tbsp butter
1 tbsp olive oil
1 pork sausage, sliced

2 cups vegetable broth
½ cup sour cream
3 green onions, chopped
2 cups water
Salt and black pepper, to taste

Directions

Sauté the green onions in melted butter over medium heat until soft and golden, about 3-4 minutes. Add celery and turnip, and cook for another 5 minutes. Pour over the vegetable broth and water over.

Bring to a boil, simmer covered, and cook for about 20 minutes until the vegetables are tender. Remove from heat. Puree the soup with a hand blender until smooth. Add sour cream and adjust the seasoning. Warm the olive oil in a skillet. Add the pork sausage and cook for 5 minutes. Serve the soup in deep bowls topped with pork sausage.

Nutritional info per serving: Calories 275, Fat: 23.1g, Net Carbs: 6.4g, Protein: 7.4g

Mushroom Cream Soup with Herbs

Prep + Cook Time: 25 minutes | Serves: 2-4

Ingredients

1 onion, chopped
½ cup crème fraiche
¼ cup butter
12 oz white mushrooms, chopped
1 tsp thyme leaves, chopped

1 tsp parsley leaves, chopped
1 tsp cilantro leaves, chopped
2 garlic cloves, minced
4 cups vegetable broth
Salt and black pepper, to taste

Directions

Add butter, onion and garlic to a large pot over high heat and cook for 3 minutes until tender. Add mushrooms, salt and pepper, and cook for 10 minutes. Pour in the broth and bring to a boil.

Reduce the heat and simmer for 10 minutes. Puree the soup with a hand blender until smooth. Stir in crème fraiche. Garnish with herbs before serving.

Nutritional info per serving: Calories 213, Fat: 18g, Net Carbs: 4.1g, Protein: 3.1g

Broccoli & Spinach Soup

Prep + Cook Time: 25 minutes | Serves: 2-4

Ingredients

2 tbsp butter
1 onion, chopped
1 garlic clove, minced
2 heads broccoli, cut in florets
2 stalks celery, chopped

4 cups vegetable broth
1 cup baby spinach
Salt and black pepper to taste
1 tbsp basil, chopped
Parmesan cheese, shaved to serve

Directions

Melt the butter in a saucepan over medium heat. Sauté the garlic and onion for 3 minutes until softened. Mix in the broccoli and celery, and cook for 4 minutes until slightly tender. Pour in the broth, bring to a boil, then reduce the heat to medium-low and simmer covered for about 5 minutes.

Drop in the spinach to wilt, adjust the seasonings, and cook for 4 minutes. Ladle soup into serving bowls. Serve with a sprinkle of grated Parmesan cheese and chopped basil.

Nutritional info per serving: Calories 123, Fat 11g, Net Carbs 3.2g, Protein 1.8g

Cheese Cream Soup with Chicken & Cilantro

Prep + Cook Time: 15 minutes | Serves: 2-4

Ingredients

1 carrot, chopped
1 onion, chopped
2 cups cooked and shredded chicken
3 tbsp butter
4 cups chicken broth

2 tbsp cilantro, chopped
1/3 cup buffalo sauce
½ cup cream cheese
Salt and black pepper, to taste

Directions

In a skillet over medium heat, warm butter and sauté carrot and onion until tender, about 5 minutes.

Add to a food processor and blend with buffalo sauce and cream cheese, until smooth. Transfer to a pot, add chicken broth and heat until hot but do not bring to a boil. Stir in chicken, salt, pepper and cook until heated through. When ready, remove to soup bowls and serve garnished with cilantro.

Nutritional info per serving: Calories 487, Fat: 41g, Net Carbs: 7.2g, Protein: 16.3g

Thick Creamy Broccoli Cheese Soup

Prep + Cook Time: 20 minutes | Serves: 2-4

Ingredients

1 tbsp olive oil
2 tbsp peanut butter
¾ cup heavy cream
1 onion, diced
1 garlic, minced
4 cups chopped broccoli

4 cups veggie broth
2 ¾ cups cheddar cheese, grated
¼ cup cheddar cheese to garnish
Salt and black pepper, to taste
½ bunch fresh mint, chopped

Directions

Warm olive oil and peanut butter in a pot over medium heat. Sauté onion and garlic for 3 minutes or until tender, stirring occasionally. Season with salt and black pepper. Add the broth and broccoli and bring to a boil.

Reduce the heat and simmer for 10 minutes. Puree the soup with a hand blender until smooth. Add in the cheese and cook about 1 minute. Stir in the heavy cream. Serve in bowls with the reserved grated cheddar cheese and sprinkled with fresh mint.

Nutritional info per serving: Calories 552, Fat: 49.5g, Net Carbs: 6.9g, Protein: 25g

Tomato Cream Soup with Basil

Prep + Cook Time: 20 minutes | Serves: 2-4

Ingredients

1 carrot, chopped
2 tbsp olive oil
1 onion, diced
1 garlic clove, minced
¼ cup raw cashew nuts, diced

14 ounces canned tomatoes
1 tsp fresh basil leaves + extra to garnish
1 cup water
Salt and black pepper to taste
1 cup crème fraîche

Directions

Warm olive oil in a pot over medium heat and sauté the onion, carrot, and garlic for 4 minutes until softened. Stir in the tomatoes, basil, water, cashew nuts, and season with salt and black pepper.

Cover and bring to simmer for 10 minutes until thoroughly cooked. Puree the ingredients with an immersion blender. Adjust to taste and stir in the crème fraîche. Serve sprinkled with basil.

Nutritional info per serving: Calories 253, Fat 23.5g, Net Carbs 6.2g, Protein 4.1g

Summer Gazpacho with Cottage Cheese

Prep + Cook Time: 15 minutes + chilling time | Serves: 2-4

Ingredients

1 green pepper, roasted
1 red pepper, roasted
1 avocado, flesh scoped out
1 garlic clove
1 spring onion, chopped
1 cucumber, chopped
½ cup olive oil

1 tbsp lemon juice
2 tomatoes, chopped
4 ounces cottage cheese, crumbled
1 small red onion, chopped
1 tbsp apple cider vinegar
Salt to taste

Directions

In a blender, put the peppers, tomatoes, avocados, red onion, garlic, lemon juice, olive oil, vinegar, half of the cucumber, a cup of water, and cottage cheese. Blitz until your desired consistency is reached; adjust the seasoning.

Transfer the mixture to a pot. Cover and chill in the fridge for at least 2 hours. Divide the soup between bowls. Serve topped with the remaining cucumber, spring onion, and an extra drizzle of olive oil.

Nutritional info per serving: Calories 373, Fat: 34.4g, Net Carbs: 7.1g, Protein: 5.8g

Zucchini & Leek Turkey Soup

Prep + Cook Time: 45 minutes | Serves: 2-4

Ingredients

1 onion, chopped
1 garlic clove, minced
3 celery stalks, chopped
2 leeks, chopped
2 tbsp butter

4 cups chicken stock
Salt and black pepper, to taste
¼ cup fresh parsley, chopped
1 large zucchini, spiralized
2 cups turkey meat, cooked and chopped

Directions

In a pot over medium heat, add in leeks, celery, onion, and garlic and cook for 5 minutes. Place in the turkey meat, black pepper, salt, and stock, and cook for 20 minutes. Stir in the zucchini, and cook turkey soup for 5 minutes. Serve in bowls sprinkled with parsley.

Nutritional info per serving: Calories 312, Fat 13g, Net Carbs 4.3g, Protein 16.3g

Vegan Coconut Green Soup
Prep + Cook Time: 30 minutes | Serves: 2-4

Ingredients

1 broccoli head, chopped
1 cup spinach
1 onion, chopped
1 garlic clove, minced
½ cup leeks
3 cups vegetable stock

½ cup coconut milk
2 tbsp coconut oil
1 bay leaf
Salt and black pepper, to taste
2 tbsp coconut yogurt

Directions

Warm coconut oil in a large pot over medium heat. Add onion, leeks, and garlic and cook for 5 minutes. Add broccoli and cook for an additional 5 minutes. Pour in the stock over and add the bay leaf. Close the lid, bring to a boil and reduce the heat. Simmer for about 10 minutes.

Add spinach and cook for 3 more minutes. Discard the bay leaf and blend the soup with a hand blender. Stir in the coconut cream, salt and black pepper. Divide among serving bowls and garnish with a swirl of coconut yogurt.

Nutritional info per serving: Calories 272, Fat: 24.5g, Net Carbs: 4.3g, Protein: 4.5g

Cauliflower Cheese Soup
Prep + Cook Time: 20 minutes | Serves: 2-4

Ingredients

½ head cauliflower, chopped
2 tbsp coconut oil
½ cup leeks, chopped
1 celery stalk, chopped
1 serrano pepper, finely chopped
1 tsp garlic puree

1 ½ tbsp flax seed meal
2 cups water
1 ½ cups coconut milk
6 ounces Monterey Jack cheese, shredded
Salt and black pepper, to taste
Fresh parsley, chopped

Directions

In a deep pan over medium heat, melt the coconut oil and sauté the serrano pepper, celery and leeks until soft, for about 5 minutes. Add in coconut milk, garlic puree, cauliflower, water and flax seed.

While covered partially, allow simmering for 10 minutes or until cooked through. Whizz with a immersion blender until smooth. Fold in the shredded cheese, and stir to ensure the cheese is completely melted and you have a homogenous mixture. Season with pepper and salt to taste.

Divide among serving bowls, decorate with parsley and serve while warm.

Nutritional info per serving: Calories 312; Fat 16g, Net Carbs 7.1g, Protein 13.8g

Sauerkraut & Corned Beef Soup

Prep + Cook Time: 20 minutes | Serves: 2-4

Ingredients

1 parsnip, chopped
1 onion, diced
3 cups beef stock
1 celery stalk, diced
1 garlic clove, minced
1 cup heavy cream

½ cup sauerkraut, shredded
½ pound corned beef, chopped
2 tbsp lard
½ cup mozzarella cheese, shredded
Salt and black pepper, to taste
Chopped chives for garnish

Directions

Melt the lard in a large pot. Add parsnip, onion, garlic, and celery, and fry for 3 minutes until tender.

Pour the beef stock over and stir in sauerkraut, salt, and black pepper. Bring to a boil. Reduce the heat to low, and add the corned beef. Cook for about 15 minutes, adjust the seasoning. Stir in heavy cream and cheese and cook for 1 minute. Garnish with chives to serve.

Nutritional info per serving: Calories 463, Fat: 41.3g, Net Carbs: 5.8g, Protein: 21.2g

Crockpot Sausage & Cheese Beer Soup

Prep + Cook Time: 8 hr | Serves: 2-4

Ingredients

2 tbsp butter
½ cup celery, chopped
½ cup heavy cream
5 oz turkey sausage, sliced
1 small carrot, chopped
2 garlic cloves, minced
4 ounces cream cheese

½ tsp red pepper flakes
1 cup beer of choice
3 cups beef stock
1 yellow onion, diced
1 cup cheddar cheese, grated
Kosher salt and black pepper, to taste
Fresh parsley, chopped, to garnish

Directions

To the crockpot, add butter, beef stock, beer, turkey sausage, carrot, onion, garlic, celery, salt, red pepper flakes, and black pepper, and stir to combine. Close the lid and cook for 6 hours on Low.

Open the lid and stir in the heavy cream, cheddar and cream cheese, and cook for 2 more hours. Ladle the soup into bowls and garnish with parsley before serving.

Nutritional info per serving: Calories 543, Fat: 44g, Net Carbs: 9.3g, Protein: 22.5g

Hearty Vegetable Soup

Prep + Cook Time: 25 minutes | Serves: 2-4

Ingredients

2 tsp olive oil
1 onion, chopped
1 garlic clove, minced
½ celery stalk, chopped

1 cup mushrooms, sliced
½ head broccoli, chopped
½ carrot, sliced
1 cup spinach, torn into pieces

Salt and black pepper, to taste
2 thyme sprigs, chopped
3 cups vegetable stock

1 tomato, chopped
½ cup almond milk

Directions

Heat olive oil in a saucepan. Add onion, celery, garlic, and carrot; sauté until translucent, stirring occasionally, about 5 minutes.

Place in spinach, mushrooms, salt, rosemary, tomatoes, bay leaves, black pepper, thyme, and vegetable stock. Simmer the mixture for 15 minutes while the lid is slightly open.

Stir in almond milk and cook for 5 more minutes.

Nutritional info per serving: Calories 167; Fat: 6.2g, Net Carbs: 7.9g, Protein: 3.2g

Zuppa Toscana with Kale

Ready in about: 30 minutes | Serves: 2-4

Ingredients

2 cups chicken broth
1 tbsp olive oil
¼ cup heavy cream
1 cup kale
3 oz pancetta, chopped
1 parsnip, chopped

1 garlic clove, minced
Salt and black pepper, to taste
¼ tsp red pepper flakes
½ onion, chopped
1 pound hot Italian sausage, chopped
2 tbsp Parmesan cheese, grated

Directions

In a pan, cook garlic, onion, pancetta, and sausage in warm olive oil over medium heat for 5 minutes. Pour in chicken broth and parsnip and simmer for 15-20 minutes. Stir in the remaining ingredients, except for the Parmesan cheese, and cook for about 5 minutes. Serve topped with Parmesan cheese.

Nutritional info per serving: Calories 543, Fat 44.9g, Net Carbs 5.6g, Protein 24g

Almond Parsnip Soup with Sour Cream

Prep + Cook Time: 25 minutes | Serves: 2-4

Ingredients

1 tbsp olive oil
1 cup onion, chopped
1 celery, chopped
2 cloves garlic, minced
2 turnips, peeled and chopped
4 cups vegetable broth

Salt and white pepper, to taste
¼ cup ground almonds
1 cup almond milk
1 tbsp fresh cilantro, chopped
4 tsp sour cream

Directions

Warm the oil in a pot over medium heat and sauté celery, garlic, and onion for 6 minutes. Stir in white pepper, broth, salt, and ground almonds. Boil the mixture.

Bring to the boil and simmer for 15 minutes. Transfer the soup to an immersion blender and puree. Serve garnished with sour cream and cilantro.

Nutritional info per serving: Calories 125; Fat: 7.1g, Net Carbs: 7.7g, Protein: 4g

Cream of Cauliflower & Leek Soup

Prep + Cook Time: 20 minutes | Serves: 2-4

Ingredients

4 cups vegetable broth
2 heads cauliflower, cut into florets
1 celery stalk, chopped
1 onion, chopped
1 cup leeks, chopped

2 tbsp butter
1 tbsp olive oil
1 cup heavy cream
½ tsp red pepper flakes

Directions

Warm butter and olive oil in a pot set over medium heat and sauté onion, leeks, and celery for 5 minutes. Stir in vegetable broth and cauliflower and bring to a boil; simmer for 30 minutes. Transfer the mixture to an immersion blender and puree; add in the heavy cream and stir.

Decorate with red pepper flakes to serve.

Nutritional info per serving: Calories 255; Fat: 21g, Net Carbs: 5.3g, Protein: 4.4g

Creamy Coconut Soup with Chicken & Celery

Prep + Cook Time: 25 minutes | Serves: 2-4

Ingredients

3 tbsp butter
1 onion, chopped
2 chicken breasts, chopped

Salt and black pepper, to taste
½ cup coconut cream
¼ cup celery, chopped

Directions

Warm butter in a pot over medium heat. Sauté the onion and celery for 3 minutes. Stir in chicken, 4 cups of water, salt and pepper, and simmer for 15 minutes. Pour in the coconut cream and stir.

Nutritional info per serving: Calories 394, Fat 24.2g, Net Carbs 6.1g, Protein 29.5g

Fresh Avocado-Cucumber Soup

Prep + Cook Time: 10 minutes + chilling time | Serves: 2-4

Ingredients

3 tbsp olive oil
1 small onion, chopped
4 large cucumbers, seeded, chopped
1 large avocado, peeled and pitted
Salt and black pepper to taste
1 ½ cups water

½ cup Greek yogurt
1 tbsp cilantro, chopped
2 limes, juiced
1 garlic clove, minced
2 tomatoes, chopped
1 chopped avocado for garnish

Directions

Pour all the ingredient, except for the tomatoes and avocado in the food processor. Puree the ingredients for 2 minutes or until smooth. Pour the mixture into a bowl. Cover and refrigerate for 2 hours. Top with avocado and tomatoes.

Nutritional info per serving: Calories 343, Fat 26.4g, Net Carbs 5.3g, Protein 10g

LUNCH & DINNER

Anchovy Caprese Pizza

Prep + Cook Time: 15 minutes | Serves: 2

Ingredients

For the Crust:

4 eggs
¼ cup buttermilk
2 tbsp flax seed meal
1 tsp chipotle pepper

¼ tsp fennel seeds, ground
Salt to taste
1 tbsp olive oil

For the Topping:

2 tbsp tomato paste
4 basil leaves
1 ball (8-oz) fresh mozzarella, sliced

2 tomatoes, sliced
2 ounces mozzarella cheese, shredded
2 anchovies, chopped

Directions

In a bowl, whisk the eggs, and add in buttermilk, flax seed, fennel seeds, chipotle pepper and salt.

Set a pan over medium heat and warm ½ tablespoon of oil. Ladle ½ of crust mixture into the pan and evenly spread out. Cook until the edges are set; then, flip the crust and cook on the other side.

Warm the remaining ½ tablespoon of oil in the pan. Do the same process with another pizza crust. Top with fresh mozzarella and tomato slices. In batches, bake in the oven for 8-10 minutes at 430 F until all the cheese melts. Garnish with anchovies and serve.

Nutritional info per serving: Calories 465, Fat: 31g, Net Carbs: 5.1g, Protein: 32g

Chorizo & Cheese Frittata

Prep + Cook Time: 25 minutes | Serves: 2

Ingredients

4 eggs
Salt and black pepper, to taste
1 chorizo sausage, sliced
1 tbsp butter
1 green onion, chopped

½ red bell pepper, crumbled
1 tsp chipotle paste
½ cup kale
¼ cup cotija cheese, shredded

Directions

Whisk the eggs with a fork in a bowl, and season with black pepper and salt. Warm butter in a skillet over medium heat. Sauté onion until soft. Add in chorizo sausage, chipotle paste, and bell pepper, and cook for 5-7 minutes. Place in kale and cook for 2 minutes. Add in the eggs.

Spread the mixture evenly over the skillet and set to the oven. Bake for 8 minutes at 370 F or until the top is set and golden. Scatter crumbled cotija cheese over and bake for 3 more minutes or until the cheese melts completely. Slice and serve while still warm.

Nutritional info per serving: Calories: 288; Fat 21g, Net Carbs 5.3g, Protein 17.2g

Ricotta Balls with Fresh Salad

Prep + Cook Time: 20 minutes | Serves: 2

Ingredients

Cheese balls

1 egg
1/3 cup ricotta cheese, crumbled
2 tbsp Grana Padano cheese, shredded

1/3 cup almond flour
1/3 tsp flax meal
Salt and black pepper, to taste

Salad:

2 cups arugula leaves
1 small cucumber, thinly sliced
1 tomato, sliced
1 green onion, sliced
4 radishes, sliced

2 tbsp mayonnaise
½ tsp mustard
1 tsp lemon juice
Salt, to taste

Directions

In a mixing dish, combine ricotta cheese, Grana Padano cheese, flax meal and almond flour. Add in the egg, salt and black pepper, and stir well. Form balls out of the mixture. Set the balls on a parchment-lined baking sheet and bake for 10 minutes at 380 F.

Lay arugula leaves on a large salad platter; add in radishes, tomato, cucumber, and green onion. In a small bowl, mix the mayonnaise, salt, lemon juice and mustard. Sprinkle this mixture over the vegetables. Add cheese balls on top and serve.

Nutritional info per serving: Calories: 255; Fat 18.7g, Net Carbs 3.9g, Protein 13.4g

Zucchini & Eggplant Steaks with Salad

Prep + Cook Time: 35 minutes | Serves: 2

Ingredients

1 eggplant, sliced
1 zucchini, sliced
¼ cup coconut oil
Juice of ½ a lemon
5 oz cheddar cheese, cut into small cubes
10 kalamata olives

2 tbsp pecans
1 oz arugula
½ cup mayonnaise
Salt to taste
½ tsp Cayenne pepper

Directions

Place the veggie slices in a colander and sprinkle with salt. Allow sitting for 10 minutes to let out the liquid.

Set the oven to broil and line a baking sheet with parchment paper. Pat the vegetable slices dry with a paper towel and arrange on the baking sheet. Brush with coconut oil and sprinkle with cayenne pepper.

Broil until golden brown on both sides, about 15 to 20 minutes. Remove to a serving platter and drizzle with the lemon juice. Arrange the cheddar cheese, kalamata olives, pecans, and arugula by the grilled veggies. Top with mayonnaise and serve.

Nutritional info per serving: Calories: 487; Fat: 32.3g; Net Carbs: 6.7g; Protein: 19.3g

Kale & Cheese Stuffed Zucchini

Prep + Cook Time: 40 minutes | Serves: 2

Ingredients

1 zucchini, halved
4 tbsp butter
2 garlic cloves, minced
1 ½ oz baby kale

Salt and black pepper to taste
2 tbsp unsweetened tomato sauce
1 cup mozzarella cheese, shredded
Olive oil for drizzling

Directions

Preheat oven to 375 F. Scoop out the pulp of the zucchini with a spoon into a plate; keep the flesh.

Grease a baking sheet with cooking spray and place the zucchini halves on top. Put the butter in a skillet and melt over medium heat. Add and sauté the garlic until fragrant and slightly browned, about 4 minutes.

Add the kale and the zucchini pulp. Cook until the kale wilts; season with salt and black pepper.

Spoon the tomato sauce into the zucchini halves and spread to coat the bottom evenly. Spoon the kale mixture into the zucchinis and sprinkle with the mozzarella cheese.

Bake in the oven for 20 to 25 minutes or until the cheese has a beautiful golden color. Plate the zucchinis when ready, drizzle with olive oil, and season with salt and black pepper.

Nutritional info per serving: Calories: 345; Fat: 24.5g; Net Carbs: 6.9g; Protein: 20.6g

Herbed Cheese Sticks with Yogurt Dip

Prep + Cook Time: 40 minutes | Serves: 2

Ingredients

8 ounces mozzarella cheese, cut into sticks
¼ cup Parmesan cheese, grated
1 tbsp almond flour
1/3 tbsp flax meal
1/3 tsp cumin powder

½ tsp dried oregano
1/3 tsp dried rosemary
1 egg
1 tbsp olive oil

Yogurt dip

1/3 cup natural yogurt
1 garlic clove
1 tsp mint, chopped

1 tbsp parsley, chopped
Sea salt to taste

Directions

In a bowl, mix the almond flour, flax meal, cumin powder, oregano, and rosemary. In a separate bowl, whisk the egg with a fork. Dip in each cheese stick into the egg, then roll in the dry mixture.

Set cheese sticks on a wax paper-lined baking sheet; freeze for 30 minutes. In a skillet over medium heat warm oil and fry cheese sticks for 5 minutes until the coating is golden brown and crisp. Set on paper towels to drain excess oil.

Mash the garlic and salt to taste into a pestle and add to the yogurt. Stir in olive oil, parsley and mint. Spread into a serving bowl and serve with the cheese sticks.

Nutritional info per serving: Calories: 354; Fat 15.9g, Net Carbs 3.7g, Protein 44.4g

Feta & Cabbage Stir-Fry

Prep + Cook Time: 45 minutes | Serves: 2

Ingredients

5 oz butter
2 ½ cups baby bok choy, quartered lengthwise
2 cups feta cheese, crumbled
Salt and black pepper to taste
1 tsp garlic powder
1 tsp onion powder

1 tbsp plain vinegar
2 garlic cloves, minced
1 tsp chili flakes
3 green onions, sliced
1 tbsp sesame oil

Directions

Melt half of the butter in a wok over medium heat, add the bok choy and stir-fry until softened.

Season with the salt, black pepper, garlic powder, onion powder, and plain vinegar. Sauté for 2 minutes and then, spoon the bok choy into a bowl; set aside.

Melt the remaining butter in the wok, add and sauté the garlic and chili flakes until fragrant. Add the green onions, feta, and bok choy, heat for 2 minutes and add the sesame oil. Serve with steamed cauli rice.

Nutritional info per serving: Calories: 641; Fat: 53g; Net Carbs: 7.8g; Protein: 31g

Awesome Beef Cheeseburgers

Prep + Cook Time: 20 minutes | Serves: 2

Ingredients

½ pound ground beef
1 spring onion, chopped
Salt, black and cayenne pepper, to taste
1 tsp yellow mustard

1 oz cheddar cheese, grated
1 tbsp olive oil
2 sprigs parsley, chopped

Directions

To a mixing bowl, add ground beef, cayenne pepper, black pepper, spring onion, parsley, and salt. Shape into 2 balls; then flatten to make burgers.

In a separate bowl, mix mustard with cheddar cheese. Split the cheese mixture between the prepared patties. Wrap the meat mixture around the cheese to ensure that the filling is sealed inside. Warm oil in a skillet over medium heat. Cook the burgers for 5 minutes on each side.

Nutritional info per serving: Calories 386; Fat: 25.5g, Net Carbs: 1.3g, Protein: 31.6g

Greek Stuffed Tomato with Cheese and Basil

Prep + Cook Time: 35 minutes | Serves: 2

Ingredients

2 tomatoes
¼ cup feta cheese, crumbled
¼ cup Greek yogurt
1 egg

1 clove garlic, minced
2 tbsp fresh dill, chopped
Salt and black pepper, to taste
2 tbsp butter, softened

Directions

Slice off top of tomatoes and scoop out pulp and seeds; reserve the tomato tops. In a bowl, mix egg, salt, butter, black pepper, chopped tomato pulp, garlic, Greek yogurt, feta, and dill.

Split the filling between tomatoes, cover each one with a tomato top and place in a greased baking dish. Bake in the oven for 30 minutes at 390 F. Place on a wire rack and allow to cool for 5 minutes; serve along with fresh rocket leaves.

Nutritional info per serving: Calories 293; Fat: 23.5g, Net Carbs: 5.1g, Protein: 12.3g

Baked Chicken Wrapped in Smoked Bacon

Prep + Cook Time: 35 minutes | Serves: 2

Ingredients

1 pound chicken breasts, flatten
1 tbsp olive oil
1 tbsp fresh parsley, chopped
1 tsp garlic paste, chopped

½ tsp sage
Salt and black pepper, to taste
½ tsp smoked paprika
2 oz smoked bacon, sliced

Directions

Mix garlic paste, sage, smoked paprika, salt, and black pepper in a small bowl; rub onto chicken and roll fillets in the smoked bacon slices.

Arrange on a greased with the olive oil baking dish, and bake for 30 minutes at 390 F. Plate the chicken and serve sprinkled with fresh parsley.

Nutritional info per serving: Calories 556, Fat: 38.5g, Net Carbs: 2.3g, Protein: 51.5g

Eggplant Pizza with Tofu

Prep + Cook Time: 45 minutes | Serves: 2

Ingredients

2 eggplants, sliced
1/3 cup butter, melted
2 garlic cloves, minced
1 red onion
12 oz tofu, chopped

7 oz tomato sauce
Salt and black pepper to taste
½ tsp cinnamon powder
1 cup Parmesan cheese, shredded
¼ cup dried oregano

Directions

Preheat oven to 400 F and line a baking sheet with parchment paper. Lay the eggplant slices in a baking sheet and brush with some butter. Bake in the oven until lightly browned, about 20 minutes.

Heat the remaining butter in a skillet and sauté the garlic and onion until fragrant and soft, about 3 minutes.

Stir in the tofu and cook for 3 minutes. Add the tomato sauce and season with salt and black pepper. Simmer for 10 minutes. Remove the eggplant from the oven and spread the tofu sauce on top.

Sprinkle with the Parmesan cheese and oregano. Bake further for 10 minutes or until the cheese has melted.

Nutritional info per serving: Calories: 657; Fat: 56.5g; Net Carbs: 11.5g; Protein: 24.5g

Vegan Caprese Gratin

Prep + Cook Time: 25 minutes | Serves: 2

Ingredients

2 tbsp olive oil
1 cup watercress
½ cup cherry tomatoes, halved
½ cup vegan mozzarella cheese, cut into pieces

1 tbsp basil pesto
½ cup vegan mayonnaise
1 oz vegan Parmesan cheese, shredded
Salt and black pepper to taste

Directions

Preheat the oven to 350 F.

In a baking dish, mix the cherry tomatoes, vegan mozzarella, basil pesto, vegan mayonnaise, half of the vegan Parmesan cheese, salt, and black pepper.

Level the ingredients with a spatula and sprinkle the remaining vegan Parmesan cheese on top. Bake for 20 minutes or until the top is golden brown. Remove and allow cooling for a few minutes. Slice and dish into plates, top with some watercress and drizzle with olive oil.

Nutritional info per serving: Calories: 450; Fat: 41g; Net Carbs: 5g; Protein: 12g

Pepperoni & Mixed Mushroom White Pizza

Prep + Cook Time: 35 minutes | Serves: 2

Ingredients

2 (1 pack) cauliflower pizza crusts
2 oz mixed mushrooms, sliced
1 tbsp basil pesto
2 tbsp olive oil

Salt and black pepper to taste
¾ cup mozzarella cheese, shredded
4 oz pepperoni, sliced

Directions

Preheat the oven to 350 F. Grease two baking dishes with cooking spray. Add in the two cauli crusts.

In a bowl, mix the mushrooms with the pesto, olive oil, salt, and black pepper.

Divide the mozzarella cheese on top of the pizza crusts. Spread the mushroom mixture and cover with the pepperoni slices. Bake the pizzas in batches until the cheese has melted, about 5 to 10 minutes.

Remove when ready, slice, and serve with baby spinach salad.

Nutritional info per serving: Calories: 512; Fat: 41.3g; Net Carbs: 4.6g; Protein: 27.5g

Spiced Halloumi with Brussels Sprouts

Prep + Cook Time: 55 minutes | Serves: 2-4

Ingredients

10 oz halloumi cheese, sliced
1 tbsp coconut oil
½ cup unsweetened coconut, shredded
1 tsp chili powder
½ tsp onion powder

½ pound Brussels sprouts, shredded
4 oz butter
Salt and black pepper to taste
Lemon wedges for serving

Directions

In a bowl, mix the shredded coconut, chili powder, salt, coconut oil and onion powder. Then, toss the halloumi slices in the spice mixture.

Heat a grill pan over medium heat and cook the coated halloumi cheese for 2-3 minutes. Transfer to a plate to keep warm. In a skillet, melt half of the butter, add, and sauté the Brussels sprouts until slightly caramelized. Then, season with salt and black pepper.

Dish the Brussels sprouts into serving plates with the halloumi cheese and lemon wedges. Melt the remaining butter in the skillet and drizzle over the Brussels sprouts and halloumi cheese. Serve immediately.

Nutritional info per serving: Calories: 574; Fat: 43.5g; Net Carbs: 4.2g; Protein: 29.5g

Habanero Coconut Pie

Prep + Cook Time: 80 minutes | Serves: 2-4

Ingredients

Filling

2 ripe avocados, peeled and chopped
1 cup mayonnaise
3 tbsp flax seed powder + 9 tbsp water
2 tbsp fresh parsley, chopped
1 habanero pepper, finely chopped

½ tsp onion powder
¼ tsp salt
½ cup ricotta cheese
1 ¼ cups Parmesan cheese, shredded

Piecrust

1 tbsp flax seed powder + 3 tbsp water
4 tbsp coconut flour
4 tbsp chia seeds
¾ cup almond flour
1 tbsp psyllium husk powder

1 tsp baking powder
1 pinch salt
3 tbsp coconut oil
4 tbsp water

Directions

Preheat the oven to 350 F.

In 2 separate bowls, mix the different portions of flax seed powder with the respective quantity of water. Allow absorbing for 5 minutes.

In a food processor, add the coconut flour, chia seeds, almond flour, psyllium husk powder, baking powder, salt, coconut oil, water, and the smaller portion of the flax egg. Blend the ingredients until the dough forms into a ball.

Line a springform pan with about 12-inch diameter of parchment paper and spread the dough in the pan. Bake for 10 to 15 minutes or until a light golden brown color is achieved.

Put the avocado in a bowl and add the mayonnaise, remaining flax egg, parsley, habanero pepper, onion powder, salt, ricotta and Parmesan cheeses. Combine well.

Remove the piecrust when ready and fill with the creamy mixture. Level the filling with a spatula and continue baking for 35 minutes or until lightly golden brown. Let cool before slicing and serving with a baby spinach salad.

Nutritional info per serving: Calories: 672; Fat: 61.3g; Net Carbs: 8.3g; Protein: 21.5g

Camembert & Chili Bacon Balls

Prep + Cook Time: 15 minutes | Serves: 2

Ingredients

1 cup bacon, finely chopped
5 oz camembert cheese, cubed
1 chili pepper, seeded and chopped

¼ tsp parsley flakes
½ tsp paprika

Directions

Fry the bacon in a pan over medium heat until crispy; about 5 minutes. Let cool for a few minutes.

Place the camembert cheese, chili pepper, parsley, and paprika in a bowl and mix to combine well. Create balls from the mixture. Set the cooled bacon in a plate. Roll the balls around to coat all sides.

Nutritional info per serving: Calories 456; Fat: 39.5g, Net Carbs: 3.6g, Protein: 22.4g

Bacon & Cauliflower Cheesy Bake

Prep + Cook Time: 15 minutes | Serves: 2-4

Ingredients

1 head cauliflower, broken into florets
1 tbsp butter
½ pound bacon, cut into strips
¼ cup buttermilk

¾ cup heavy cream
1 garlic clove, minced
½ cup mozzarella cheese, crumbled
1 tbsp fresh rosemary, chopped

Directions

Preheat oven to 350 F. Boil cauliflower in saucepan until tender, about 7-8 minutes. Drain and pour in a baking pan.

Set a frying pan over medium heat and melt the butter, brown the bacon for 3 minutes and set aside. Add in the heavy cream, garlic and buttermilk, and cook until warmed fully. Take the reserved bacon back to the pan. Fold in mozzarella cheese and stir well. Pour the sauce over the cauliflower and insert in the oven. Bake for 20 minutes until the top is golden. Serve sprinkled with rosemary.

Nutritional info per serving: Calories 355, Fat: 28g, Net Carbs: 6.5g, Protein: 16g

Mushroom & Zucchini with Spinach Dip

Prep + Cook Time: 20 minutes | Serves: 2-4

Ingredients

Spinach Dip

3 oz spinach, chopped
1 ripe avocado, halved and pitted
2 tbsp fresh lemon juice
1 garlic clove, minced

2 oz pecans
Salt and black pepper to taste
¾ cup olive oil

Zucchini

2 zucchinis, sliced
Salt and black pepper to taste
2 tbsp butter, melted

½ pound mushrooms, sliced
2 tbsp olive oil

Directions

Place the spinach in a food processor along with the avocado pulp, lemon juice, garlic, and pecans. Blend the ingredients until smooth and then, season with salt and black pepper. Add the olive oil and process a little more.

Pour the pesto into a bowl and set aside. Place the zucchinis and mushrooms in a bowl. Season with salt, black pepper and the olive oil.

Preheat a grill pan over medium heat and cook both the mushroom and zucchini slices until browned on both sides. Plate the veggies and serve with spinach dip.

Nutritional info per serving: Calories: 683; Fat: 72g; Net Carbs: 5.5g; Protein: 5.3g

Chargrilled Halloumi with Avocado & Eggs

Prep + Cook Time: 20 minutes | Serves: 2-4

Ingredients

8 oz halloumi cheese, sliced
4 tsp olive oil
6 eggs, beaten
Sea salt to taste

¼ tsp red pepper flakes, crushed
1 avocado, pitted and sliced
10 cherry tomatoes, halved
4 tbsp pine nuts, toasted

Directions

Preheat your grill to medium. Drizzle the halloumi slices with some olive oil. Grill for 3 minutes each side until charred.

In a frying pan, warm 1 tablespoon of oil and cook the eggs. Stir well to create large and soft curds. Season with salt and red pepper flakes. Put the eggs and grilled cheese on a serving bowl. Serve alongside tomatoes and avocado, decorated with pine nuts.

Nutritional info per serving: Calories 553; Fat: 44g, Net Carbs: 7.2g, Protein: 27g

Bacon & Brussels Sprouts Bake

Prep + Cook Time: 25 minutes | Serves: 2-4

Ingredients

3 tbsp butter
1 cup bacon, chopped
1 ½ lb halved Brussels sprouts
5 garlic cloves, minced

1 ¼ cups heavy cream
1 ¼ cups cheddar cheese, shredded
¼ cup Parmesan cheese, shredded
Salt and black pepper to taste

Directions

Preheat the oven to 400 F. Melt the butter in a large skillet over medium heat and fry the bacon until crispy, about 5 minutes. Remove onto a plate and set aside. Pour the Brussels sprouts and garlic into the skillet and sauté until fragrant and slightly golden.

Mix in heavy cream and simmer for 4 minutes. Add bacon and combine well. Pour the sauté into a baking dish, and sprinkle with cheddar and Parmesan cheeses. Bake for 10 minutes or until golden brown on top. Serve with tomato salad.

Nutritional info per serving: Calories: 587; Fat: 51g; Net Carbs: 9.5g; Protein: 23g

Feta & Baby Spinach Lasagna

Prep + Cook Time: 65 minutes | Serves: 2-4

Ingredients

2 tbsp butter
1 onion, chopped
1 garlic clove, minced
2 ½ cups feta, crumbled
3 tbsp tomato paste

½ tbsp dried oregano
Salt and black pepper to taste
½ cup water
1 cup baby spinach

Keto pasta

Flax egg: 8 tbsp flax seed powder + 1 ½ cups water
1 ½ cups cream cheese

1 tsp salt
5 tbsp psyllium husk powder

Cheese topping

2 cups heavy cream
5 oz mozzarella cheese, shredded
2 oz Parmesan cheese, grated

Salt and black pepper
½ cup fresh parsley, chopped

Directions

Melt the butter in a pot over medium heat. Add in the onion and garlic, and sauté until fragrant and soft, about 3 minutes. Mix in the tomato paste, oregano, salt, and black pepper.

Pour the water into the pot, stir, and simmer the ingredients until most of the liquid has evaporated.

While cooking the sauce, make the lasagna sheets. Preheat the oven to 300 F and mix the flax seed powder with the water in a medium bowl to make flax egg. Allow sitting to thicken for 5 minutes.

Combine the flax egg with the cream cheese and salt. Add the psyllium husk powder a bit at a time while whisking and allow the mixture to sit for a few more minutes.

Line a baking sheet with parchment paper and spread the mixture in. Cover with another parchment paper and use a rolling pin to flatten the dough into the sheet. Bake the batter in the oven for 10 to 12 minutes, remove after, take off the parchment papers, and slice the pasta into sheets that fit your baking dish.

In a bowl, combine the heavy cream and two-thirds of the mozzarella cheese. Fetch out 2 tablespoons of the mixture and reserve. Mix in the Parmesan cheese, salt, black pepper, and parsley. Set aside.

Grease a baking dish with cooking spray and lay in one-third of the pasta sheet; spread half of the tomato paste on top, add another one-third set of the pasta sheets, the remaining tomato paste and the rest of the pasta sheets.

Grease a baking dish with cooking spray, layer a single line of pasta, spread with some tomato sauce, 1/3 of the spinach, 1/3 of the feta cheese, and ¼ of the heavy cream mixture. Season with salt and pepper.

Repeat layering the ingredients twice in the same manner making sure to top the final layer with the heavy cream mixture and the reserved cream cheese.

Bake in the oven for 30 minutes at 400 F or until the lasagna has a beautiful brown surface. Remove the dish; allow cooling for a few minutes, and slice. Serve the lasagna with a green salad.

Nutritional info per serving: Calories: 732; Fat: 59.6g; Net Carbs: 8.3g; Protein: 43.2g

Chicken Balls with Spaghetti Squash

Prep + Cook Time: 65 minutes | Serves: 2-4

Ingredients

1 pound butternut squash, halved
½ pound ground chicken
Salt and black pepper to taste
½ cup pork rinds, crushed
1 garlic clove, minced
1 shallot, chopped
1 stalk celery, chopped
2 tbsp parsley, chopped

3 tbsp olive oil
1 red bell pepper, sliced
1 egg
1 cup sugar-free tomato sauce
1 tsp dried oregano
½ cup + 2 tbsp Pecorino cheese, grated
Grated Parmesan cheese for garnishing

Directions

Preheat the oven to 450 F. Scoop the seeds out of the squash halves with a spoon. Sprinkle with salt and brush with 1 tbsp of olive oil.

Place in a baking dish and roast for 30 minutes. Scrape the pulp into strands. Remove the spaghetti strands to a bowl and toss with 2 tbsp of pecorino cheese. Put the ground chicken in a bowl; pour in garlic, shallot, pork rinds, egg, and a ½ cup of Pecorino cheese; mix well. Mold out meatballs from the mixture and place them on a baking sheet. Bake the meatballs for just 10 minutes, but not done.

Place a pot over medium heat and warm the remaining olive oil. Stir in the tomato sauce, celery, red bell pepper, and salt to taste. Let the sauce cook on low-medium heat for 5 minutes, remove, and add in the meatballs. Continue cooking for 15 minutes. Spoon the meatballs with sauce over the spaghetti, sprinkle with Parmesan cheese and parsley to serve.

Nutritional info per serving: Calories 424, Fat 28g, Net Carbs 7.2g, Protein 21g

Zucchini Balls with Bacon & Capers

Prep + Cook Time: 3 hours 20 minutes | Serves: 2-4

Ingredients

2 zucchinis, shredded
2 bacon slices, chopped
½ cup cream cheese, at room temperature
1 cup fontina cheese
¼ cup capers
1 clove garlic, crushed

½ cup grated Parmesan cheese
½ tsp poppy seeds
¼ tsp dried dill weed
½ tsp onion powder
Salt and black pepper, to taste
1 cup crushed pork rinds

Directions

Preheat oven to 360 F.

Thoroughly mix zucchinis, capers, ½ of Parmesan cheese, garlic, cream cheese, bacon, and fontina cheese until well combined. Shape the mixture into balls. Refrigerate for 3 hours.

In a mixing bowl, mix the remaining Parmesan cheese, crushed pork rinds, dill, black pepper, onion powder, poppy seeds, and salt. Roll cheese ball in Parmesan mixture to coat. Arrange in a greased baking dish in a single layer and bake in the oven for 15-20 minutes, shaking once.

Nutritional info per serving: Calories 398; Fat: 25g, Net Carbs: 6.2g, Protein: 31g

Gorgonzola & Ricotta Stuffed Red Peppers

Prep + Cook Time: 45 minutes | Serves: 2-4

Ingredients

2 tbsp olive oil
4 red bell peppers, halved and seeded
1 cup ricotta cheese
½ cup gorgonzola cheese, crumbled
2 cloves garlic, minced

1 ½ cups tomatoes, chopped
1 tsp dried basil
Salt and black pepper, to taste
½ tsp oregano

Directions

Preheat oven to 350 F and lightly grease the sides and bottom of a baking dish with cooking spray.

In a bowl, mix garlic, tomatoes, gorgonzola and ricotta cheeses. Stuff the pepper halves and remove to the baking dish. Season with oregano, salt, cayenne pepper, black pepper and basil. Drizzle with olive oil and bake for 40 minutes until the peppers are tender.

Nutritional info per serving: Calories 541; Fat: 42.7g, Net Carbs: 7.3g, Protein: 25.7g

Sausage & Cauliflower Bake

Prep + Cook Time: 35 minutes | Serves: 2-4

Ingredients

1 pound pork sausage, sliced
2 oz butter
1 onion, chopped
½ cup celery stalks, finely chopped
1 green bell pepper, chopped

Salt and black pepper
1 small head cauliflower, cut into florets
1 cup mayonnaise
4 oz Parmesan cheese, shredded
1 tsp red chili flakes

Directions

Preheat the oven to 400 F and grease a baking dish with cooking spray.

In a pan over medium heat, warm butter, and cook onion, celery, and bell pepper for 5 minutes until tender. Add in the sausage and continue cooking for 4-5 minutes. Season with salt and pepper.

In a bowl, mix the cauliflower, mayonnaise, Parmesan cheese, and red chili flakes. Pour the mixture into the baking dish, add the sausage mixture, and mix to be evenly distributed. Bake in the oven until golden brown, about 20 minutes; serve warm.

Nutritional info per serving: Calories: 611; Fat: 47.3g; Net Carbs: 7.4g; Protein: 31.5g

Baked Sausage with Roasted Peppers & Fresh Salad

Prep + Cook Time: 25 minutes | Serves: 2-4

Ingredients

1 cucumber, sliced
1 large tomato, chopped
Salt and black pepper to taste
2 tsp dried parsley
2 red bell peppers

1 pound sausages, sliced
1 tbsp butter, melted
1 tsp dried basil
1 tbsp mayonnaise
2 tbsp Greek yogurt

Directions

Preheat the oven's broiler to 420 F and line a baking sheet with parchment paper.

Arrange the bell peppers and sausages on the baking sheet, drizzle with the melted butter, and season with basil, salt, and black pepper. Bake in the oven for 20 minutes.

Meanwhile, in a salad bowl, combine the Greek yogurt, mayonnaise, cucumber, tomato, salt, black pepper and parsley; set aside.

When the bake is ready, remove from the oven and serve with the salad.

Nutritional info per serving: Calories: 623; Fat: 48.5g; Net Carbs: 6.3g; Protein: 32.2g

Butternut Squash Bolognese

Prep + Cook Time: 45 minutes | Serves: 2-4

Ingredients

Bolognese

2 tbsp olive oil
1 onion, chopped
1 garlic clove, minced
1 small carrot, chopped
½ pound ground beef
2 tbsp tomato paste

1 ½ cups tomatoes, crushed
1 tbsp dried basil
12 oz butternut squash
2 tbsp butter
Salt and black pepper to taste

Directions

Pour the olive oil into a saucepan and heat over medium heat. Add in the onion, garlic and carrot. Sauté for 3 minutes or until the onion is soft and the carrot caramelized.

Pour in the ground beef, tomato paste, tomatoes, salt, black pepper and basil. Stir and cook for 15 minutes, or simmer for 30 minutes. Mix in some water if the mixture is too thick and simmer further for 20 minutes.

Melt the butter in a skillet over medium heat and toss the butternut squash quickly in the butter, for about 1 minute only. Season with salt and black pepper. Divide the butternut squash into serving plates and spoon the sauce on top. Serve the dish immediately.

Nutritional info per serving: Calories: 335; Fat: 23.5g; Net Carbs: 9.5g; Protein: 16.5g

Avocado Boats Stuffed with Crabmeat & Yogurt

Prep + Cook Time: 25 minutes | Serves: 2-4

Ingredients

4 oz crabmeat
2 avocados
3 oz cream cheese

2 tbsp chives, chopped
1 tsp smoked paprika

Directions

Halve the avocados. In a bowl, mix paprika with cream cheese. Fill the avocado halves with crabmeat and top with the paprika cream cheese. Decorate with chives and serve.

Nutritional info per serving: Calories 506, Fat: 43.4g, Net Carbs: 3.8g, Protein: 17.7g

Sliced Turkey Breast with Garlic & Cheese

Prep + Cook Time: 20 minutes | Serves: 2-4

Ingredients

1 tbsp olive oil
1 pound turkey breasts, sliced
2 garlic cloves, minced
½ cup sour cream
1/3 cup water

2 tbsp tomato paste
1 cup provolone cheese, shredded
Salt and black pepper to taste
1 tsp dried oregano

Directions

Fry the turkey and garlic in warm olive oil for 5-6 minutes in a pan over medium heat; set aside. Stir in the water, tomato paste, and sour cream; and cook until thickened.

Season with salt, black pepper, and oregano. Return the turkey to the pan, and spread the shredded cheese over. Let sit for 5 minutes while covered or until the cheese melts. Serve right away.

Nutritional info per serving: Calories 398; Fat: 25g, Net Carbs: 3.3g, Protein: 35.7g

Green Pork Bake

Prep + Cook Time: 45 minutes | Serves: 2-4

Ingredients

1 pound ground pork
1 onion, chopped
1 garlic clove, minced
½ green beans, chopped
Salt and black pepper to taste

1 zucchini, sliced
¼ cup heavy cream
5 eggs
½ cup Monterey Jack cheese, grated

Directions

In a bowl, mix onion, green beans, ground pork, garlic, black pepper and salt. Layer the meat mixture on the bottom of a small greased baking dish. Spread zucchini slices on top.

In a separate bowl, combine cheese, eggs and heavy cream. Top with this creamy mixture and bake for 40 minutes at 360 F, until the edges and top become brown.

Nutritional info per serving: Calories 335; Fat: 21.3g, Net Carbs: 3.9g, Protein: 27.7g

Four-Cheese Pizza

Prep + Cook Time: 15 minutes | Serves: 2-4

Ingredients

1 tbsp olive oil
½ cup Monterey Jack cheese, shredded
1 ¼ cups mozzarella cheese, shredded
½ cup brie cheese
½ cup gorgonzola cheese
2 garlic cloves, chopped

2 green bell peppers, sliced
½ cup tomato sauce
1 tsp oregano
2 tbsp basil, chopped
6 black olives for garnish

Directions

Mix all cheeses in a bowl. Set a pan over medium heat and warm olive oil. Spread the bottom with the cheese mixture and cook for 5 minutes until cooked through.

Scatter garlic, oregano, and tomato sauce over the crust. Sprinkle the bell peppers and cook for 2 more minutes. Top with basil and olives to serve.

Nutritional info per serving: Calories 316, Fat: 26g, Net Carbs: 4.6g, Protein: 7.9g

Basil & Chicken Meatball Bake

Prep + Cook Time: 35 minutes | Serves: 2-4

Ingredients

1 pound chicken sausages, casing removed
1 egg
½ carrot, grated
1 garlic clove, minced
1 onion, chopped

1 tbsp basil, chopped
Salt and black pepper, to taste
2 tbsp olive oil
1 cup Pecorino cheese, shredded

Directions

Combine all ingredients except for cheese and olive oil, in a bowl. Form meatballs from the mixture.

Heat olive oil in a large frying pan over a medium heat and cook the meatballs for 3-4 minutes until browned. Set them on a parchment-lined baking sheet, top with Pecorino cheese and bake for 10 minutes at 370 F until all cheese melts. Scatter basil over to serve.

Nutritional info per serving: Calories 689; Fat: 42g, Net Carbs: 3.3g, Protein: 62g

Roasted Chicken with Creamy Topping

Prep + Cook Time: 50 minutes | Serves: 2-4

Ingredients

1 pound chicken legs
¼ cup mascarpone cheese
4 tbsp sour cream
1 tbsp butter, softened

2 tbsp chives, chopped
1 tbsp cilantro, chopped
Sea salt and black pepper, to taste

Directions

Brush the chicken with melted butter, coat with salt and black pepper, and arrange in a baking dish. Bake in the oven for 35-40 minutes at 360 F until crispy and browned.

In a mixing bowl, mix the rest of the ingredients to form the topping. Serve alongside the prepared chicken legs.

Nutritional info per serving: Calories 235; Fat: 21g, Net Carbs: 1.3g, Protein: 5.4g

Chicken Pizza with Sundried Tomatoes

Prep + Cook Time: 35 minutes | Serves: 2-4

Ingredients

1 ½ cups almond flour
1 ½ tbsp olive oil

1 tsp salt
2 eggs

Pesto chicken topping

½ pound chicken breasts, cut into strips
Salt and black pepper to taste
1 ½ tbsp olive oil
6 sundried tomatoes, sliced

1 ½ cups basil pesto
1 cup mozzarella cheese, grated
1 tbsp fresh basil leaves
A pinch of red pepper flakes

Directions

Preheat the oven to 350 F. To prepare the pizza crust, in a bowl, mix almond flour, olive oil, salt, and eggs until a dough forms. Form the dough into a ball and place it in between two full parchment papers on a flat surface.

Roll it out into a circle and slide into a pizza pan; remove the parchment paper. Bake the dough for 20 minutes.

Season the chicken with salt and pepper. Heat olive oil in a pan over medium heat and fry the chicken on all sides for 5 minutes. Apply 2/3 of the pesto on the pizza crust and sprinkle half of the mozzarella cheese on it.

Toss the chicken in the remaining pesto and spread it on top of the pizza. Sprinkle with the remaining mozzarella and sundried tomatoes, and put the pizza back in the oven to bake for 9 minutes. When it is ready, remove from the oven to cool slightly, garnish with the basil leaves and sprinkle with red pepper flakes. Slice and serve.

Nutritional info per serving: Calories 512, Fat 29g, Net Carbs 4.2g, Protein 28g

Vegetable Patties

Prep + Cook Time: 35 minutes | Serves: 2-4

Ingredients

1 tbsp olive oil
1 onion, chopped
1 garlic clove, minced
½ head cauliflower, grated
1 carrot, shredded
3 tbsp coconut flour

½ cup Gruyere cheese, shredded
½ cup Parmesan cheese, grated
2 eggs, beaten
½ tsp dried rosemary
Salt and black pepper, to taste

Directions

Cook onion and garlic in warm olive oil over medium heat, until soft, for about 3 minutes. Stir in grated cauliflower and carrot and cook for a minute; allow cooling and set aside.

To the cooled vegetables, add the rest of the ingredients; form balls from the mixture, then, press each ball to form burger patty. Set oven to 400 F and bake the burgers for 20 minutes. Flip and bake for another 10 minutes or until the top becomes golden brown.

Nutritional info per serving: Calories 421; Fat: 31g, Net Carbs: 6.9g, Protein: 15g

VEGAN & VEGETABLES

Vegan Sandwich with Tofu & Lettuce Slaw

Prep + Cook Time: 10 minutes + marinade time | Serves: 2

Ingredients

¼ pound firm tofu, sliced
2 low carb buns

1 tbsp olive oil

Marinade

2 tbsp olive oil
Salt and black pepper to taste
1 tsp allspice
½ tbsp xylitol

1 tsp thyme, chopped
1 habanero pepper, seeded and minced
2 green onions, thinly sliced
1 garlic clove

Lettuce slaw

½ small iceberg lettuce, shredded
½ carrot, grated
½ red onion, grated
2 tsp liquid stevia

1 tbsp lemon juice
2 tbsp olive oil
½ tsp Dijon mustard
Salt and black pepper to taste

Directions

Put the tofu slices in a bowl.

In a food processor, blend the marinade ingredients for a minute. Cover the tofu with this mixture and place in the fridge to marinate for 1 hour. In a large bowl, combine the lemon juice, stevia, olive oil, Dijon mustard, salt, and pepper. Stir in the lettuce, carrot, and onion; set aside.

Heat 1 teaspoon of oil in a skillet over medium heat and cook the tofu on both sides for 6 minutes in total. Remove to a plate. In the buns, add the tofu and top with the slaw. Close the buns and serve.

Nutritional info per serving: Calories 687, Fat 58.5g, Net Carbs 10.5g, Protein 21.3g

Chili & Blue Cheese Stuffed Mushrooms

Prep + Cook Time: 30 minutes | Serves: 2

Ingredients

1 tbsp olive oil
4 portobello mushrooms, stems removed
1 cup blue cheese, crumbled
2 sprigs fresh thyme, chopped

½ chili pepper chopped
Salt and black pepper to taste
2 tbsp ground walnuts

Directions

Preheat the oven to 360 F.

Place the mushrooms on a lined baking sheet. In a bowl, add the blue cheese, chili pepper, and thyme and mix to combine. Fill the mushrooms with the blue cheese mixture, top with walnuts, drizzle with olive oil and bake for 20 minutes. Serve with mixed leaf salad.

Nutritional info per serving: Calories 368, Fat: 31.5g, Net Carbs: 3.9g, Protein: 18g

Fresh Coconut Milk Shake with Blackberries

Prep + Cook Time: 5 minutes | Serves: 2

Ingredients

½ cup water
1 ½ cups coconut milk
2 cups fresh blackberries

¼ tsp vanilla extract
1 tbsp vegan protein powder

Directions

In a blender, combine all the ingredients and blend well until you attain a uniform and creamy consistency. Divide in glasses and serve!

Nutritional info per serving: Calories 253; Fat: 22g, Net Carbs: 5.6g, Protein: 3.3g

Burritos Wraps with Avocado & Cauliflower

Prep + Cook Time: 5 minutes | Serves: 2

Ingredients

1 tbsp butter
½ head cauliflower, cut into florets
2 zero carb flatbread
1 cup yogurt

1 cup tomato salsa
1 avocado, sliced
1 tbsp cilantro, chopped

Directions

Put the cauliflower in a food processor and pulse until it resembles rice. In a skillet, melt the butter and add the cauli rice. Sauté for 4-5 minutes until cooked through. Season with salt and black pepper.

On flatbread, spread the yogurt all over and distribute the salsa on top. Top with cauli rice and scatter the avocado slices and cilantro on top. Fold and tuck the burritos and cut into two.

Nutritional info per serving: Calories 457, Fat 31.3g, Net Carbs 9.6g, Protein 15.8g

Pizza Bianca with Mushrooms

Prep + Cook Time: 17 minutes | Serves: 2

Ingredients

2 tbsp olive oil
4 eggs
2 tbsp water
1 jalapeño pepper, diced
¼ cup mozzarella cheese, shredded

2 chives, chopped
2 cups egg Alfredo sauce
½ tsp oregano
½ cup mushrooms, sliced

Directions

Preheat oven to 360 F.

In a bowl, whisk eggs, water, and oregano. Heat the olive oil in a large skillet. Pour in the egg mixture and cook until set, flipping once. Remove and spread the alfredo sauce and jalapeño pepper all over. Top with mozzarella cheese, mushrooms and chives. Bake for 5-10 minutes until the cheese melts.

Nutritional info per serving: Calories 312, Fat: 23.5g, Net Carbs: 2.4g, Protein: 17.2g

Hot Pizza with Tomatoes, Cheese & Olives

Prep + Cook Time: 30 minutes | Serves: 2

Ingredients

2 tbsp psyllium husk
1 cup cheddar cheese
2 tbsp cream cheese

2 tbsp Pecorino cheese
1 tsp oregano
½ cup almond flour

Topping

1 tomato, sliced
4 oz cheddar cheese, sliced
¼ cup tomato sauce

1 jalapeño pepper, sliced
½ cup black olives
2 tbsp basil, chopped

Directions

Preheat the oven to 375 F.

Microwave the cheddar cheese in an oven-proof bowl. In a separate bowl, combine cream cheese, pecorino cheese, psyllium husk, almond flour, and oregano. Add in the melted cheddar cheese and mix with your hands to combine.

Divide the dough in two. Roll out the two crusts in circles and place on a lined baking sheet. Bake for about 10 minutes.

Spread the tomato sauce over the crust and top with the cheddar cheese slices, jalapeño pepper, and tomato slices. Return to the oven and bake for another 10 minutes.

Garnish with black olives and basil.

Nutritional info per serving: Calories 576, Fat: 42.3g, Net Carbs: 7.5g, Protein: 32.4g

Spicy Vegetarian Burgers with Fried Eggs

Prep + Cook Time: 20 minutes | Serves: 2

Ingredients

1 garlic clove, minced
2 portobello mushrooms, chopped
1 cup cauli rice
1 tbsp peanut butter
1 tbsp basil, chopped
1 tbsp oregano
Salt to taste

1 jalapeño pepper, minced
¼ red onion, sliced
2 eggs
2 low carb buns
2 tbsp mayonnaise
2 lettuce leaves

Directions

Sauté the mushrooms and cauli rice in warm peanut butter for 5 minutes. Remove to a bowl and add in garlic, oregano, basil, jalapeño pepper, and salt and mix well to obtain a dough. Make medium-sized burgers from the dough.

Cook the burgers in the same butter for 2 minutes per side and transfer to a serving plate. Reduce the heat and fry the eggs. Cut the low carb buns in half.

Add the lettuce leaves, burgers, eggs, red onion, and mayonnaise. Top with the other bun half.

Nutritional info per serving: Calories 456, Fat: 37.5g, Net Carbs: 9.3g, Protein: 19g

Grilled Cauliflower Steaks with Haricots Vert

Prep + Cook Time: 20 minutes | Serves: 2

Ingredients

2 tbsp olive oil
1 head cauliflower, sliced lengthwise into 'steaks'
2 tbsp chili sauce
1 tsp hot paprika
1 tsp oregano

Salt and black pepper to taste
1 shallot, chopped
1 bunch haricots vert, trimmed
1 tbsp fresh lemon juice
1 tbsp cilantro, chopped

Directions

Preheat grill to medium heat. Steam the haricots vert in salted water over medium heat for 6 minutes. Drain, remove to a bowl and toss with lemon juice.

In a bowl, mix the olive oil, chili sauce, hot paprika, and oregano. Brush the cauliflower steaks with the mixture. Place them on the grill, close the lid and grill for 6 minutes.

Flip the cauliflower and cook further for 6 minutes. Remove the grilled caulis to a plate; sprinkle with salt, black pepper, shallots and cilantro. Serve with the steamed haricots vert.

Nutritional info per serving: Calories 234, Fat 15.9g, Net Carbs 8.4g, Protein 5.2g

Tofu & Vegetable Stir-Fry

Prep + Cook Time: 10 minutes + marinade time | Serves: 2

Ingredients

2 tbsp olive oil
1 ½ cups extra firm tofu, pressed and cubed
1 ½ tbsp flax seed meal
Salt and black pepper, to taste
1 garlic clove, minced

1 tbsp soy sauce, sugar-free
½ head broccoli, break into florets
1 tsp onion powder
1 cup mushrooms, sliced
1 tbsp sesame seeds

Directions

In a bowl, add onion powder, tofu, salt, soy sauce, black pepper, flaxseed, and garlic. Toss the mixture to coat and allow to marinate for 20-30 minutes.

In a pan, warm oil over medium heat, add in broccoli, mushrooms and tofu mixture and stir-fry for 6-8 minutes. Serve sprinkled with sesame seeds.

Nutritional info per serving: Calories 423; Fat: 31g, Net Carbs: 7.3g, Protein: 25.5g

Chili Lover's Frittata with Spinach & Cheese

Prep + Cook Time: 17 minutes | Serves: 2

Ingredients

2 tbsp olive oil
1 cup spinach, chopped
2 red and yellow chilies, roasted and chopped
1 tbsp red wine vinegar
1 tbsp parsley, chopped

4 eggs
¼ cup Parmesan cheese, grated
2 tbsp goat cheese, crumbled
½ cup salad greens

Directions

In a bowl, mix the vinegar, half of the olive oil, and chilies. Coat the salad greens with the dressing.

In another bowl, whisk the eggs with salt, black pepper, parsley, spinach, and Parmesan cheese.

Heat the remaining oil in the cast iron over medium heat and pour the egg mixture along with half of the goat cheese. Let cook for 3 minutes and when it is near done, sprinkle the remaining goat cheese on it, and transfer the cast iron to the oven.

Bake the frittata for 4 more minutes at 400 F. Garnish the frittata with salad greens and serve.

Nutritional info per serving: Calories 316, Fat 28.3g, Net Carbs 4.1g, Protein 9.5g

Spicy Cauliflower Falafel

Prep + Cook Time: 15 minutes | Serves: 2

Ingredients

4 tbsp olive oil
1 head cauliflower, cut into florets
1/3 cup silvered ground almonds
½ tsp ground cumin
1 tsp parsley, chopped

Salt to taste
1 tsp chili pepper
3 tbsp coconut flour
2 eggs

Directions

Blitz the cauliflower in a food processor until a grain meal consistency is formed. Transfer to a bowl, add in the ground almonds, ground cumin, parsley, salt, chili pepper, and coconut flour, and mix until evenly combined.

Beat the eggs in a bowl and mix with the cauli mixture. Shape ¼ cup each into patties and set aside.

Warm olive oil in a frying pan over medium heat and fry the patties for 5 minutes on each side to be firm and browned. Remove onto a wire rack to cool, share into serving plates, and serve.

Nutritional info per serving: Calories 343, Fat 31.2g, Net Carbs 3.7g, Protein 8.5g

Mediterranean Eggplant Squash Pasta

Prep + Cook Time: 15 minutes | Serves: 2

Ingredients

2 tbsp butter
1 cup cherry tomatoes
2 tbsp parsley, chopped
1 eggplant, cubed
¼ cup Parmesan cheese

3 tbsp scallions, chopped
1 cup green beans
1 tsp lemon zest
10 oz butternut squash, spirals

Directions

In a saucepan over medium heat, add the butter to melt. Cook the spaghetti squash for 4-5 minutes and remove to a plate. In the same saucepan, cook eggplant for 5 minutes until tender.

Add the tomatoes and green beans, and cook for 5 more minutes. Stir in parsley, zest, and scallions, and remove the pan from heat. Stir in spaghetti squash and Parmesan cheese to serve.

Nutritional info per serving: Calories 388, Fat: 17.8g, Net Carbs: 9.6g, Protein: 12g

Spiral Zucchini Noodles with Cheesy Sauce

Prep + Cook Time: 20 minutes | Serves: 2

Ingredients

2 tbsp olive oil
1 (28-ounce) can tomatoes, crushed
2 garlic cloves, minced
1 cup kale
1 onion, chopped

1 pound zucchinis, spiralized
¼ cup Parmesan cheese, shredded
10 kalamata olives, halved
2 tbsp basil, chopped
Salt and black pepper to taste

Directions

Heat the olive oil in a pan over medium heat. Add zucchinis and cook for about 5 minutes. Transfer to a serving platter. In the same pan, sauté onion and garlic for 3 minutes.

Add in tomatoes, kale, salt, and pepper, reduce the heat and simmer for 8-10 minutes until thickened. Pour the sauce over zucchini noodles, scatter Parmesan cheese all over and top with olives and basil.

Nutritional info per serving: Calories 388, Fat: 25.4g, Net Carbs: 6.8g, Protein: 15.5g

Cajun Flavored Stuffed Mushrooms

Prep + Cook Time: 35 minutes | Serves: 2

Ingredients

2 tbsp coconut oil
½ head broccoli, cut into florets
1 pound cremini mushrooms, stems removed
1 onion, chopped
¼ cup almonds, chopped

1 garlic clove, minced
1 bell pepper, chopped
1 tsp cajun seasoning mix
Salt and black pepper, to taste
1 cup Parmesan cheese, shredded

Directions

Blend the broccoli in a food processor until they become small rice-like granules.

Set oven to 360 F. Bake mushroom caps until tender for 8 to 12 minutes. In a skillet, melt the coconut oil; stir in bell pepper, garlic, and onion and sauté until fragrant. Place in black pepper, salt, and cajun seasoning mix. Fold in broccoli rice and almonds.

Equally separate the filling mixture among mushroom caps. Add a topping of Parmesan cheese and bake for 17 more minutes. Serve warm.

Nutritional info per serving: Calories 423; Fat: 25.4g, Net Carbs: 9.5g, Protein: 21.7g

Keto Tortilla Wraps with Vegetables

Prep + Cook Time: 10 minutes | Serves: 2

Ingredients

2 tsp olive oil
2 low carb tortillas
1 green onion, sliced
1 bell pepper, sliced
¼ tsp hot chilli powder
1 large avocado, sliced

1 cup cauli rice
Salt and black pepper to taste
¼ cup sour cream
1 tbsp Mexican salsa
1 tbsp cilantro, chopped

Directions

Warm the olive oil in a skillet and sauté the green onion and bell pepper until they start to brown on the edges, for about 4 minutes; remove to a bowl. To the same pan, add in the cauli rice and stir-fry for 4-5 minutes. Combine with the onion and bell pepper mixture, season with salt, black pepper, and chili powder. Let cool for a few minutes.

Add in avocado, sour cream, and Mexican salsa and stir. Top with cilantro. Fold in the sides of each tortilla, and roll them in and over the filling to be enclosed. Wrap with foil, cut in halves, and serve.

Nutritional info per serving: Calories 373, Fat 31.2g, Net Carbs 8.6g, Protein 7.6g

Roasted Cauliflower Gratin

Prep + Cook Time: 21 minutes | Serves: 2-4

Ingredients

1/3 cup butter
2 tbsp melted butter
1 onion, chopped
2 heads cauliflower, cut into florets
Salt and black pepper to taste

¼ cup almond milk
½ cup almond flour
1 ½ cups cheddar cheese, grated
1 tbsp ground almonds
1 tbsp parsley, chopped

Directions

Steam the cauliflower in salted water for 4-5 minutes. Drain and set aside.

Melt the 1/3 cup of butter in a saucepan over medium heat and sauté the onion for 3 minutes. Add the cauliflower, season with salt and black pepper and mix in almond milk. Simmer for 3 minutes.

Mix the remaining melted butter with the almond flour. Stir into the cauliflower as well as half of the cheese. Sprinkle the top with the remaining cheese and ground almonds, and bake for 10 minutes until golden brown on the top. Serve sprinkled with parsley.

Nutritional info per serving: Calories 455, Fat 38.3g, Net Carbs 6.5g, Protein 16.3g

Basil Spinach & Zucchini Lasagna

Prep + Cook Time: 40 minutes | Serves: 2-4

Ingredients

2 zucchinis, sliced
Salt and black pepper to taste
2 cups feta cheese
2 cups mozzarella cheese, shredded

3 cups tomato sauce
1 cup spinach
1 tbsp basil, chopped

Directions

Mix the feta, mozzarella cheese, salt, and black pepper to evenly combine and spread ¼ cup of the mixture at the bottom of a greased baking dish. Layer 1/3 of the zucchini slices on top, spread 1 cup of tomato sauce over and scatter a 1/3 cup of spinach on top.

Repeat the layering process two more times to exhaust the ingredients while making sure to layer with the last ¼ cup of cheese mixture finally. Bake for 35 minutes until the cheese has a nice golden brown color. Remove the dish, sit for 5 minutes and serve sprinkled with basil.

Nutritional info per serving: Calories 411, Fat 41.3g, Net Carbs 3.2g, Protein 6.5g

Broccoli & Asparagus Flan

Prep + Cook Time: 65 minutes | Serves: 2-4

Ingredients

A bunch of asparagus, stems trimmed
1 cup broccoli florets
1 cup water
½ cup whipping cream
1 cup almond milk
3 eggs
2 tbsp tarragon, chopped

Salt and black pepper to taste
A small pinch of nutmeg
2 tbsp Parmesan cheese, grated
3 cups water
2 tbsp butter, melted
1 tbsp butter, softened

Directions

Steam asparagus and broccoli in salted water over medium heat for 6 minutes. Drain and cut the tips of the asparagus and reserve for garnishing. Chop the remaining asparagus into small pieces.

In a blender, add the chopped asparagus, broccoli, whipping cream, almond milk, tarragon salt, nutmeg, black pepper and Parmesan cheese and process until smooth. Pour the mixture through a sieve into a bowl and whisk the eggs into it.

Preheat the oven to 350 F. Grease ramekins with softened butter and share the asparagus mixture among the ramekins. Pour the melted butter over each one and top with 2-3 asparagus tips.

Pour the remaining water into a baking dish, place in the ramekins, and insert in the oven. Bake for 45 minutes or until their middle parts are no longer watery. Garnish the flan with the asparagus tips and serve.

Nutritional info per serving: Calories 298, Fat 24,6g, Net Carbs 4.5g, Protein 17.5g

Grilled Vegetables & Tempeh Shish Kebab

Prep + Cook Time: 26 minutes + marinade time | Serves: 2-4

Ingredients

2 tbsp olive oil
10 oz tempeh, cut into chunks
1 ½ cups water
1 red onion, cut into chunks
1 red bell pepper, cut chunks

1 yellow bell pepper, cut into chunks
1 cup zucchini, sliced
1 cup barbecue sauce, sugar-free
2 tbsp chives

Directions

In a pot over medium heat, pour the water. Bring to boil, remove from heat and add the tempeh. Cover the pot and let tempeh steam for 5 minutes to remove its bitterness. Drain the tempeh after.

Pour the barbecue sauce in a bowl, add the tempeh to it, and coat with the sauce. Cover the bowl and marinate in the fridge for 2 hours. Preheat grill to medium heat. Thread the tempeh, yellow bell pepper, red bell pepper, zucchini, and onion.

Brush the grate of the grill with olive oil, place the skewers on it, and brush with barbecue sauce. Cook the skewers for 3 minutes on each side while rotating and brushing with more barbecue sauce.

Once ready, transfer the kabobs to a plate and serve sprinkled with chives.

Nutritional info per serving: Calories 228, Fat 15g, Net Carbs 3.6g, Protein 13.2g

Grilled Tofu Kabobs with Arugula Salad

Prep + Cook Time: 40 minutes + marinade time | Serves: 2-4

Ingredients

14 oz firm tofu, cut into strips
4 tsp sesame oil
1 lemon, juiced
5 tbsp soy sauce, sugar-free

3 tsp garlic powder
4 tbsp coconut flour
½ cup sesame seeds

Arugula salad:

4 cups arugula, chopped
2 tsp extra virgin olive oil
2 tbsp pine nuts

Salt and black pepper to season
1 tbsp balsamic vinegar

Directions

Stick the tofu strips on the skewers, height-wise and place onto a plate.

In a bowl, mix sesame oil, lemon juice, soy sauce, garlic powder, and coconut flour. Pour the soy sauce mixture over the tofu, and turn in the sauce to be adequately coated. Cover the dish with cling film and marinate in the fridge for 2 hours.

Heat the griddle pan over high heat. Coat the tofu in the sesame seeds and grill in the griddle pan to be golden brown on both sides, about 12 minutes in total.

Arrange the arugula on a serving plate. Drizzle over olive oil and balsamic vinegar, and season with salt and black pepper. Sprinkle with pine nuts and place the tofu kabobs on top to serve.

Nutritional info per serving: Calories 411, Fat 32.9g, Net Carbs 7.1g, Protein 21.6g

Sticky Tofu with Cucumber & Tomato Salad

Prep + Cook Time: 40 minutes | Serves: 2-4

Ingredients

2 tbsp olive oil
12 ounces tofu
1 cup green onions, chopped

1 garlic clove, minced
2 tbsp vinegar
1 tbsp sriracha sauce

Salad

1 tbsp fresh lemon juice
2 tbsp extra virgin olive oil
Sea salt and black pepper, to taste
1 tsp fresh dill weed

1 cup Greek yogurt
1 cucumber, sliced
2 tomatoes, sliced

Directions

Pat the tofu dry with kitchen paper and cut into slices. Put tofu slices, garlic, sriracha sauce, vinegar, and scallions in a bowl; allow to settle for approximately 30 minutes. Set oven to medium heat and add oil in a nonstick skillet to warm. Cook tofu for 5 minutes until golden brown.

In a salad plate, arrange tomatoes and cucumber slices, season with salt and black pepper, drizzle lemon juice and extra virgin olive oil and scatter dill all over. Top with the tofu and serve.

Nutritional info per serving: Calories 371; Fat: 30.9g, Net Carbs: 7.7g, Protein: 17.3g

Stewed Vegetables

Prep + Cook Time: 32 minutes | Serves: 2-4

Ingredients

2 tbsp butter
1 shallot, chopped
1 garlic clove, minced
1 tsp paprika
1 carrot, chopped
2 tomatoes, chopped

1 head cabbage, shredded
2 cups green beans, chopped
2 bell peppers, sliced
Salt and black pepper to taste
2 tbsp parsley, chopped
1 cup vegetable broth

Directions

Melt butter in a saucepan over medium heat and sauté onion and garlic to be fragrant, for 2 minutes.

Stir in bell peppers, carrot, cabbage, and green beans, paprika, salt, and pepper, add the vegetable broth and tomatoes, stir again, and cook the vegetables on low heat for 25 minutes to soften. Serve the stew sprinkled with parsley.

Nutritional info per serving: Calories 310, Fat 26.4g, Net Carbs 6g, Protein 8g

Grilled Halloumi with Cauli-Rice & Almonds

Prep + Cook Time: 5 minutes | Serves: 2-4

Ingredients

2 tbsp olive oil
4 oz halloumi, sliced
1 cauliflower head, grated
¼ cup oregano, chopped
¼ cup parsley, chopped

¼ cup mint, chopped
½ lemon juiced
2 tbsp almonds, chopped
Salt and black pepper to taste
1 avocado, sliced to garnish

Directions

Heat a grill pan over medium heat. Drizzle the halloumi cheese with olive oil and add in the pan. Grill for 2 minutes on each side to be golden brown, set aside.

To make the cauli rice, add in the cauliflower and cook for 5-6 minutes until slightly cooked but crunchy. Stir in the cilantro, parsley, mint, lemon juice, salt and black pepper. Garnish the rice with avocado slices and almonds and serve with grilled halloumi.

Nutritional info per serving: Calories 255, Fat 23g, Net Carbs 3.3g, Protein 7.6g

Portobello Bun Mushroom Burgers

Prep + Cook Time: 15 minutes | Serves: 2-4

Ingredients

2 tbsp olive oil
4 portobello mushroom caps
1 clove garlic
Salt and black pepper to taste
½ cup roasted red peppers, sliced
2 tomatoes, sliced

1 cup guacamole
1 zucchini, sliced
¼ cup feta cheese, crumbled
1 tbsp red wine vinegar
2 tbsp pitted kalamata olives, chopped
½ tsp dried oregano

Directions

Crush the garlic with salt in a bowl using the back of a spoon. Stir in 1 tablespoon of oil and brush the mushrooms and each inner side of the buns with the mixture.

Place the mushrooms in a preheated pan and grill them on both sides for 8 minutes until tender. Drizzle the zucchini with a little bit of olive oil, season with salt and pepper, and grill on both sides for 5-6 minutes.

In a bowl, mix the red peppers, olives, feta cheese, vinegar, oregano, and remaining oil; toss them. Assemble the burger: spread some guacamole on a slice of a mushroom bun, add 1-2 zucchini slices, a scoop of the vegetable mixture, a slice of tomato and another slice of mushroom bun.

Nutritional info per serving: Calories 221, Fat 18.8g, Net Carbs 4.3g, Protein 4.5g

Soy Chorizo & Cabbage Bake

Prep + Cook Time: 25 minutes | Serves: 2-4

Ingredients

1 pound soy chorizo, sliced
1 head green cabbage, cut into wedges
4 tbsp butter, melted
1 tsp garlic powder

Salt and black pepper to taste
2 tbsp Parmesan cheese, grated
1 tbsp parsley, chopped

Directions

Preheat oven to 390 F and grease a baking tray with cooking spray. Mix the butter, garlic, salt, and black pepper until evenly combined in a bowl.

Brush the mixture on all sides of the cabbage wedges. Place on the baking sheet, add in the soy chorizo and bake for 20 minutes to soften the cabbage. Sprinkle with Parmesan cheese and parsley.

Nutritional info per serving: Calories 268, Fat 19.3g, Net Carbs 4g, Protein 17.5g

One-Pot Mushroom Stroganoff

Prep + Cook Time: 15 minutes | Serves: 2-4

Ingredients

3 tbsp cashew butter
1 onion, chopped
4 cups baby bella mushrooms, cubed
2 cups vegetable broth

½ cup heavy cream
½ cup Parmesan cheese, grated
1 ½ tbsp dried Italian seasoning
Salt and black pepper to taste

Directions

Melt the cashew butter in a saucepan over medium heat, sauté the onion for 3 minutes until soft.

Stir in the mushrooms and cook until tender, for about 3 minutes. Add the vegetable broth, mix, and bring to boil for 4 minutes until the liquid reduces slightly.

Pour in the heavy cream and Parmesan cheese. Stir to melt the cheese. Also, mix in the Italian seasoning. Season with salt and pepper, simmer for 40 seconds and turn the heat off. Ladle stroganoff over a bed of spaghetti squash and serve.

Nutritional info per serving: Calories 255, Fat 21g, Net Carbs 5.4g, Protein 7.8g

Vegetable Stew

Prep + Cook Time: 25 minutes | Serves: 2-4

Ingredients

2 tbsp olive oil
1 turnip, chopped
1 onion, chopped
2 garlic cloves, pressed
½ cup celery, chopped
1 carrot, chopped
1 cup wild mushrooms, sliced
2 tbsp dry white wine

2 tbsp rosemary, chopped
1 thyme sprig, chopped
4 cups vegetable stock
½ tsp chili pepper
1 tsp smoked paprika
2 tomatoes, chopped
1 tbsp flax seed meal

Directions

Cook onion, carrot, celery, mushrooms, paprika, chili pepper, and garlic in warm oil over medium heat for 5-6 minutes until tender; set the vegetables aside.

Stir in wine to deglaze the stockpot's bottom. Place in thyme and rosemary. Pour in tomatoes, vegetable stock, reserved vegetables and turnip and allow to boil.

On low heat, allow the mixture to simmer for 15 minutes while covered. Stir in flax seed meal to thicken the stew. Plate into individual bowls and serve.

Nutritional info per serving: Calories 164; Fat: 11.3g, Net Carbs: 8.2g, Protein: 3.3g

Sauteed Tofu with Pistachios

Prep + Cook Time: 15 minutes | Serves: 2-4

Ingredients

2 tbsp olive oil
8 oz firm tofu, cubed
1 tbsp tomato paste
1 tbsp balsamic vinegar

1 tsp garlic powder
1 tsp onion powder
Salt and black pepper to taste
1 cup pistachios, chopped

Directions

Heat the oil in a skillet over medium heat and cook the tofu for 3 minutes while stirring to brown.

Mix the tomato paste, garlic powder, onion powder, and vinegar; add to the tofu. Stir, season with salt and black pepper, and cook for another 4 minutes.

Add the pistachios. Stir and cook on low heat for 3 minutes to be fragrant.

Nutritional info per serving: Calories 335, Fat 27g, Net Carbs 6.3g, Protein 16.5g

Zucchini Spaghetti with Avocado & Capers

Prep + Cook Time: 15 minutes | Serves: 2-4

Ingredients

2 tbsp olive oil
4 zucchinis, julienned or spiralized
½ cup pesto
2 avocados, sliced

¼ cup capers
¼ cup basil, chopped
¼ cup sun-dried tomatoes, chopped

Directions

Cook zucchini spaghetti in half of the warm olive oil over medium heat for 4 minutes.

Transfer to a plate. Stir in pesto, basil, salt, tomatoes, and capers. Top with avocado slices.

Nutritional info per serving: Calories 449, Fat: 42g, Net Carbs: 8.4g, Protein: 6.3g

Mushroom & Cheese Cauliflower Risotto

Prep + Cook Time: 15 minutes | Serves: 2-4

Ingredients

3 tbsp olive oil
1 onion, chopped
¼ cup vegetable broth
1/3 cup Parmesan cheese
4 tbsp heavy cream

3 tbsp chives, chopped
2 pounds mushrooms, sliced
1 large head cauliflower, break into florets
2 tbsp parsley, chopped

Directions

In a food processor, pulse the cauliflower florets until you attain a rice-like consistency.

Heat 2 tbsp oil in a saucepan. Add the mushrooms and cook over medium heat for about 3 minutes, set aside. Heat the remaining oil and cook the onion for 2 minutes.

Stir in the cauliflower and broth, and cook until the liquid is absorbed, about 7-8 minutes. Stir in the heavy cream and Parmesan cheese. Top with chives and parsley to serve.

Nutritional info per serving: Calories 255, Fat: 21g, Net Carbs: 5.3g, Protein: 10.3g

Avocado Boats

Prep + Cook Time: 10 minutes | Serves: 2-4

Ingredients

2 avocados, halved and stoned
1 tomato, chopped
1 cucumber, chopped
¼ cup walnuts, ground
2 carrots, chopped

1 garlic clove
1 tsp lemon juice
1 tbsp soy sauce
Salt and black pepper, to taste

Directions

To make the filling, in a mixing bowl, mix soy sauce, tomato, carrots, avocado pulp, cucumber, lemon juice, walnuts, and garlic.

Add black pepper and salt. Plate the mixture into the avocado halves. Scatter walnuts over to serve.

Nutritional info per serving: Calories 272; Fat: 25g, Net Carbs: 6.1g, Protein: 4g

Basil Tofu with Cashew Nuts

Prep + Cook Time: 13 minutes | Serves: 2-4

Ingredients

3 tsp olive oil
1 cup extra firm tofu, cubed
¼ cup cashew nuts
1 ½ tbsp coconut aminos
3 tbsp vegetable broth
1 garlic clove, minced

1 tsp cayenne pepper
½ tsp turmeric powder
Salt and black pepper, to taste
2 tsp sunflower seeds
10 basil leaves, torn
1 tbsp balsamic vinegar

Directions

Warm olive oil in a frying pan over medium heat. Add in tofu and fry until golden, turning once, for about 6 minutes. Pour in the cashew nuts and cook for 2 minutes. Stir in the remaining ingredients except for the balsamic vinegar and basil, set heat to medium-low and cook for 5 more minutes.

Drizzle with the balsamic vinegar, season to taste, sprinkle with basil and serve.

Nutritional info per serving: Calories 245; Fat: 19.6g, Net Carbs: 5.5g, Protein: 12.3g

Stuffed Mushrooms

Prep + Cook Time: 30 minutes | Serves: 2-4

Ingredients

2 tbsp olive oil
¼ tsp chilli flakes
1 cup gorgonzola cheese, crumbled
1 onion, chopped
1 garlic clove, minced

1 pound mushrooms, stems removed
Salt and black pepper, to taste
¼ cup walnuts, toasted and chopped
2 tbsp parsley, chopped

Directions

Put to a pan over medium heat and warm the olive oil. Sauté garlic and onion, until soft, for about 5 minutes. Sprinkle with black pepper and salt, and remove to a bowl.

Add in walnuts and gorgonzola cheese and stir until heated through. Divide the filling among the mushroom caps and set on a greased baking sheet.

Bake in the oven for 30 minutes at 360 F and remove to a wire rack to cool slightly. Add fresh parsley and serve.

Nutritional info per serving: Calories 139; Fat: 11.2g, Net Carbs: 7.4g, Protein: 4.8g

Steamed Bok Choy with Thyme & Garlic

Prep + Cook Time: 25 minutes | Serves: 2-4

Ingredients

2 pounds Bok choy, sliced
2 tbsp coconut oil
2 tbsp soy sauce, sugar-free
1 tsp garlic, minced

½ tsp thyme, chopped
½ tsp red pepper flakes, crushed
Salt and black pepper, to the taste

Directions

In a pot, steam bok choy in salted water over medium heat, for 6 minutes; drain and set aside. Place a pan over medium heat and warm the coconut oil. Add in garlic and cook until soft.

Stir in the bok choy, red pepper, soy sauce, black pepper, salt, and thyme and cook until everything is heated through, for about 1-2 minutes.

Nutritional info per serving: Calories 132; Fat: 9.5g, Net Carbs: 3.5g, Protein: 4.9g

Stir-Fried Brussels Sprouts with Tofu & Leeks

Prep + Cook Time: 20 minutes | Serves: 2-4

Ingredients

2 tbsp olive oil
2 garlic cloves, minced
1 leek, sliced
10 ounces tofu, crumbled
2 tbsp water
2 tbsp soy sauce, sugar-free

1 tbsp tomato puree
½ pound Brussels sprouts, halved
½ red chilli, seeded and sliced
Salt and black pepper, to taste
Lime wedges to serve

Directions

In a saucepan over medium heat, warm the oil. Add the leek and garlic and cook until tender, about 2-3 minutes. Place in the soy sauce, water, red chilli and tofu.

Cook for 5 minutes until the tofu starts to brown. Add in Brussels sprouts, season with black pepper and salt, and cook for 10 minutes while stirring frequently. Garnish with lime wedges to serve.

Nutritional info per serving: Calories 183; Fat: 12.5g, Net Carbs: 7.7g, Protein: 13.2g

Colorful Peppers Stuffed with Mushrooms & "Rice"

Prep + Cook Time: 40 minutes | Serves: 2-4

Ingredients

2 tbsp olive oil
1 head cauliflower, grated
2 pounds mixed bell peppers, tops removed
1 cup mushrooms, sliced
1 onion, chopped
1 cup celery, chopped

1 garlic clove, minced
1 tsp dried oregano
1 tsp chili powder
2 tomatoes, pureed
Sea salt and pepper, to taste
2 tbsp parsley, chopped

Directions

Preheat oven to 360 F and lightly oil a casserole dish.

Warm the olive oil over medium heat in a pan. Add in garlic, celery, and onion and sauté until soft and translucent. Stir in chili powder, tomatoes, mushrooms, oregano, parsley, and cauliflower rice. Cook for 6 minutes until the cauliflower rice becomes tender. Season with salt and black pepper.

Split the cauliflower mixture among the bell peppers. Set in the casserole dish and bake for 30 minutes until the skin of the peppers starts to brown. Serve with full-fat Greek yogurt.

Nutritional info per serving: Calories: 233; Fat 8g, Net Carbs 8.4g, Protein 7.6g,

Fennel & Celeriac with Chili Tomato Sauce

Prep + Cook Time: 20 minutes | Serves: 2-4

Ingredients

2 tbsp olive oil
1 garlic clove, crushed
½ celeriac, sliced

½ fennel bulb, sliced
¼ cup vegetable stock
Sea salt and black pepper, to taste

Sauce

2 tomatoes, halved
2 tbsp olive oil
½ cup onions, chopped
2 cloves garlic, minced

1 chili, minced
1 bunch fresh basil, chopped
1 tbsp fresh cilantro, chopped
Salt and black pepper, to taste

Directions

Set a pan over medium-high heat and warm olive oil. Add in garlic and sauté for 1 minute. Stir in celeriac and fennel slices, stock and cook until softened. Sprinkle with black pepper and salt.

Brush olive oil to the tomato halves. Microwave for 15 minutes; get rid of any excess liquid. Remove the cooked tomatoes to a food processor; add the rest of the ingredients for the sauce and puree to obtain the desired consistency. Serve the celeriac and fennel topped with tomato sauce.

Nutritional info per serving: Calories 145; Fat: 15g, Net Carbs: 5.3g, Protein: 2.1g

Steamed Asparagus with Feta

Prep + Cook Time: 30 minutes | Serves: 2-4

Ingredients

1 pound asparagus, cut off stems
2 tbsp olive oil
1 cup feta cheese, crumbled
2 garlic cloves, minced
1 tsp cajun spice mix

1 tsp mustard
1 bell pepper, chopped
¼ cup vegetable broth
Salt and black pepper, to taste

Directions

Steam asparagus in salted water in a pot over medium heat until tender for 10 minutes; then drain.

Heat olive oil in a pan over medium heat and place in garlic; cook for 30 seconds until soft. Stir in the rest of the ingredients, including reserved asparagus, and cook for an additional 4 minutes. Serve topped with feta cheese in a platter.

Nutritional info per serving: Calories 211; Fat: 16.5g, Net Carbs: 2.8g, Protein: 8.8g

Roasted Pumpkin with Almonds & Cheddar

Prep + Cook Time: 45 minutes | Serves: 2-4

Ingredients

2 tbsp olive oil
1 large pumpkin, peeled and sliced
½ cup almonds, ground

½ cup cheddar cheese, grated
2 tbsp thyme, chopped

Directions

Preheat the oven to 360 F.

Arrange the pumpkin slices on a baking dish, drizzle with olive oil, and bake for 35 minutes. Mix the almonds and cheese, and when the pumpkin is ready, remove it from the oven, and sprinkle the cheese mixture all over. Bake for 5 more minutes. Sprinkle with thyme to serve.

Nutritional info per serving: Calories 154, Fat 8.6g, Net Carbs 5.1g, Protein 4.5g

Smoked Vegetable Bake with Parmesan

Prep + Cook Time: 35 minutes | Serves: 2-4

Ingredients

2 tbsp olive oil
1 onion, chopped
1 celery, chopped
2 carrots, sliced
½ pound artichokes, halved
1 cup vegetable broth

1 tsp turmeric
Salt and black pepper, to taste
½ tsp liquid smoke
1 cup Parmesan cheese, shredded
2 tbsp chives, chopped

Directions

Preheat oven to 360 F and grease a baking dish with olive oil. Place in the artichokes, onion, and celery. Combine vegetable broth with turmeric, black pepper, liquid smoke, and salt.

Spread this mixture over the vegetables and bake for about 25 minutes. Sprinkle with Parmesan cheese and return in the oven to bake for another 5 minutes until the cheese melts. Decorate with fresh chives and serve.

Nutritional info per serving: Calories 231; Fat: 15.5g, Net Carbs: 9.3g, Protein: 11g

Sauteed Spinach with Spicy Tofu

Prep + Cook Time: 25 minutes | Serves: 2-4

Ingredients

2 tbsp olive oil
14 ounces block tofu, pressed and cubed
1 celery stalk, chopped
1 bunch scallions, chopped
1 tsp cayenne pepper
1 tsp garlic powder

2 tbsp Worcestershire sauce
Salt and black pepper, to taste
1 pound spinach, chopped
½ tsp turmeric powder
¼ tsp dried basil

Directions

In a large skillet over medium heat, warm 1 tablespoon of olive oil. Stir in tofu cubes and cook for 8 minutes. Place in scallions and celery; cook for 5 minutes until soft. Stir in cayenne, Worcestershire sauce, black pepper, salt, and garlic; cook for 3 more minutes; set aside.

In the same pan, warm the remaining 1 tablespoon of oil. Add in spinach and the remaining seasonings and cook for 4 minutes. Mix in tofu mixture and serve warm.

Nutritional info per serving: Calories 205; Fat: 12.5g, Net Carbs: 7.8g, Protein: 7.7g

Traditional Greek Eggplant Casserole

Prep + Cook Time: 50 minutes | Serves: 2-4

Ingredients

2 large eggplants, cut into strips
½ cup celery, chopped
½ cup carrots, chopped
1 white onion, chopped
1 egg
1 tomato, chopped

1 tsp olive oil
2 cups grated Parmesan, divided into 2
1 cup feta cheese, crumbled
2 cloves garlic, minced
1 tsp Greek seasoning
Salt and black pepper to taste

Sauce:

1 cup heavy cream
2 tbsp butter, melted
½ cup mozzarella cheese, grated

1 tsp Greek seasoning
2 tbsp almond flour

Directions

Preheat the oven to 350 F. Heat olive oil in a skillet over medium heat and sauté the onion, garlic, tomato, celery, and carrots for 5 minutes; set aside to cool.

Mix the egg, 1 cup of Parmesan cheese, feta cheese, and salt in a bowl; set aside.

Pour the heavy cream in a pot and bring to heat over a medium fire while continually stirring. Stir in the remaining Parmesan cheese, and 1 teaspoon of Greek seasoning; set aside.

Spread a small amount of the cream sauce at the bottom of the baking dish and place the eggplant strips in a single layer on top of the sauce. Spread a layer of feta cheese on the eggplants, sprinkle some veggies on it, and repeat the layering process from the sauce until all the ingredients are exhausted.

In a small bowl, evenly mix the melted butter, almond flour, and 1 teaspoon of Greek seasoning. Spread the top of the mousaka layers with this mixture and sprinkle with mozzarella cheese. Cover the dish with foil and place it in the oven to bake for 25 minutes. Remove the foil and bake for 5 minutes until the cheese is slightly burned. Slice the mousaka and serve warm.

Nutritional info per serving: Calories 612, Fat 33.5g, Net Carbs 13.5g, Protein 36.6g

Poppy Seed Coleslaw

Prep + Cook Time: 3 hours 15 minutes | Serves: 2-4

Ingredients

Dressing

2 tbsp olive oil
1 cup poppy seeds
2 cups water
2 tbsp green onions, chopped
1 garlic clove, minced

1 lime, freshly squeezed
Salt and black pepper, to taste
¼ tsp dill, minced
1 tbsp yellow mustard

Salad

½ head white cabbage, shredded
1 carrot, shredded
1 shallot, sliced

2 tbsp Kalamata olives, pitted

Directions

In a food processor, place olive oil, water, green onion, mustard, dill, lime juice, salt, and black pepper to taste. Pulse until well incorporated. Add in poppy seeds and mix well.

Place cabbage, carrot, and onion in a bowl and mix to combine. Transfer to a salad plate, pour the dressing over and top with kalamata olives to serve.

Nutritional info per serving: Calories 235; Fat: 17.3g, Net Carbs: 6.4g, Protein: 8.1g

Tofu & Hazelnut Loaded Zucchini

Prep + Cook Time: 50 minutes | Serves: 2-4

Ingredients

2 tbsp olive oil
12 ounces firm tofu, drained and crumbled
2 garlic cloves, pressed
½ cup onions, chopped
2 cups crushed tomatoes
¼ tsp dried oregano

Salt and black pepper to taste
¼ tsp chili pepper
2 zucchinis, cut into halves, scoop out the insides
¼ cup hazelnuts, chopped
2 tbsp cilantro, chopped

Directions

Sauté onion, garlic, and tofu in olive oil for 5 minutes until softened. Place in scooped zucchini flesh, 1 cup of tomatoes, oregano, and chili pepper. Season with salt, and pepper and cook for 6 minutes.

Preheat oven to 390 F. Pour the remaining tomatoes in a baking dish. Spoon the tofu mixture into the zucchini shells. Arrange the zucchini boats in the baking dish. Bake for about 30 minutes. Sprinkle with hazelnuts and continue baking for 5 to 6 more minutes. Scatter with cilantro to serve.

Nutritional info per serving: Calories 234; Fat: 18.3g, Net Carbs: 5.9g, Protein: 12.5g

Parsnip & Carrot Strips with Walnut Sauce

Prep + Cook Time: 15 minutes | Serves: 2-4

Ingredients

2 tbsp olive oil
2 carrots, cut into strips
2 parsnips, cut into strips

½ cup water
Salt and black pepper to taste
1 tsp rosemary, chopped

Walnut sauce

½ cup walnuts
3 tbsp nutritional yeast
Salt and black pepper, to taste

¼ tsp onion powder
½ tsp garlic powder
¼ cup olive oil

Directions

Set a pan over medium heat and warm oil; cook the parsnips and carrots for 1 minute as you stir. Add in water and cook for an additional 6 minutes. Sprinkle with rosemary, salt, and pepper; transfer to a serving platter.

Place all sauce ingredients in a food processor and pulse until you attain the required consistency. Pour the sauce over the vegetables and serve.

Nutritional info per serving: Calories 338; Fat: 28.6g, Net Carbs: 9.7g, Protein: 6.5g

Cauliflower & Celery Bisque

Prep + Cook Time: 30 minutes | Serves: 2-4

Ingredients

2 tbsp olive oil
1 onion, finely chopped
1 garlic clove, minced
1 head cauliflower, cut into florets
½ cup celery, chopped

4 cups vegetable broth
½ cup heavy cream
Salt and black pepper to taste
1 tbsp parsley, chopped

Directions

Set a large pot over medium heat and warm the olive oil. Add celery, garlic and onion and sauté until translucent, about 5 minutes. Place in vegetable broth and cauliflower.

Bring to a boil, reduce the heat and simmer for 15-20 minutes. Transfer the soup to an immersion blender and blend to achieve the required consistency; top with parsley to serve.

Nutritional info per serving: Calories 187; Fat: 13.5g, Net Carbs: 5.6g, Protein: 4.1g

Balsamic Roasted Vegetables with Feta & Almonds

Prep + Cook Time: 45 minutes | Serves: 2-4

Ingredients

4 tbsp olive oil
1 red bell pepper, sliced
1 green bell pepper, sliced
1 orange bell pepper, sliced
½ head broccoli, cut into florets
2 zucchinis, sliced
8 white pearl onions, peeled

2 garlic cloves, halved
2 thyme sprigs, chopped
1 tsp dried sage, crushed
2 tbsp balsamic vinegar
Sea salt and cayenne pepper, to taste
1 cup feta cheese, crumbled
½ cup almonds, toasted and chopped

Directions

Preheat oven to 375 F. Mix all vegetables with olive oil, seasonings, and balsamic vinegar; shake well. Spread the vegetables out in a baking dish and roast in the oven for 40 minutes or until tender, flipping once halfway through.

Remove from the oven to a serving plate. Scatter the feta cheese and almonds all over and serve.

Nutritional info per serving: Calories 276; Fat: 23.3g, Net Carbs: 7.9g, Protein: 8.1g

Cauliflower-Kale Dip

Prep + Cook Time: 10 minutes | Serves: 2-4

Ingredients

¼ cup olive oil
1 pound cauliflower, cut into florets
2 cups kale
Salt and black pepper, to taste

1 garlic clove, minced
1 tbsp sesame paste
1 tbsp fresh lime juice
½ tsp garam masala

Directions

In a large pot filled with salted water over medium heat, steam cauliflower until tender for 5 minutes. Add in the kale and continue to cook for another 2-3 minutes.

Drain, transfer to a blender and pulse until smooth. Place in garam masala, oil, black pepper, fresh lime juice, garlic, salt and sesame paste. Blend the mixture until well combined. Decorate with some additional olive oil and serve.

Nutritional info per serving: Calories 185; Fat: 16.5g, Net Carbs: 3.9g, Protein: 3.5g

Tofu & Vegetable Casserole
Prep + Cook Time: 45 minutes | Serves: 2-4

Ingredients

10 oz tofu, pressed and cubed
2 tsp olive oil
1 cup leeks, chopped
1 garlic clove, minced
½ cup celery, chopped
½ cup carrot, chopped
1 ½ pounds Brussels sprouts, shredded
1 habanero pepper, chopped

2 ½ cups mushrooms, sliced
1 ½ cups vegetable stock
2 tomatoes, chopped
2 thyme sprigs, chopped
1 rosemary sprig, chopped
2 bay leaves
Salt and ground black pepper to taste

Directions

Set a pot over medium heat and warm oil. Add in garlic and leeks and sauté until soft and translucent, about 3 minutes. Add in tofu and cook for another 4 minutes. Add the habanero pepper, celery, mushrooms, and carrots. Cook as you stir for 5 minutes. Stir in the rest of the ingredients.

Simmer for 25 to 35 minutes or until cooked through. Remove and discard the bay leaves.

Nutritional info per serving: Calories 328; Fat: 18.5g, Net Carbs: 9.7g, Protein: 21g

Cauliflower-Based Waffles with Zucchini & Cheese
Prep + Cook Time: 45 minutes | Serves: 2

Ingredients

2 green onions
1 tbsp olive oil
2 eggs
1/3 cup Parmesan cheese
1 cup zucchini, shredded and squeezed

1 cup mozzarella cheese, grated
½ head cauliflower
1 tsp garlic powder
1 tbsp sesame seeds
2 tsp thyme, chopped

Directions

Chop the cauliflower into florets, toss the pieces a the food processor and pulse until rice is formed. Remove to a clean kitchen towel and press to eliminate excess moisture. Return to the food processor and add zucchini, spring onions, and thyme; pulse until smooth and transfer to a bowl.

Stir in the rest of the ingredients and mix to combine. Leave to rest for 10 minutes. Heat waffle iron and spread in the mixture, evenly. Cook until golden brown, for about 5 minutes.

Nutritional info per serving: Calories 336, Fat: 21g, Net Carbs: 7.2g, Protein: 32.6g

Pumpkin & Bell Pepper Noodles with Avocado Sauce

Prep + Cook Time: 15 minutes | Serves: 2-4

Ingredients

½ pound pumpkin, spiralized
½ pound bell peppers, spiralized
2 tbsp olive oil
2 avocados, chopped
1 lemon, juiced and zested
2 tbsp sesame oil

2 tbsp cilantro, chopped
1 onion, chopped
1 jalapeño pepper, deveined and minced
Salt and black pepper, to taste
2 tbsp pumpkin seeds

Directions

Toast the pumpkin seeds in a dry nonstick skillet, stirring frequently for a minute until golden; set aside. Add in oil and sauté bell peppers and pumpkin for 8 minutes. Remove to a serving platter.

Combine avocados, sesame oil, onion, jalapeño pepper, lemon juice, and lemon zest in a food processor and pulse to obtain a creamy mixture. Adjust the seasoning and pour over the vegetable noodles, top with the pumpkin seeds and serve.

Nutritional info per serving: Calories 673; Fat: 59g, Net Carbs: 9.8g, Protein: 22.9g

Curried Cauliflower & Mushrooms Traybake

Prep + Cook Time: 30 minutes | Serves: 2-4

Ingredients

1 head cauliflower, cut into florets
1 cup mushrooms, halved
4 garlic cloves, minced
1 red onion, sliced
2 tomatoes, chopped

¼ cup coconut oil, melted
1 tsp chili paprika paste
½ tsp curry powder
Salt and black pepper, to taste

Directions

Set oven to 380 F and grease a baking dish with the coconut oil.

In a large bowl, toss the cauliflower and mushrooms, garlic, onion, tomatoes, chili paprika paste, curry, black pepper, and salt. Spread out on the baking dish and roast for 20-25 minutes, turning once. Place in a plate and drizzle over the cooking juices to serve.

Nutritional info per serving: Calories 171; Fat: 15.7g, Net Carbs: 6.9g, Protein: 3.5g

Tasty Tofu & Swiss Chard Dip

Prep + Cook Time: 10 minutes | Serves: 2-4

Ingredients

2 tbsp mayonnaise
2 cups Swiss chard
½ cup tofu, pressed, drained, crumbled
¼ cup almond milk
1 tsp nutritional yeast

1 garlic clove, minced
2 tbsp olive oil
Salt and pepper to taste
½ tsp paprika
½ tsp mint leaves, chopped

Directions

Fill a pot with salted water and boil Swiss chard over medium heat for 5-6 minutes, until wilted.

Puree the remaining ingredients, except for the mayonnaise, in a food processor. Season with salt and black pepper. Stir in the Swiss chard and mayonnaise to get a homogeneous mixture.

Nutritional info per serving: Calories 136; Fat: 11g, Net Carbs: 6.3g, Protein: 3.1g

One-Pot Ratatouille with Pecans

Prep + Cook Time: 47 minutes | Serves: 2-4

Ingredients

2 tbsp olive oil
1 eggplant, sliced
1 zucchini, sliced
1 red onion, sliced
14 oz canned tomatoes
1 red bell peppers, sliced
1 yellow bell pepper, sliced

1 cloves garlic, sliced
¼ cup basil leaves, chop half
2 sprigs thyme
1 tbsp balsamic vinegar
½ lemon, zested
¼ cup pecans, chopped
Salt and black pepper to taste

Directions

Place a casserole pot over medium heat and warm the olive oil. Sauté the eggplants, zucchinis, and bell peppers for 5 minutes. Spoon the veggies into a large bowl.

In the same pan, sauté garlic, onion, and thyme leaves for 5 minutes and return the cooked veggies to the pan along with the canned tomatoes, balsamic vinegar, chopped basil, salt, and pepper to taste. Stir and cover the pot, and cook the ingredients on low heat for 30 minutes.

Stir in the remaining basil leaves, lemon zest, and adjust the seasoning to serve.

Nutritional info per serving: Calories 188, Fat 13g, Net Carbs 8.3g, Protein 4.5g

Baked Parsnip Chips with Yogurt Dip

Prep + Cook Time: 20 minutes | Serves: 2-4

Ingredients

3 tbsp olive oil
1/3 cup natural yogurt
1 tsp lime juice
1 tbsp parsley, chopped

Salt and black pepper, to taste
1 garlic clove, minced
2 cups parsnips, sliced

Directions

Preheat the oven to 300 F. Set parsnip slices on a baking sheet; toss with garlic powder, 1 tbsp of olive oil, and salt. Bake for 15 minutes, tossing once halfway through, until slices are crisp and slightly browned.

In a bowl, mix yogurt, lime juice, black pepper, 2 tbsp of olive oil, garlic, and salt until well combined. Serve the chips with yogurt dip.

Nutritional info per serving: Calories 176; Fat: 12.7g, Net Carbs: 8.7g, Protein: 1.9g

Roasted Cauliflower with Bell Peppers & Onion

Prep + Cook Time: 40 minutes | Serves: 2-4

Ingredients

1 pound cauliflower, cut into florets
2 bell peppers, halved
¼ cup olive oil
2 onions, quartered

Salt and black pepper, to taste
½ tsp cayenne pepper
1 tsp curry powder

Directions

Preheat oven to 425 F. Line a large baking sheet with parchment paper and spread out the cauliflower, onion, and bell peppers. Sprinkle olive oil, curry powder, black pepper, salt and cayenne pepper and toss to combine well.

Roast for 35 minutes as you toss in intervals until they start to brown.

Nutritional info per serving: Calories 186; Fat: 15.1g, Net Carbs: 8.2g, Protein: 3.9g

Oven-Roasted Asparagus with Romesco Sauce

Prep + Cook Time: 15 minutes | Serves: 2-4

Ingredients

1 pound asparagus spears, trimmed
2 tbsp olive oil

Salt and black pepper, to taste
½ tsp paprika

Romesco sauce

2 red bell peppers, roasted
2 tsp olive oil
2 tbsp almond flour
½ cup scallions, chopped
1 garlic clove, minced

1 tbsp lemon juice
½ tsp chili pepper
Salt and black pepper, to taste
2 tbsp rosemary, chopped

Directions

In a food processor, pulse together the bell peppers, salt, black pepper, garlic, lemon juice, scallions, almond flour, 2 tsp of olive oil and chili pepper. Mix evenly and set aside.

Preheat oven to 390 F and line a baking sheet with parchment paper. Add asparagus spears to the baking sheet. Toss with 2 tbsp of olive oil, paprika, black pepper, and salt. Bake until cooked through for 9 minutes. Transfer to a serving plate, pour the sauce over and garnish with rosemary to serve.

Nutritional info per serving: Calories 145; Fat: 11g, Net Carbs: 5.9g, Protein: 4.1g

Parmesan Brussels Sprouts with Onion

Prep + Cook Time: 45 minutes | Serves: 2-4

Ingredients

1 ½ pounds Brussels sprouts, halved
2 large red onions, sliced
2 tbsp olive oil

Salt and black pepper, to taste
1 tbsp fresh chives, chopped
2 tbsp Parmesan cheese, shredded

Directions

Set oven to 400 F and spread Brussel sprout halves and onion slices on a baking sheet. Season with black pepper and drizzle with olive oil; toss to coat.

Roast in the oven for 30 minutes, until the vegetables become soft. Sprinkle with Parmesan cheese and bake for 5-10 more minutes until the cheese melts. Serve scattered with chives.

Nutritional info per serving: Calories: 179; Fat 9g, Net Carbs 8.6g, Protein 7.5g

Chocolate Nut Granola

Prep + Cook Time: 1 hour | Serves: 2-4

Ingredients

¼ cup cocoa powder
1/3 tbsp coconut oil, melted
¼ cup almond flakes
¼ cup almond milk
¼ tbsp xylitol
1/8 tsp salt
1/3 tsp lime zest

¼ tsp ground cinnamon
¼ cup pecans, chopped
¼ cup almonds, slivered
1 tbsp pumpkin seeds
2 tbsp sunflower seeds
2 tbsp flax seed

Directions

Preheat oven to 300 F and line a baking dish with parchment paper. Set aside.

Mix almond flakes, cocoa powder, ground cinnamon, almonds, xylitol, pumpkin seeds, sunflower seeds, flax seed, and salt in a bowl.

In a separate bowl, whisk coconut oil, almond milk and lemon zest until combined. Pour over the other mixture and stir to coat.

Lay the mixture in an even layer onto the baking dish. Bake for 50 minutes, making sure that you shake gently in intervals of 15 minutes. Let cool completely before serving.

Nutritional info per serving: Calories 273; Fat: 26.2g, Net Carbs: 8.9g, Protein: 4.6g

Mozzarella & Bell Pepper Avocado Cups

Prep + Cook Time: 10 minutes | Serves: 2-4

Ingredients

2 avocados
½ cup fresh mozzarella, chopped
2 tbsp olive oil
2 cups green bell peppers, chopped
1 onion, chopped

½ tsp garlic puree
Salt and black pepper, to taste
½ tomato, chopped
2 tbsp basil, chopped

Directions

Halve the avocados and scoop out 2 teaspoons of flesh; set aside.

Sauté olive oil, garlic, onion, and bell peppers in a skillet over medium heat for 5 minutes until tender. Remove to a bowl and leave to cool. Mix in the reserved avocado, tomato, salt, mozzarella, and black pepper. Fill the avocado halves with the mixture and serve sprinkled with basil.

Nutritional info per serving: Calories 273; Fat: 22.5g, Net Carbs: 6.9g, Protein: 8.3g

Green Mac and Cheese

Prep + Cook Time: 15 minutes | Serves: 2-4

Ingredients

4 zucchinis, spiralized
2 tbsp butter, melted
Salt and black pepper, to taste
1 cup heavy cream

1 cup cream cheese
1 tsp garlic paste
½ tsp onion flakes

Directions

Shake zucchinis with melted butter, salt and pepper. Cook in a saucepan over medium heat for 5-6 minutes. Remove to a serving plate.

In the same pan, pour the heavy cream, garlic paste, and cream cheese and heat through, stirring frequently. Reduce heat to low and simmer for 2-3 minutes until thickened. Adjust the seasoning.

Coat the zucchinis in the cheese sauce and serve immediately in serving bowls.

Nutritional info per serving: Calories 686; Fat: 72g, Net Carbs: 3.9g, Protein: 10g

Roasted Tomatoes with Vegan Cheese Crust

Prep + Cook Time: 15 minutes | Serves: 2-4

Ingredients

3 tomatoes, sliced
2 tbsp olive oil
½ cup pepitas seeds
1 tbsp nutritional yeast

Salt and black pepper, to taste
1 tsp garlic puree
2 tbsp parsley. chopped

Directions

Preheat oven to 380 F and grease a baking pan with olive oil. Drizzle olive oil over the tomatoes.

In a food processor, add pepitas seeds, nutritional yeast, garlic puree, salt and pepper, and pulse until the desired consistency is attained. Press the mixture firmly onto each slice of tomato. Set the tomato slices on the prepared baking pan and bake for 10 minutes. Serve sprinkled with parsley.

Nutritional info per serving: Calories 165; Fat: 14.7g, Net Carbs: 3.2g, Protein: 6.2g

MEAT RECIPES

Veggie Beef Stew with Root Mash

Prep + Cook Time: 1 hour 50 minutes | Serves: 2

Ingredients

1 tbsp olive oil
1 parsnip, chopped
1 garlic clove, minced
1 onion, chopped
1 celery stalk, chopped
½ pound stewing beef, cut into chunks
Salt and black pepper to taste
1 ¼ cups beef stock

2 bay leaves
1 carrot, chopped
½ tbsp fresh rosemary, chopped
1 tomato, chopped
2 tbsp red wine
½ cauliflower head, cut into florets
½ celeriac, chopped
2 tbsp butter

Directions

In a pot, cook the celery, onion, and garlic, in warm oil over medium heat for 5 minutes. Stir in the beef chunks, and cook for 3 minutes. Season with salt and black pepper.

Deglaze the bottom of the pot by adding the red wine. Add in the carrot, parsnip, beef stock, tomato, and bay leaves. Boil the mixture, reduce the heat to low and cook for 1 hour and 30 minutes.

Meanwhile, heat a pot with water over medium heat. Place in the celeriac, cover and simmer for 10 minutes. Add in the cauliflower florets, cook for 15 minutes, drain everything and combine with butter, pepper and salt. Mash using a potato masher and split the mash between 2 plates.

Top with vegetable mixture and stewed beef, sprinkle with rosemary and serve.

Nutritional info per serving: Calories 465, Fat 24.5g, Net Carbs 9.8g, Protein 32g

Asian Spiced Beef with Broccoli

Prep + Cook Time: 30 minutes | Serves: 2

Ingredients

½ cup coconut milk
2 tbsp coconut oil
¼ tsp garlic powder
¼ tsp onion powder
½ tbsp coconut aminos
1 pound beef steak, cut into strips

Salt and black pepper, to taste
1 head broccoli, cut into florets
½ tbsp thai green curry paste
1 tsp ginger paste
1 tbsp cilantro, chopped
½ tbsp sesame seeds

Directions

Warm coconut oil in a pan over medium heat, add in the beef, season with garlic powder, black pepper, salt, ginger paste, and onion powder and cook for 4 minutes. Mix in the broccoli and stir-fry for 5 minutes.

Pour in the coconut milk, coconut aminos, and thai curry paste and cook for 15 minutes. Serve sprinkled with cilantro and sesame seeds.

Nutritional info per serving: Calories 623, Fat 43.2g, Net Carbs 2.3g, Protein 53.5g

Flank Steak Roll

Prep + Cook Time: 42 minutes | Serves: 2

Ingredients

1 lb flank steak
Salt and black pepper to taste
½ cup ricotta cheese, crumbled

½ cup baby kale, chopped
1 serrano pepper, chopped
1 tbsp basil leaves, chopped

Directions

Wrap the steak in plastic wraps, place on a flat surface, and gently run a rolling pin over to flatten. Take off the wraps. Sprinkle with half of the ricotta cheese, top with kale, serrano pepper, and the remaining cheese. Roll the steak over on the stuffing and secure with toothpicks.

Place in the greased baking sheet and cook for 30 minutes at 390 F, flipping once until nicely browned on the outside and the cheese melted within. Cool for 3 minutes, slice and serve with basil.

Nutritional info per serving: Calories 445, Fat 21g, Net Carbs 2.8g, Protein 53g

Grilled Beef on Skewers with Fresh Salad

Prep + Cook Time: 25 minutes | Serves: 2

Ingredients

1 lb sirloin steak, boneless, cubed
¼ cup ranch dressing
1 red onion, sliced
½ tbsp white wine vinegar
1 tbsp extra virgin olive oil

2 ripe tomatoes, sliced
2 tbsp fresh parsley, chopped
1 cucumber, sliced
Salt to taste

Directions

Thread the beef cubes on the skewers, about 4 to 5 cubes per skewer. Brush half of the ranch dressing on the skewers (all around).

Preheat grill to 400 F and place the skewers on the grill grate to cook for 6 minutes. Turn the skewers once and cook further for 6 minutes.

Brush the remaining ranch dressing on the meat and cook them for 1 more minute on each side.

In a salad bowl mix together red onion, tomatoes, and cucumber, sprinkle with salt, vinegar, and extra virgin olive oil; toss to combine. Top the salad with skewers and scatter the parsley all over.

Nutritional info per serving: Calories 423, Fat 24g, Net Carbs 2.4g, Protein 45.1g

Grilled Steak with Herb Butter & Green Beans

Prep + Cook Time: 20 minutes | Serves: 2

Ingredients

2 ribeye steaks
2 tbsp unsalted butter
1 tsp olive oil
½ cup green beans, sliced

Salt and ground pepper, to taste
1 tbsp fresh thyme, chopped
1 tbsp fresh rosemary, chopped
1 tbsp fresh parsley, chopped

Directions

Brush the steaks with olive oil and season with salt and black pepper. Preheat a grill pan over high heat and cook the steaks for about 4 minutes per side; set aside. Steam the green beans for 3-4 minutes until tender. Season with salt.

Melt the butter in the pan and stir-fry the herbs for 1 minute; then mix in the green beans. Transfer over the steaks and serve.

Nutritional info per serving: Calories 576, Fat: 39g, Net Carbs: 4.3g, Protein: 51g

King Size Burgers

Prep + Cook Time: 25 minutes | Serves: 2

Ingredients

2 tbsp olive oil
1 pound ground beef
2 green onions, chopped
1 garlic clove, minced
1 tbsp thyme

2 tbsp almond flour
2 tbsp cup beef broth
½ tbsp chopped parsley
½ tbsp Worcestershire sauce

Directions

Grease a baking dish with the olive oil.

Combine all ingredients except for the parsley in a bowl. Mix well with your hands and make 2 patties out of the mixture. Arrange on a lined baking sheet. Bake at 370 F, for about 18 minutes, until nice and crispy. Serve sprinkled with parsley.

Nutritional info per serving: Calories 363, Fat: 26g, Net Carbs: 3.1g, Protein: 25.4g

Portobello Mushroom Beef Cheeseburgers

Prep + Cook Time: 15 minutes | Serves: 2

Ingredients

2 tbsp olive oil
½ lb ground beef
½ tsp fresh parsley, chopped
½ tsp sugar-free Worcestershire sauce

Salt and black pepper to taste
2 slices mozzarella cheese
2 portobello mushroom caps

Directions

In a bowl, mix the beef, parsley, Worcestershire sauce, salt and black pepper with your hands until evenly combined. Make medium-sized patties out of the mixture.

Preheat a grill to 400 F and coat the mushroom caps with olive oil, salt and black pepper.

Lay portobello caps, rounded side up and burger patties onto the hot grill pan and cook for 5 minutes. Turn the mushroom caps and continue cooking for 1 minute.

Lay a mozzarella slice on top each patty. Continue cooking until the mushroom caps are softened and the turkey patties are no longer pink in the center, 4 to 5 minutes more. Flip the patties and top with cheese. Cook for another 2-3 minutes to be well done while the cheese melts onto the meat. Remove the patties and sandwich into two mushroom caps each.

Nutritional info per serving: Calories 505, Fat 38.5g, Net Carbs 3.2g, Protein 38g

Grilled Beef Steaks & Vegetable Medley

Prep + Cook Time: 30 minutes | Serves: 2

Ingredients

2 sirloin beef steaks
Salt and black pepper to taste
2 tbsp olive oil
1 ½ tbsp balsamic vinegar
¼ lb asparagus, trimmed

½ cup mushrooms, sliced
½ cup snow peas
1 red bell pepper, seeded, cut into strips
1 small onion, quartered
1 garlic clove, sliced

Directions

In a bowl, put asparagus, mushrooms, snow peas, bell pepper, onion, and garlic.

Mix salt, pepper, olive oil, and balsamic vinegar in a small bowl, and pour half of the mixture over the vegetables; stir to combine and set aside. To the remaining oil mixture, add in the beef and toss to coat well.

Preheat a grill pan over high heat. Place the steaks in the grill pan and sear both sides for 2 minutes each, then continue cooking for 6 minutes on each side.

When done, remove the beef onto a plate; set aside.

Now, pour the vegetables and marinade in the pan; and cook for 5 minutes, turning once. Turn the heat off and share the vegetables into plates.

Top with each piece of beef, the sauce from the pan, and serve warm.

Nutritional info per serving: Calories 488, Fat 31g, Net Carbs 4.1g, Protein 57g

Beef Roast with Red Wine & Vegetables

Prep + Cook Time: 2 hours 20 minutes | Serves: 2

Ingredients

1 tbsp olive oil
1 lb brisket
½ cup carrots, peeled
1 red onion, quartered
2 stalks celery, cut into chunks

1 garlic clove, minced
Salt and black pepper to taste
1 bay leaf
1 tbsp fresh thyme, chopped
1 cup red wine

Directions

Season the brisket with salt and pepper. Brown the meat on both sides in warm olive oil over medium heat for 6-8 minutes. Transfer to a deep casserole dish.

In the dish, arrange the carrots, onion, garlic, celery, and bay leaf around the brisket and pour the beer all over it. Cover the pot and cook the ingredients in the oven for 2 hours at 370 F.

When ready, remove the casserole. Transfer the beef to a chopping board and cut it into thick slices. Serve the beef and vegetables with a drizzle of the sauce.

Nutritional info per serving: Calories 446, Fat 21.3g, Net Carbs 5.6g, Protein 52.6g

Beef Burgers with Iceberg Lettuce & Avocado

Prep + Cook Time: 15 minutes | Serves: 2

Ingredients

½ pound ground beef
1 green onion, chopped
½ tsp garlic powder
1 tbsp butter
Salt and black pepper to taste
1 tbsp olive oil

½ tsp Dijon mustard
2 low carb buns, halved
2 tbsp mayonnaise
½ tsp balsamic vinegar
2 tbsp iceberg lettuce, chopped
1 avocado, sliced

Directions

In a bowl, mix together the beef, green onion, garlic powder, mustard, salt, and black pepper; create 2 burgers. Heat the butter and olive oil in a skillet and cook the burgers for about 3 minutes per side.

Fill the buns with lettuce, mayonnaise, balsamic vinegar, burgers, and avocado slices to serve.

Nutritional info per serving: Calories 778, Fat: 62g, Net Carbs: 5.6g, Protein: 34g

Cilantro Beef Balls with Mascarpone

Prep + Cook Time: 45 minutes | Serves: 2-4

Ingredients

1 garlic clove, minced
1 pound ground beef
1 small onion, chopped
1 jalapeño pepper, chopped
2 tsp cilantro
½ tsp allspice
1 tsp cumin

Salt and black pepper, to taste
1 tbsp butter + 1 ½ tbsp melted
½ cup mascarpone cheese, at room temperature
¼ tsp turmeric
¼ tsp baking powder
1 cup flax meal
¼ cup coconut flour

Directions

Puree onion with garlic, jalapeño pepper, and ¼ cup water in a blender.

Set a pan over medium heat, add in 1 tbsp butter and cook the beef for 3 minutes. Stir in the onion mixture, and cook for 2 minutes.

Stir in cilantro, salt, cumin, turmeric, allspice, and black pepper, and cook for 3 minutes.

In a bowl, combine coconut flour, flax meal, and baking powder. In a separate bowl, combine the melted butter with the mascarpone cheese.

Combine the 2 mixtures to obtain a dough. Form balls from this mixture, set them on a parchment paper, and roll each into a circle.

Split the beef mix on one-half of the dough circles, cover with the other half, seal edges, and lay on a lined sheet.

Bake for 25 minutes in the oven at 350 F.

Nutritional info per serving: Calories 434, Fat 26.3g, Net Carbs 8.6g, Protein 32.7g

Traditional Scottish Beef Dish with Parsnips

Prep + Cook Time: 40 minutes | Serves: 2-4

Ingredients

2 tbsp olive oil
12 oz canned corn beef, cubed
1 onion, chopped
4 parsnips, peeled and chopped
1 carrot, chopped
1 garlic clove, minced

Salt and black pepper to taste
1 cup vegetable broth
2 tsp rosemary leaves
1 tbsp sugar-free Worcestershire sauce
½ small cabbage, shredded

Directions

Add the onion, garlic, carrots, rosemary, and parsnips to a warm olive oil over medium heat. Stir and cook for a minute. Pour in the vegetable broth and Worcestershire sauce.

Stir the mixture and cook the ingredients on low heat for 25 minutes. Stir in the cabbage and corn beef, season with salt and pepper, and cook further for 10 minutes.

Nutritional info per serving: Calories 321, Fat 16.7g, Net Carbs 2.3g, Protein 13.4g

Traditional Bolognese Sauce with Zoodles

Prep + Cook Time: 35 minutes | Serves: 2-4

Ingredients

2 cups zoodles
1 pound ground beef
2 garlic cloves
1 onion, chopped
1 tsp oregano

1 tsp sage
1 tsp rosemary
7 oz canned chopped tomatoes
2 tbsp olive oil

Directions

Cook the zoodles in warm olive oil over medium heat for 3-4 minutes and remove to a serving plate. To the same pan, add onion and garlic and cook for 3 minutes. Add beef and cook until browned, about 4-5 minutes. Stir in the herbs and tomatoes. Cook for 15 minutes and serve over the zoodles.

Nutritional info per serving: Calories 336, Fat: 21g, Net Carbs: 7.3g, Protein: 29g

Juicy Beef with Rosemary & Thyme

Prep + Cook Time: 25 minutes | Serves: 2-4

Ingredients

2 garlic cloves, minced
2 tbsp butter
2 tbsp olive oil
1 tbsp fresh rosemary, chopped
1 pound beef rump steak, sliced
Salt and black pepper, to taste
1 shallot, chopped
½ cup heavy cream

½ cup beef stock
1 tbsp mustard
2 tsp soy sauce, sugar-free
2 tsp lemon juice
1 tsp xylitol
A sprig of rosemary
A sprig of thyme

Directions

Set a pan to medium heat, warm in a tbsp of olive oil and stir in the shallot; cook for 3 minutes. Stir in the stock, soy sauce, xylitol, thyme sprig, cream, mustard and rosemary sprig, and cook for 8 minutes. Stir in butter, lemon juice, pepper and salt. Get rid of the rosemary and thyme. Set aside.

In a bowl, combine the remaining oil with black pepper, garlic, rosemary, and salt. Toss in the beef to coat, and set aside for some minutes.

Heat a pan over medium-high heat, place in the beef steak, cook for 6 minutes, flipping halfway through; set aside and keep warm. Plate the beef slices, sprinkle over the sauce, and enjoy.

Nutritional info per serving: Calories 441, Fat 31g, Net Carbs 4.6g, Protein 28.5g

Spicy Hot Grilled Spare Ribs

Prep + Cook Time: 32 minutes | Serves: 2-4

Ingredients

4 tbsp BBQ sauce , sugar-free
2 tbsp olive oil
2 tbsp xylitol
Salt and black pepper to taste

3 tsp hot chili powder
1 tsp garlic powder
1 lb spare ribs

Directions

Preheat oven to 400 F. In a bowl, mix the xylitol, salt, pepper, canola oil, hot chili powder and garlic powder. Brush on the meaty sides of the ribs and wrap in foil. Sit for 30 minutes to marinate.

Place wrapped ribs on a baking sheet, and cook for 40 minutes to be cooked through. Remove ribs and aluminium foil, brush with BBQ sauce, and brown under the broiler for 10 minutes. Slice to serve.

Nutritional info per serving: Calories 406, Fat 34.1g, Net Carbs 3.4g, Protein 25.5g

Skirt Steak with Cauli Rice & Green Beans

Prep + Cook Time: 22 minutes | Serves: 2-4

Ingredients

3 cups green beans, chopped
2 cups cauli rice
2 tbsp ghee
1 tbsp olive oil

1 lb skirt steak
Salt and black pepper to taste
4 fresh eggs
Hot sauce (sugar-free) for topping

Directions

Put the cauli rice and green beans in a bowl, sprinkle with a little water, and steam in the microwave for 90 seconds to be tender. Share into bowls.

Warm the ghee and olive oil in a skillet, season the beef with salt and black pepper, and brown for 5 minutes on each side. Use a perforated spoon to ladle the meat onto the vegetables.

Wipe out the skillet and return to medium heat, crack in an egg, season with salt and pepper and cook until the egg white has set, but the yolk is still runny 3 minutes. Remove egg onto the vegetable bowl and fry the remaining 3 eggs. Add to the other bowls. Drizzle with hot sauce and serve.

Nutritional info per serving: Calories 334, Fat 25.3g, Net Carbs 6.3g, Protein 14g

Casserole with Beef Sausage & Okra

Prep + Cook Time: 60 minutes | Serves: 2-4

Ingredients

1 cup okra, trimmed
1 tbsp olive oil
1 celery stalk, chopped
¼ cup almond flour
1 egg
1 pound beef sausage, chopped
Salt and black pepper, to taste
½ tbsp dried parsley

¼ tsp red pepper flakes
¼ cup Parmesan cheese, grated
2 green onions, chopped
½ tsp garlic powder
¼ tsp dried oregano
½ cup ricotta cheese
½ cup marinara sauce, sugar-free
1 cup cheddar cheese, shredded

Directions

In a bowl, combine the sausage, pepper, pepper flakes, oregano, egg, Parmesan cheese, green onions, almond flour, salt, parsley, celery, and garlic powder. Form balls, lay them on a lined baking sheet, place in the oven at 390 F, and bake for 15 minutes.

Remove the balls from the oven and cover with half of the marinara sauce and okra. Pour ricotta cheese all over followed by the rest of the marinara sauce. Scatter the cheddar cheese and bake in the oven for 10 minutes. Allow the meatballs casserole to cool before serving.

Nutritional info per serving: Calories 479, Fat 31g, Net Carbs 4.3g, Protein 39.5g

Mini Beef & Mushroom Meatloaf

Prep + Cook Time: 1 hour and 15 minutes | Serves: 2-4

Ingredients

Meatloaf:

1 pound ground beef
½ onion, chopped
1 tbsp almond milk
1 tbsp almond flour
1 garlic clove, minced

1 cup sliced mushrooms
1 small egg
Salt and black pepper to taste
1 tbsp parsley, chopped
1/3 cup Parmesan cheese, grated

Glaze:

1/3 cup balsamic vinegar
¼ tbsp xylitol
¼ tsp tomato paste

¼ tsp garlic powder
¼ tsp onion powder
1 tbsp ketchup, sugar-free

Directions

Grease a loaf pan with cooking spray and set aside. Preheat oven to 390 F.

Combine all meatloaf ingredients in a large bowl. Press this mixture into the prepared loaf pan. Bake in the oven for about 30 minutes.

To make the glaze, whisk all ingredients in a bowl. Pour the glaze over the meatloaf. Put the meatloaf back in the oven and cook for 20 more minutes. Let meatloaf sit for 10 minutes before slicing.

Nutritional info per serving: Calories 311, Fat: 21.3g, Net Carbs: 5.5g, Protein: 24.2g

Ragout with Beef Bell Pepper & Green Beans

Prep + Cook Time: 1 hour 52 minutes | Serves: 2-4

Ingredients

2 tbsp olive oil
1 lb chuck steak, trimmed and cubed
Salt and black pepper to taste
2 tbsp almond flour
4 green onions, diced
½ cup dry white wine
1 yellow bell pepper, seeded and diced

1 cup green beans, chopped
2 tsp Worcestershire sauce, sugar-free
4 oz tomato puree
3 tsp smoked paprika
1 cup beef broth
Parsley leaves to garnish

Directions

Dredge the meat in the almond flour and set aside.

Place a large skillet over medium heat, add 1 tablespoon of oil to heat and then sauté the green onion, green beans, and bell pepper for 3 minutes. Stir in the paprika and the remaining olive oil.

Add the beef and cook for 10 minutes while turning them halfway. Stir in white wine, let it reduce by half, about 3 minutes, and add Worcestershire sauce, tomato puree, and beef broth.

Let the mixture boil for 2 minutes, then reduce the heat to lowest and let simmer for 1 ½ hours; stirring now and then. Adjust the taste and dish the ragout. Serve garnished with parsley leaves.

Nutritional info per serving: Calories 334, Fat 22g, Net Carbs 3.9g, Protein 35.3g

Zucchini Noodle Beef Lasagna

Prep + Cook Time: 1 hour 15 minutes | Serves: 2-4

Ingredients

2 tbsp olive oil
½ red chili, chopped
1 lb ground beef
3 large zucchinis, sliced lengthwise
2 garlic cloves, minced
1 shallot, chopped
1 cup tomato sauce

Salt and black pepper to taste
2 tsp sweet paprika
1 tsp dried thyme
1 tsp dried basil
1 cup mozzarella cheese, shredded
1 cup chicken broth

Directions

Heat the oil in a skillet and cook the beef for 4 minutes while breaking any lumps as you stir. Top with shallot, garlic, chilli, tomatoes, salt, paprika and black pepper. Stir and cook for 5 more minutes.

Lay 1/3 of the zucchinis slices in a greased baking dish. Top with 1/3 of the beef mixture and repeat the layering process two more times with the same quantities. Season with basil and thyme. Pour in the chicken broth.

Sprinkle the mozzarella cheese on top and tuck the baking dish in the oven. Bake for 35 minutes at 380 F. Remove the lasagna and let it rest for 10 minutes before serving.

Nutritional info per serving: Calories 451, Fat 22.8g, Net Carbs 6.8g, Protein 42g

Veggie Chuck Roast Beef in Oven

Prep + Cook Time: 1 hour 40 minutes | Serves: 2-4

Ingredients

2 tbsp olive oil
1 pound beef chuck roast, cubed
1 cup canned diced tomatoes
1 carrot, chopped
Salt and black pepper, to taste
½ pound mushrooms, sliced
1 celery stalk, chopped

1 bell pepper, sliced
1 onion, chopped
1 bay leaf
½ cup beef stock
1 tbsp fresh rosemary, chopped
½ tsp dry mustard
1 tbsp almond flour

Directions

Preheat oven to 350 F.

Set a pot over medium heat, warm olive oil and brown the beef on each side for 4-5 minutes. Stir in tomatoes, onion, mustard, carrot, mushrooms, bell pepper, celery, and stock. Season with salt and pepper.

In a bowl, combine ½ cup of water with flour and stir in the pot. Transfer to a baking dish and bake for 90 minutes, stirring at intervals of 30 minutes. Scatter the rosemary over and serve warm.

Nutritional info per serving: Calories 325, Fat 17.8g, Net Carbs 5.6g, Protein 31.5g

Sunday Gratin with Beef & Cheese

Prep + Cook Time: 30 minutes | Serves: 2-4

Ingredients

2 tbsp olive oil
1 onion, chopped
1 pound ground beef
2 garlic cloves, minced
Salt and black pepper, to taste

1 cup mozzarella cheese, shredded
1 cup fontina cheese, shredded
14 oz canned tomatoes, chopped
2 tbsp sesame seeds, toasted
20 dill pickle slices

Directions

Preheat the oven to 390 F. Heat olive oil in a pan over medium heat, place in the beef, garlic, salt, onion, and black pepper, and cook for 5 minutes. Remove and set to a baking dish, stir in half of the tomatoes and mozzarella cheese. Lay the pickle slices on top, spread over the fontina cheese and sesame seeds, and place in the oven to bake for 20 minutes.

Nutritional info per serving: Calories 523, Fat 43g, Net Carbs 6.5g, Protein 36.5g

Beef Fajitas with Colorful Bell Peppers

Prep + Cook Time: 35 minutes + marinade time | Serves: 2-4

Ingredients

2 tbsp olive oil
2 lb skirt steak, cut in halves
2 tbsp Cajun seasoning
Salt to taste

2 large white onion, chopped
¼ cup cheddar cheese, shredded
1 cup mixed bell peppers, chopped
12 low carb tortillas

Directions

Rub the steak with Cajun seasoning and marinate in the fridge for one hour.

Preheat grill to 400 F and cook steak for 6 minutes on each side, flipping once until lightly browned. Remove from heat and cover with foil to sit for 10 minutes, before slicing.

Heat the olive oil in a skillet over medium heat and sauté the onion and bell peppers for 5 minutes or until soft. Cut steak against the grain into strips and share on the tortillas. Top with the veggies and cheddar cheese, and serve.

Nutritional info per serving: Calories 512, Fat 32g, Net Carbs 4.7g, Protein 25g

Cilantro Beef Curry with Cauliflower

Prep + Cook Time: 26 minutes | Serves: 2-4

Ingredients

1 tbsp olive oil
½ lb ground beef
1 garlic clove, minced
1 tsp turmeric
1 tbsp cilantro, chopped
1 tbsp ginger paste

½ tsp garam masala
5 oz canned whole tomatoes
1 head cauliflower, cut into florets
Salt and chili pepper to taste
¼ cup water

Directions

Heat oil in a saucepan over medium heat, add the beef, garlic, ginger paste, and garam masala. Cook for 5 minutes while breaking any lumps.

Stir in the tomatoes and cauliflower, season with salt, turmeric, and chili pepper, and cook covered for 6 minutes. Add the water and bring to a boil over medium heat for 10 minutes or until the water has reduced by half. Spoon the curry into serving bowls and serve sprinkled with cilantro.

Nutritional info per serving: Calories 365, Fat 31.6g, Net Carbs 3.5g, Protein 19.5g

Ground Beef Stew with Majoram & Basil

Prep + Cook Time: 30 minutes | Serves: 2-4

Ingredients

2 tbsp olive oil
¼ cup red wine
1 pound ground beef
1 onion, chopped
2 garlic cloves, minced
14 ounces canned diced tomatoes

1 tbsp dried basil
1 tbsp dried marjoram
Salt and black pepper, to taste
2 carrots, sliced
2 celery stalks, chopped
1 cup vegetable broth

Directions

Put a pan over medium heat, add in the olive oil, onion, carrots, celery, and garlic, and sauté for 5 minutes. Place in the beef and cook for 6 minutes. Stir in the tomatoes, carrots, red wine, vegetable broth, black pepper, marjoram, basil, and salt, and simmer for 15 minutes. Serve and enjoy!

Nutritional info per serving: Calories 274, Fat 14.3g, Net Carbs 6.2g, Protein 29.5g

Casserole with Beef & Cauliflower

Prep + Cook Time: 30 minutes | Serves: 2-4

Ingredients

2 tbsp olive oil
1 pound ground beef
Salt and black pepper to taste
½ cup cauli rice
1 tbsp parsley, chopped

½ tsp dried oregano
1 cup kohlrabi, chopped
5 oz can diced tomatoes
¼ cup water
½ cup mozzarella cheese, shredded

Directions

Put beef in a pot and season with salt and black pepper and cook over medium heat for 6 minutes until no longer pink. Add cauli rice, kohlrabi, tomatoes, and water. Stir and bring to boil covered for 5 minutes to thicken the sauce. Adjust the taste with salt and black pepper.

Spoon the beef mixture into the baking dish and spread evenly. Sprinkle with cheese and bake in the oven for 15 minutes at 380 F until cheese has melted and it's golden brown. Remove and cool for 4 minutes, and serve sprinkled with parsley.

Nutritional info per serving: Calories 391, Fat 23.6g, Net Carbs 7.3g, Protein 19.5g

Beef, Broccoli & Rosemary Slow-Cooked Stew

Prep + Cook Time: 4 hours 15 minutes | Serves: 2-4

Ingredients

2 tbsp olive oil
1 pound ground beef
½ cup leeks, chopped
1 head broccoli, cut into florets
Salt and black pepper, to taste
1 tsp yellow mustard

1 tsp Worcestershire sauce
2 tomatoes, chopped
8 ounces tomato sauce
1 tbsp fresh rosemary, chopped
½ tsp dried oregano

Directions

Coat the broccoli with black pepper and salt. Set them into a bowl, drizzle over the olive oil, and toss to combine. In a separate bowl, combine the beef with Worcestershire sauce, leeks, salt, mustard, and black pepper, and stir well. Press on the slow cooker's bottom.

Scatter in the broccoli, add the tomatoes, oregano, and tomato sauce. Cook for 4 hours on high; covered. Serve the casserole with scattered rosemary.

Nutritional info per serving: Calories 677, Fat 42.1g, Net Carbs 8.3g, Protein 63g

Beef Roast with Serrano Pepper Gravy

Prep + Cook Time: 1 hour 25 minutes | Serves: 2-4

Ingredients

2 pounds beef roast
1 cup mushrooms, sliced
1 ½ cups beef stock

1 ounce onion soup mix
½ cup basil dressing
2 serrano peppers, shredded

Directions

Preheat the oven to 350 F.

In a bowl, combine the stock with the basil dressing and onion soup mixture. Place the beef roast in a pan, stir in the stock mixture, mushrooms, and serrano peppers; cover with aluminum foil.

Set in the oven and bake for 1 hour. Take out the foil and continue baking for 15 minutes. Allow the roast to cool, then slice, and serve alongside a topping of the gravy.

Nutritional info per serving: Calories 722, Fat 51g, Net Carbs 5.1g, Protein 71g

Jerked Beef Stew

Prep + Cook Time: 1 hour 10 minutes | Serves: 2-4

Ingredients

1 onion, chopped
2 tbsp olive oil
1 tsp ginger paste
1 tsp soy sauce
1 pound beef stew meat, cubed
1 red bell pepper, seeded and chopped
½ scotch bonnet pepper, chopped
2 green chilies, chopped

1 cup tomatoes, chopped
1 tbsp fresh cilantro, chopped
1 garlic clove, minced
¼ cup vegetable broth
Salt and black pepper, to taste
¼ cup black olives, chopped
1 tsp jerk seasoning

Directions

Brown the beef on all sides in warm olive oil over medium heat; remove and set aside. Stir-fry in the red bell peppers, green chilies, jerk seasoning, garlic, scotch bonnet pepper, onion, ginger paste, and soy sauce, for about 5-6 minutes. Pour in the tomatoes and broth, and cook for 1 hour.

Stir in the olives, adjust the seasonings and serve sprinkled with fresh cilantro.

Nutritional info per serving: Calories 235, Fat 13.4g, Net Carbs 2.8g, Protein 25.8g

Leek & Beef Bake

Prep + Cook Time: 50 minutes | Serves: 2-4

Ingredients

3 tbsp olive oil
1 pound beef steak racks
2 leeks, sliced
Salt and black pepper, to taste

½ cup apple cider vinegar
1 tsp Italian seasoning
1 tbsp xylitol

Directions

Preheat the oven to 420 F.

In a bowl, mix the leeks with 2 tbsp of oil, xylitol, and vinegar, toss to coat well, and set to a baking dish. Season with Italian seasoning, black pepper and salt, and cook in the oven for 15 minutes.

Sprinkle pepper and salt to the beef, place into an oiled pan over medium heat, and cook for a couple of minutes. Place the beef to the baking dish with the leeks, and bake for 20 minutes.

Nutritional info per serving: Calories 234, Fat 12g, Net Carbs 4.8g, Protein 15.5g

Roasted Pumpkin Filled with Beef & Mushrooms

Prep + Cook Time: 1 hour 15 minutes | Serves: 2-4

Ingredients

1 ½ lb pumpkin, pricked with a fork
Salt and black pepper, to taste
1 garlic clove, minced
1 onion, chopped
½ cup mushrooms, sliced

28 ounces canned diced tomatoes
¼ tsp cayenne pepper
½ tsp dried thyme
1 pound ground beef
1 cup cauli rice

Directions

Preheat the oven to 430 F. Lay the pumpkin on a lined baking sheet and bake in the oven for 40 minutes. Cut in half, set aside to cool, deseed, scoop out most of the flesh and let sit. Heat a greased pan over high heat, add in garlic, mushrooms, onion and beef, and cook until the meat browns.

Stir in green pepper, salt, thyme, tomatoes, black pepper, and cayenne, and cook for 10 minutes; stir in flesh and cauli rice. Stuff the squash halves with beef mixture, and bake in the oven for 10 minutes.

Nutritional info per serving: Calories 422, Fat 20g, Net Carbs 9.8g, Protein 33.4g

Winter Beef Stew

Prep + Cook Time: 40 minutes | Serves: 2-4

Ingredients

3 tsp olive oil
1 pound ground beef
1 cup beef stock
14 ounces canned tomatoes with juice
1 carrot, chopped
1 celery stick, chopped
1 pound butternut squash, chopped

1 tbsp Worcestershire sauce
2 bay leaves
Salt and black pepper, to taste
3 tbsp fresh parsley, chopped
1 onion, chopped
1 tsp dried sage
1 garlic clove, minced

Directions

Cook the onion, garlic, celery, carrot, and beef, in warm oil over medium heat for 10 minutes. Add in butternut squash, Worcestershire sauce, bay leaves, beef stock, canned tomatoes, and sage, and bring to a boil.

Reduce heat, and simmer for 20 minutes. Adjust the seasonings. Remove and discard the bay leaves and serve sprinkled with parsley.

Nutritional info per serving: Calories 353, Fat 16.5g, Net Carbs 6.6g, Protein 26.1g

Spiced Roast Beef

Prep + Cook Time: 70 minutes | Serves: 2-4

Ingredients

2 lb beef brisket
½ tsp celery salt
1 tsp chili powder
2 tbsp olive oil
1 tbsp sweet paprika

A pinch of cayenne pepper
½ tsp garlic powder
½ cup beef stock
3 onions, cut into quarters
¼ tsp dry mustard

Directions

Grease a baking dish with cooking spray and preheat oven to 360 F. In a bowl, combine the paprika with dry mustard, chili powder, salt, garlic powder, cayenne pepper, and celery salt. Rub the meat with this mixture.

Set a pan over medium heat and warm olive oil, place in the beef, and sear until brown. Remove to the baking dish. Pour in the stock, add onions and bake for 60 minutes. Set the beef to a cutting board, and leave to cool before slicing. Take the juices from the baking dish and strain, sprinkle over the meat to serve.

Nutritional info per serving: Calories 483, Fat 22g, Net Carbs 5.1g, Protein 49.7g

Juicy Beef Meatballs

Prep + Cook Time: 30 minutes | Serves: 2-4

Ingredients

1 pound ground beef
Salt and black pepper, to taste
½ tsp garlic powder
1 ¼ tbsp coconut aminos
1 cup beef stock
¾ cup almond flour

1 tbsp fresh parsley, chopped
1 onion, sliced
2 tbsp butter
1 tbsp olive oil
¼ cup sour cream

Directions

Preheat the oven to 390 F and grease a baking dish. In a bowl, combine beef with salt, garlic powder, almond flour, parsley, 1 tbsp of coconut aminos, black pepper, ¼ cup of beef stock. Form patties and place on the baking sheet. Bake for 18 minutes.

Set a pan with the butter and olive oil over medium heat, stir in the onion, and cook for 3 minutes. Stir in the remaining beef stock, sour cream, and remaining coconut aminos, and bring to a simmer. Adjust the seasoning with black pepper and salt. Serve the meatballs topped with onion sauce.

Nutritional info per serving: Calories 441, Fat 24g, Net Carbs 5.7g, Protein 31g

Mexican Inspired Beef Chili

Prep + Cook Time: 45 minutes | Serves: 2-4

Ingredients

2 tbsp olive oil
1 onion, chopped
2 pounds ground beef
15 oz canned tomatoes, chopped
½ cup pickled jalapeños, chopped
1 tsp chipotle chili paste
1 garlic clove, minced

3 celery stalks, chopped
2 tbsp coconut aminos
Salt and black pepper, to taste
2 tbsp cumin
1 tsp onion powder
1 tsp garlic powder
1 tsp chopped cilantro

Directions

Put a pan over medium heat and warm olive oil, add in the onion, celery, garlic, beef, black pepper, and salt; cook until the meat browns. Stir in the rest of the ingredients, except for cilantro and cook for 30 minutes. Sprinkle with cilantro and serve.

Nutritional info per serving: Calories 441, Fat 24.3g, Net Carbs 3.8g, Protein 16.5g

Burgundy Beef with Mushrooms

Prep + Cook Time: 60 minutes + marinated time | Serves: 2-4

Ingredients

3 tbsp olive oil
1 tbsp parsley, chopped
1 cup red wine
1 tsp dried thyme
Salt and black pepper, to taste
1 bay leaf
1 cup beef stock

1 pound stewed beef, cubed
12 pearl onions, halved
1 tomato, chopped
2 oz pancetta, chopped
2 garlic cloves, minced
½ pound mushrooms, chopped

Directions

Heat a pan over high heat, stir in the pancetta and beef and cook until lightly browned; set aside.

Place in the onions, mushrooms, and garlic, and cook for 5 minutes. Pour in the wine to deglaze the bottom of the pan and add beef stock, bay leaf, and tomato. Season with salt, black pepper and thyme. Return the meat and pancetta, cover and cook for 50 minutes. Serve sprinkled with parsley.

Nutritional info per serving: Calories 367, Fat 24g, Net Carbs 4.7g, Protein 33g

Cocktail Chili Beef Meatballs

Prep + Cook Time: 45 minutes | Serves: 2-4

Ingredients

2 tbsp olive oil
2 tbsp thyme
½ cup pork rinds, crushed
1 egg
Salt and black pepper, to taste
1½ pounds ground beef

10 ounces canned onion soup
1 tbsp almond flour
2 tbsp chili sauce
¼ cup free-sugar ketchup
3 tsp Worcestershire sauce
½ tsp dry mustard

Directions

In a bowl, combine 1/3 cup of the onion soup with the beef, pepper, thyme, pork rinds, egg, and salt.

Shape meatballs from the beef mixture. Heat olive oil in a pan over medium heat and place in the meatballs to brown on both sides.

In a bowl, combine the rest of the soup with the almond flour, dry mustard, ketchup, Worcestershire sauce, and ¼ cup of water. Pour this over the beef meatballs, cover the pan, and cook for 20 minutes.

Nutritional info per serving: Calories 341, Fat 21g, Net Carbs 5.6g, Protein 23.5g

Thyme Beef & Bacon Casserole

Prep + Cook Time: 45 minutes | Serves: 2-4

Ingredients

2 tbsp olive oil
2 tbsp ghee
1 cup pumpkin, chopped
½ cup celery, chopped

3 slices bacon, chopped
1 pound beef meat for stew, cubed
1 garlic clove, minced
1 onion, chopped

1 tbsp red vinegar
2 cups beef stock
1 tbsp tomato puree
1 cinnamon stick

1 lemon peel strip
3 thyme sprigs, chopped
Salt and black pepper, to taste

Directions

Put a saucepan over medium heat and warm oil, add in the celery, garlic and onion, and cook for 3 minutes. Stir in the beef and bacon, and cook until slightly brown. Pour in the vinegar, ghee, lemon peel strip, beef stock, tomato puree, cinnamon stick and pumpkin. Cover and cook for 25 minutes. Get rid of the lemon peel and cinnamon stick. Adjust the seasoning and sprinkle with thyme to serve.

Nutritional info per serving: Calories 552, Fat 41g, Net Carbs 4.5g, Protein 32.3g

Stewed Veal with Vegetables

Prep + Cook Time: 2 hours | Serves: 2-4

Ingredients

2 tbsp olive oil
1 pound veal shoulder, cubed
1 onion, chopped
1 garlic clove, minced
Salt and black pepper, to taste
½ cup white wine
1 tsp sweet paprika

2 cups tomatoes, chopped
1 carrot, chopped
1 turnip, chopped
½ cup celery, chopped
1 cup mushrooms, chopped
½ cup green beans, chopped
1 tsp dried oregano

Directions

Set a pot over medium heat and warm the oil. Brown the veal for 5-6 minutes. Stir in the onion, celery and garlic, and cook for 3 minutes. Place in the wine to deglaze the bottom for 1-2 minutes.

Add in oregano, paprika, carrot, tomatoes, 1 cup of water, turnip, mushrooms, salt, and pepper, and bring to a boil. Reduce the heat to low and cook for 1 hour. Add in green beans and cook for 5 minutes.

Nutritional info per serving: Calories 495, Fat 22.3g, Net Carbs 6.8g, Protein 51.4g

Red Wine Lamb with Mint & Sage

Prep + Cook Time: 40 minutes | Serves: 2-4

Ingredients

1 tbsp olive oil
1 pound lamb chops
½ tbsp sage
½ tsp mint

½ onion, sliced
1 garlic clove, minced
¼ cup red wine
Salt and black pepper, to taste

Directions

Heat the olive oil in a pan. Add onion and garlic and cook for 3 minutes, until soft. Rub the sage and mint over the lamb chops. Cook the lamb for about 3 minutes per side; set aside.

Pour the red wine and 1 cup of water into the pan, bring the mixture to a boil. Cook until the liquid is reduced by half. Add the chops in the pan, reduce the heat, and let simmer for 30 minutes.

Nutritional info per serving: Calories 402, Fat: 29.6g, Net Carbs: 3.8g, Protein: 14.7g

Lamb Chops with Garlic-Lime Vinaigrette

Prep + Cook Time: 25 minutes | Serves: 2

Ingredients

4 lamb chops
4 tsp olive oil
Salt and black pepper to taste
½ tsp red pepper flakes
1 tbsp lime juice

1 tbsp fresh mint
1 garlic clove, pressed
1 tbsp parsley
½ tsp smoked paprika

Directions

Heat a griddle pan over high heat. Brush the lamb with 2 tbsp of olive oil and sprinkle with salt and black pepper. Grill the lamb chops for about 3-5 minutes per side.

Whisk together the remaining olive oil, red pepper flakes, lime juice, mint, garlic, parsley, and smoked paprika in a jar; shake until smooth and creamy.

Serve the lamb chops topped with the vinaigrette.

Nutritional info per serving: Calories 365, Fat: 29g, Net Carbs: 2.1g, Protein: 25.3g

Stuffed Lamb Shoulder

Prep + Cook Time: 1 hour | Serves: 2-4

Ingredients

2 tbsp olive oil
1 lb rolled lamb shoulder, boneless
1 ½ cups basil leaves, chopped
5 tbsp macadamia nuts, chopped

½ cup green olives, pitted and chopped
2 garlic cloves, minced
Salt and black pepper to taste

Directions

In a bowl, combine the basil, macadamia nuts, olives, and garlic. Season the lamb with salt and black pepper. Spread with the previously prepared mixture, roll up the lamb and tie it together using 3 to 4 strings of butcher's twine. Place the lamb onto a greased with olive oil baking dish and cook in the oven for 10 minutes at 420 F. Reduce the heat to 350 F and continue cooking for 40 minutes.

When ready, transfer the meat to a cleaned chopping board, and let it rest for 10 minutes before slicing.

Nutritional info per serving: Calories 5573 Fat 41g, Net Carbs 3.1g, Protein 37g

Lamb Kebabs with Mint Yogurt

Prep + Cook Time: 20 minutes | Serves: 2

Ingredients

1 pound ground lamb
¼ tsp cinnamon
1 tsp garlic powder
1 tsp onion powder
Salt and black pepper, to taste

1 cup natural yogurt
2 tbsp mint, chopped

Directions

Preheat your grill to medium heat. Place lamb, cinnamon, onion powder, salt, and black pepper in a bowl. Mix with hands to combine well. Divide the meat into pieces. Shape all meat portions around previously-soaked skewers and grill the kebabs for about 5 minutes per side.

In a separate bowl, put the yogurt, garlic powder, mint, and salt and stir to combine.

Nutritional info per serving: Calories 543, Fat: 33.5g, Net Carbs: 4.7g, Protein: 52.5g

Pork Chops with Creamy Bacon & Mushrooms

Prep + Cook Time: 50 minutes | Serves: 2

Ingredients

2 oz bacon, chopped
1 cup mushrooms, sliced
1 garlic clove, chopped
1 shallot, chopped
1 cup heavy cream

½ pound pork chops, boneless
1 tsp ground nutmeg
¼ cup coconut oil
Salt and black pepper to taste
1 tbsp parsley, chopped

Directions

In a frying pan over medium heat, cook the bacon for 2-3 minutes and set aside. In the same pan, warm the oil, add in the onions, garlic and mushrooms, and cook for 4 minutes. Stir in the pork chops, season with salt, black pepper and nutmeg, and sear until browned, about 2 minutes per side.

Preheat oven to 360 F and insert the pan in the oven to bake for 25 minutes. Remove the pork chops to a bowl and cover with foil.

Place the pan over medium heat, pour in the heavy cream over the mushroom mixture, add in the reserved bacon and cook for 5 minutes; remove from heat. Spread the bacon/mushroom sauce over pork chops, sprinkle with parsley and serve.

Nutritional info per serving: Calories 765, Fat 71g, Net Carbs 3.8g, Protein 32g

Barbecued Pork Chops

Prep + Cook Time: 20 minutes | Serves: 2

Ingredients

2 pork loin chops, boneless
½ cup BBQ sauce, sugar-free
Salt and black pepper to taste
1 tbsp erythritol
½ tsp ginger powder

½ tsp onion powder
½ tsp garlic powder
1 tsp red pepper flakes
2 thyme sprigs, chopped

Directions

Mix black pepper, salt, ginger powder, onion powder, garlic powder and red pepper flakes, and rub the pork chops on all sides. Preheat the grill to 450 F and cook the meat for 2 minutes per side.

Reduce the heat and brush the BBQ sauce on the meat, cover and grill for another 5 minutes. Open the lid, turn the meat and brush again with barbecue sauce. Continue cooking covered for 5 minutes. Remove the meat to a serving platter and serve sprinkled with thyme.

Nutritional info per serving: Calories 412, Fat 34.6g, Net Carbs 1.1g, Protein 34.1g

Baked Pork Sausage with Vegetables

Prep + Cook Time: 50 minutes | Serves: 2

Ingredients

1 tbsp olive oil
½ pound pork sausages
2 tomatoes, chopped
1 small onion, sliced
½ medium carrot, sliced
1 tsp smoked paprika

1 red bell peppers, sliced
1 sprig rosemary, chopped
1 garlic clove, minced
1 tbsp balsamic vinegar
Salt and black pepper to taste

Directions

Preheat the oven to 360 F.

Heat olive oil in a casserole and add the tomatoes, bell peppers, garlic, carrot, onion and balsamic vinegar, and cook for 8-10 minute until softened and lightly golden. Season with salt, smoked paprika and black pepper.

Arrange the sausages on top of the veggies. Put the pan in the oven and bake for 20-25 minutes until the sausages have browned to a desired color. Serve sprinkled with rosemary.

Nutritional info per serving: Calories 411, Fat 32g, Net Carbs 6.5g, Protein 14.7g

Green Chimichurri Sauce with Grilled Pork Steaks

Prep + Cook Time: 64 minutes | Serves: 2

Ingredients

1 garlic clove, minced
½ tsp white wine vinegar
2 tbsp parsley leaves, chopped
2 tbsp cilantro leaves, chopped

2 tbsp extra-virgin olive oil
8 oz pork loin steaks
Salt and black pepper to season
2 tbsp sesame oil

Directions

To make the sauce: in a bowl, mix the parsley, cilantro and garlic. Add the vinegar, extra-virgin olive oil, and salt, and combine well. Preheat a grill pan over medium heat.

Rub the pork with sesame oil, and season with salt and pepper. Grill the meat for 4-5 minutes on each side until no longer pink in the center. Put the pork on a serving plate and spoon chimichurri sauce over, to serve.

Nutritional info per serving: Calories 452, Fat 33.6g, Net Carbs 2.3g, Protein 32.8g

Pork Chops with Basil Tomato Sauce

Prep + Cook Time: 50 minutes | Serves: 2

Ingredients

2 pork chops
½ tbsp fresh basil, chopped
1 garlic clove, minced
1 tbsp olive oil

7 ounces canned diced tomatoes
½ tbsp tomato paste
Salt and black pepper, to taste
½ red chili, finely chopped

Directions

Season the pork with salt and black pepper. Set a pan over medium heat and warm oil, place in the pork chops, cook for 3 minutes, turn and cook for another 3 minutes; remove to a bowl. Add in the garlic and cook for 30 seconds.

Stir in the tomato paste, tomatoes, and chili; bring to a boil, and reduce heat to medium-low. Place in the pork chops, cover the pan and simmer everything for 30 minutes. Remove the pork chops to plates and sprinkle with fresh oregano to serve.

Nutritional info per serving: Calories 425, Fat 25g, Net Carbs 2.5g, Protein 39g

Pork Steaks with Carrot & Broccoli

Prep + Cook Time: 40 minutes | Serves: 2

Ingredients

1 tbsp olive oil
1 tbsp butter
2 pork steaks, bone-in
½ cup water
Salt and black pepper, to taste

2 garlic cloves, minced
1 tbsp fresh parsley, chopped
½ head broccoli, cut into florets
1 carrot, sliced
½ lemon, sliced

Directions

Heat oil and butter over high heat. Add in the pork steaks, season with pepper and salt, and cook until browned; set to a plate. In the same pan, add garlic, carrot and broccoli and cook for 4 minutes.

Pour the water, lemon slices, salt, and black pepper, and cook everything for 5 minutes. Return the pork steaks to the pan and cook for 10 minutes. Serve the steaks sprinkled with sauce with parsley.

Nutritional info per serving: Calories 674, Fat 46g, Net Carbs 7.5g, Protein 51.4g

Roasted Pork Stuffed with Ham & Cheese

Prep + Cook Time: 40 minutes + marinade time | Serves: 2

Ingredients

2 tbsp olive oil
Zest and juice from 1 lime
1 garlic clove, minced
2 tbsp fresh cilantro, chopped
2 tbsp fresh mint, chopped
Salt and black pepper, to taste

1 tsp cumin
2 pork loin steaks
1 pickle, chopped
2 oz smoked ham, sliced
2 oz Gruyere cheese sliced
1 tbsp mustard

Directions

Start with making the marinade: combine the lime zest, oil, black pepper, cumin, cilantro, lime juice, garlic, mint and salt, in a food processor. Place the steaks in the marinade, and toss well to coat; set aside for some hours in the fridge.

Arrange the steaks on a working surface, split the pickles, mustard, cheese, and ham on them, roll, and secure with toothpicks. Heat a pan over medium heat, add in the pork rolls, cook each side for 2 minutes and remove to a baking sheet. Bake in the oven at 350 F for 25 minutes.

Nutritional info per serving: Calories 433, Fat 38.3g, Net Carbs 4.2g, Protein 24.3g

Tender Pork Loin Steaks with Mustard Sauce

Prep + Cook Time: 15 minutes | Serves: 2

Ingredients

½ tbsp butter
½ tbsp olive oil
2 pork loin chops
½ tsp Dijon mustard
½ tbsp soy sauce

½ tsp lemon juice
2 tsp cumin seeds
½ tbsp water
Salt and black pepper, to taste
½ cup chives, chopped

Directions

Set a pan over medium heat and warm butter and olive oil, add in the pork chops, season with salt, and pepper, cook for 4 minutes, turn and cook for additional 4 minutes. Remove the pork chops to a plate and keep warm.

In a bowl, mix the water with lemon juice, cumin seeds, mustard and soy sauce. Pour the mustard sauce in the same pan and simmer for 5 minutes. Spread over pork, top with chives and serve.

Nutritional info per serving: Calories 382, Fat 21.5g, Net Carbs 1.2g, Protein 38g

Spicy Pork with Capers & Olives

Prep + Cook Time: 20 minutes + chilling time | Serves: 2

Ingredients

2 pork chops
1 tbsp olive oil
1 garlic clove, minced
¼ tbsp chili powder
¼ tsp cumin

Salt and black pepper, to taste
½ tsp hot pepper sauce
¼ cup capers
6 black olives, sliced

Directions

Preheat grill over medium heat. In a mixing bowl, combine olive oil, cumin, salt, hot pepper sauce, black pepper, garlic and chili powder. Place in the pork chops, toss to coat, and refrigerate for 4 hours.

Arrange the pork on a preheated grill, cook for 7 minutes, turn, add in the capers, and cook for another 2 minutes. Place onto serving plates and sprinkle with olives to serve.

Nutritional info per serving: Calories 415, Fat 25.8g, Net Carbs 1.8g, Protein 43.6g

Cheese Stuffing Pork Rolls with Bacon

Prep + Cook Time: 40 minutes | Serves: 2

Ingredients

1 tbsp olive oil
2 oz bacon, sliced
1 tbsp fresh parsley, chopped
2 pork chops, boneless and flatten
¼ cup ricotta cheese
1 tbsp pine nuts

1 spring onion, chopped
1 garlic clove, minced
1 tbsp Parmesan cheese, grated
5 ounces canned diced tomatoes
Salt and black pepper to taste
½ tsp herbes de Provence

Directions

Put the pork chops on a flat surface. Set the bacon slices on top, then divide the ricotta cheese, pine nuts, and Parmesan cheese. Roll each pork piece and secure with a toothpick.

Set a pan over medium heat and warm oil. Cook the pork rolls until browned, and remove to a plate.

Add in the spring onion and garlic, and cook for 5 minutes. Place in the stock and cook for 3 minutes. Get rid of the toothpicks from the rolls and return them to the pan. Stir in the black pepper, salt, tomatoes and herbes de Provence. Bring to a boil, set heat to medium-low, and cook for 20 minutes while covered. Sprinkle with parsley to serve.

Nutritional info per serving: Calories 631, Fat 42g, Net Carbs 7.1g, Protein 44g

Mediterranean Pork Chops

Prep + Cook Time: 45 minutes | Serves: 2

Ingredients

1 garlic clove, minced
2 pork chops, bone-in
Salt and black pepper, to taste
1 tsp dried oregano

¼ cup kalamata olives, pitted and sliced
2 tbsp olive oil
2 tbsp vegetable broth
¼ cup feta cheese, crumbled

Directions

Preheat the oven to 425 F.

Rub pork chops with pepper and salt, and add in a roasting pan. Stir in the garlic, olives, olive oil, broth, and oregano, set in the oven and bake for 10 minutes. Reduce heat to 350 F and roast for 25 minutes. Slice the pork, divide among plates, and sprinkle with pan juices and feta cheese all over.

Nutritional info per serving: Calories 533, Fat 38.2g, Net Carbs 1.9g, Protein 41g

Pork Chops with Peanut Sauce

Prep + Cook Time: 35 minutes + marinade time | Serves: 2

Ingredients

1/3 cup cilantro
1/3 cup mint
1 onion, chopped
¼ cup peanuts
3 tbsp olive oil

Salt, to taste
2 pork chops
2 garlic cloves, minced
Juice and zest from 1 lemon

Directions

Preheat oven to 250 F.

In a food processor, combine the cilantro with olive oil, mint, peanuts, salt, lemon zest, garlic, and onion. Rub the pork with this mixture, place in a bowl, and refrigerate for 1 hour while covered.

Remove the chops and set to a greased baking dish, sprinkle with lemon juice, and bake for 30 minutes in the oven.

Nutritional info per serving: Calories 643, Fat 47g, Net Carbs 6.1g, Protein 45.4g

Rosemary Buttered Pork Chops

Prep + Cook Time: 25 minutes | Serves: 2

Ingredients

½ tbsp olive oil
2 tbsp butter
1 tbsp rosemary
2 pork chops

Salt and black pepper, to taste
A pinch of paprika
½ tsp chili powder

Directions

Rub the pork chops with olive oil, salt, black pepper, paprika, and chili powder. Heat a grill over medium, add in the pork chops and cook for 10 minutes, flipping once halfway through.

Remove to a serving plate. In a pan over low heat, warm the butter until it turns nutty brown. Pour over the pork chops, sprinkle with rosemary and serve.

Nutritional info per serving: Calories 363, Fat 21.4g, Net Carbs 3.8g, Protein 38.5g

Pork Kofte with Tomato Passata & Basil

Prep + Cook Time: 45 minutes | Serves: 2

Ingredients

½ lb ground pork
1 tbsp olive oil
1 tbsp pork rinds, crushed
1 garlic clove, minced
1 shallot, chopped
1 small egg
1/3 tsp paprika

Salt and black pepper to taste
1 tbsp parsley, chopped
½ cup tomato sauce, sugar-free
½ tsp oregano
1/3 cup Italian blend kinds of cheeses
1 tbsp basil, chopped to garnish

Directions

In a bowl, mix the ground pork, shallot, pork rinds, garlic, egg, paprika, oregano, parsley, salt, and black pepper, just until combined. Form balls of the mixture and place them in an oiled baking pan; drizzle with olive oil. Bake in the oven for 18 minutes at 390 F.

Pour the tomato sauce all over the meatballs. Sprinkle with the Italian blend cheeses, and put it back in the oven to bake for 10-15 minutes until the cheese melts.

Once ready, take out the pan and garnish with basil. Delicious when served with cauliflower mash.

Nutritional info per serving: Calories 586, Fat 38g, Net Carbs 7.3g, Protein 39.2g

Mushroom Pork Chops with Steamed Broccoli

Prep + Cook Time: 1 hour and 15 minutes | Serves: 2

Ingredients

1 shallot, chopped
2 (10.5-ounce) cans mushroom soup
2 pork chops
½ cup sliced mushrooms

Salt and black pepper, to taste
1 tbsp parsley
½ head broccoli, cut into florets

Directions

Steam the broccoli in salted water over medium heat for 6-8 minutes until tender. Set aside.

Preheat the oven to 370 F. Season the pork chops with salt and pepper, and place in a greased baking dish. Combine the mushroom soup, mushrooms and onion, in a bowl. Pour this mixture over the pork chops. Bake for 45 minutes. Sprinkle with parsley and serve with broccoli.

Nutritional info per serving: Calories 412, Fat: 31g, Net Carbs: 7.2g, Protein: 20.3g

Citrus Pork with Sauteed Cabbage & Tomatoes

Prep + Cook Time: 27 minutes | Serves: 2

Ingredients

3 tbsp olive oil
2 tbsp lemon juice
1 garlic clove, pureed
2 pork loin chops
1/3 head cabbage, shredded
1 tomato, chopped

1 tbsp white wine
Salt and black pepper to taste
¼ tsp cumin
¼ tsp ground nutmeg
1 tbsp parsley

Directions

In a bowl, mix the lemon juice, garlic, salt, pepper and olive oil. Brush the pork with the mixture.

Preheat grill to high heat. Grill the pork for 2-3 minutes on each side until cooked through. Remove to serving plates. Warm the remaining olive oil in a pan and cook in cabbage for 5 minutes until tender.

Drizzle with white wine, sprinkle with cumin, nutmeg, salt and pepper. Add in the tomatoes, cook for another 5 minutes, stirring occasionally. Ladle the sautéed cabbage to the side of the chops and serve sprinkled with parsley.

Nutritional info per serving: Calories 565, Fat 36.7g, Net Carbs 6.1g, Protein 43g

Pork Chops with Creamy Bacon Sauce

Prep + Cook Time: 30 minutes | Serves: 2

Ingredients

2 oz bacon, chopped
2 pork chops
Salt and black pepper to taste

2 sprigs fresh thyme
2 tbsp heavy cream
½ tsp Dijon mustard

Directions

Brown bacon in a large skillet on medium heat for 5 minutes to be crispy. Remove to a paper towel-lined plate to soak up excess fat.

Season pork chops with salt and black pepper, and brown in the bacon fat for 4 minutes on each side. Remove to the bacon plate. Stir in the thyme, 2 tbsp of water, mustard, and heavy cream and simmer for 5 minutes. Season with salt and black pepper. Return the chops and bacon, and cook further for another 10 minutes. Garnish with thyme leaves.

Nutritional info per serving: Calories 422, Fat 35.3g, Net Carbs 2.8g, Protein 21.5g

Caramelized Onion over Pork Burgers

Prep + Cook Time: 20 minutes | Serves: 2

Ingredients

2 tbsp olive oil
½ pound ground pork
Salt and black pepper to taste
½ tsp chili pepper
1 tbsp parsley

1 white onion, sliced into rings
½ tbsp balsamic vinegar
1 drop liquid stevia
1 tomato, sliced into rings
1 tbsp mayonnaise

Directions

Warm half of the oil in a skillet over medium heat, sauté the onions for 2 minutes to be soft, and stir in the balsamic vinegar and liquid stevia. Cook for 30 seconds stirring once or twice until caramelized; remove to a plate.

Combine the pork, salt, black pepper and chili pepper in a bowl, and mold out 2 patties.

Heat the remaining olive oil in a skillet over medium heat and fry the patties for 4 to 5 minutes on each side until golden brown on the outside. Remove to a plate and sit for 3 minutes.

In each tomato slice, place half of the mayonnaise and a patty, and top with some onion rings. Cover with another tomato slice and serve.

Nutritional info per serving: Calories 510, Fat 41.2g, Net Carbs 2.6g, Protein 31g

Herb Pork Chops with Cranberry Sauce

Prep + Cook Time: 2 hours 40 minutes | Serves: 2

Ingredients

2 pork chops
½ tsp garlic powder
Salt and black pepper, to taste
1 tsp fresh basil, chopped
A drizzle of olive oil
½ onion, chopped
½ cup white wine
Juice of ½ lemon

1 bay leaf
1 cup chicken stock
Fresh parsley, chopped, for serving
1 cup cranberries
½ tsp fresh rosemary, chopped
½ cup xylitol
½ cup water
½ tsp harissa paste sriracha sauce

Directions

Preheat oven to 360 F. In a bowl, combine the pork chops with basil, salt, garlic powder, and black pepper. Heat a pan with a drizzle of oil over medium heat, place in the pork, and cook until browned, about 4-5 minutes; set aside.

Stir in the onion and cook for 2 minutes. Place in the bay leaf and wine, and cook for 4 minutes. Pour in lemon juice, and chicken stock, and simmer for 5 minutes. Return the pork and cook for 10 minutes. Cover the pan and place it in the oven for 2 hours.

Set a pan over medium-high heat, add in the cranberries, rosemary, sriracha sauce, water and xylitol, and bring to a simmer for 15 minutes. Remove the pork chops from the oven and discard the bay leaf. Pour the sauce over the pork and serve sprinkled with parsley.

Nutritional info per serving: Calories 450, Fat 23.5g, Net Carbs 7.3g, Protein 42g

Grilled Pork Chops with Balsamic Sauce

Prep + Cook Time: 20 minutes + marinade time | Serves: 2

Ingredients

2 pork loin chops, boneless
1 tbsp rosemary, chopped
1 tbsp balsamic vinegar
1 garlic clove, minced
2 tbsp olive oil
Salt and black pepper to taste

Directions

Put the pork in a deep dish. Add in the balsamic vinegar, rosemary, garlic, olive oil, salt, and black pepper, and toss to coat. Cover the dish with plastic wrap and marinate the pork for 1 to 2 hours.

Preheat grill to medium heat. Remove the pork when ready, reserve the marinade and grill covered for 10 minutes per side. Remove the pork chops and let them sit for 4 minutes on a serving plate.

In a saucepan over medium heat, pour in the reserved marinade, add in 3 tbsp water and bring to a boil for 2-3 minutes until the liquid becomes thickened.

Top the chops with the sauce and serve.

Nutritional info per serving: Calories 421, Fat 25g, Net Carbs 2.3g, Protein 41g

Fried Pork with Blackberry Gravy

Prep + Cook Time: 17 minutes | Serves: 2

Ingredients

2 tbsp olive oil
1 lb pork chops
Salt and black pepper to taste
1 cup blackberries
2 tbsp chicken broth
½ tbsp rosemary leaves, chopped
1 tbsp balsamic vinegar
1 tsp Worcestershire sauce, sugar-free

Directions

Place the blackberries in a bowl and mash them with a fork until jam-like. Pour into a saucepan, add the chicken broth and rosemary. Bring to boil on low heat for 4 minutes. Stir in balsamic vinegar and Worcestershire sauce. Simmer for 1 minute.

Heat oil in a skillet over medium heat, season the pork with salt and black pepper, and cook for 5 minutes on each side.

Put on serving plates and spoon sauce over the pork chops.

Nutritional info per serving: Calories 732, Fat 41.5g, Net Carbs 6.9g, Protein 56.3g

Stir-Fried Pork with Bell Peppers

Prep + Cook Time: 23 minutes | Serves: 2-4

Ingredients

2 tbsp olive oil
2 lb pork loin, cut into strips
Salt and chili pepper to taste
1 tsp fresh ginger, grated

2 garlic cloves, minced
2 tbsp soy sauce, sugar-free
1 red bell pepper, sliced
1 green bell pepper, sliced

Directions

In a bowl, mix salt, chili pepper, ginger, garlic and soy sauce. Pour the pork into the bowl and toss to coat. Warm the olive oil in a wok and add in the pork to cook for 6 minutes until no longer pink.

Stir in the bell peppers and cook for 5 minutes. Adjust the taste with salt and black pepper, and spoon the stir-fry to a serving plate. Serve immediately.

Nutritional info per serving: Calories 568, Fat 36.9g, Net Carbs 1.6g, Protein 52.5g

Leek & Bacon Gratin

Prep + Cook Time: 35 minutes | Serves: 2-4

Ingredients

1 pound leeks, trimmed and sliced
3 oz bacon, chopped
2 cups baby spinach
4 oz halloumi cheese, cut into cubes
2 garlic cloves, minced
1 cup buttermilk

1 tomato, chopped
2 tbsp water
1 cup grated mozzarella cheese
½ tsp dried oregano
Salt and black pepper to taste

Directions

Place a cast iron pan over medium heat and fry the bacon for 4 minutes, then add garlic and leeks and cook for 5-6 minute.

In a bowl, mix the buttermilk, tomato, and water, and add to the pan. Stir in the spinach, halloumi, oregano, salt, and pepper to taste. Sprinkle the mozzarella cheese on top and transfer the pan to the oven. Bake for 20 minutes or until the cheese is golden.

When ready, remove the pan and serve the gratin warm.

Nutritional info per serving: Calories 350, Fat 27g, Net Carbs 5.3g, Protein 16g

Roasted Pork Loin Garnish with Brussels Sprouts

Prep + Cook Time: 40 minutes | Serves: 2-4

Ingredients

½ pound Brussels sprouts, chopped
2 tbsp olive oil
Salt and black pepper, to taste
1 ½ pounds pork loin
A pinch of dry mustard

1 tsp hot red pepper flakes
½ tsp ginger, minced
2 garlic cloves, minced
½ lemon sliced
¼ cup water

Directions

Preheat oven to 380 F. In a bowl, combine the ginger with salt, mustard, and black pepper. Add in meat, toss to coat. Heat the oil in a saucepan over medium heat, brown the pork on all sides, for 8 minutes. Transfer to the oven and roast for 1 hour. To the saucepan, add Brussels sprouts, lemon slices, garlic, and water; cook for 10 minutes. Serve on a platter, sprinkled with pan juices on top.

Nutritional info per serving: Calories 422, Fat 22.4g, Net Carbs 4.1g, Protein 43.4g

Yellow Squash & Pork Traybake

Prep + Cook Time: 38 minutes | Serves: 2-4

Ingredients

1 lb ground pork
1 large yellow squash, thinly sliced
Salt and black pepper to taste
1 garlic clove, minced
2 red onions, chopped
1 cup broccoli, chopped

1 (15 oz) can diced tomatoes
½ cup pork rinds, crushed
¼ cup parsley, chopped
2 cups cottage cheese
2 tbsp olive oil
1/3 cup chicken broth

Directions

Heat the olive oil in a skillet over medium heat, add the pork, season it with salt and pepper, and cook for 3 minutes or until no longer pink. Stir occasionally while breaking any lumps apart.

Add the garlic, half of the red onions, broccoli, and 2 tablespoons of pork rinds. Continue cooking for 3 minutes. Stir in the tomatoes, half of the parsley, and chicken broth. Cook further for 3 minutes.

Mix the remaining parsley and cottage cheese and set aside. Sprinkle the bottom of a baking dish with 3 tbsp of pork rinds; top with half of the squash and a season of salt, 2/3 of the pork mixture, and the cheese mixture. Repeat the layering process a second time to exhaust the ingredients.

Cover the baking dish with foil and put in the oven to bake for 20 minutes at 380 F. Remove the foil and brown the top of the casserole with the broiler side of the oven for 2 minutes.

Nutritional info per serving: Calories 423, Fat 27g, Net Carbs 3.1g, Protein 33g

Pork Medallions & Fresh Rosemary

Prep + Cook Time: 55 minutes | Serves: 2-4

Ingredients

2 onions, chopped
4 oz bacon, chopped
½ cup vegetable stock

Salt and black pepper, to taste
2 tbsp fresh rosemary, chopped
1 pound pork tenderloin, cut into medallions

Directions

Fry the bacon in a pan over medium heat, until crispy, and remove to a plate. Add in onions, black pepper, and salt, and cook for 5 minutes; set to the same plate with bacon.

Add the pork medallions to the pan, season with pepper and salt, brown for 3 minutes on each side, turn, reduce heat to medium, and cook for 7 minutes. Stir in the stock and cook for 2 minutes. Return the bacon and onions to the pan and cook for 1 minute. Plate and garnish with fresh rosemary.

Nutritional info per serving: Calories 325, Fat 17g, Net Carbs 5.5g, Protein 34.5g

Stewed Pork With Cauliflower and Broccoli

Prep + Cook Time: 35 minutes | Serves: 2-4

Ingredients

2 tbsp olive oil
1 red bell pepper, seeded and chopped
1 pound stewed pork, cubed
Salt and black pepper, to taste
2 cups cauliflower florets
2 cups broccoli florets

1 onion, chopped
14 ounces canned diced tomatoes
¼ tsp garlic powder
1 tbsp tomato puree
1 ½ cups water
2 tbsp parsley, chopped

Directions

In a pan, heat olive oil and cook the pork over medium heat for 5 minutes, until browned. Place in the bell pepper, and onion, and cook for 4 minutes. Stir in the water, tomatoes, broccoli, cauliflower, tomato paste, and garlic powder; bring to a simmer and cook for 20 minutes while covered. Adjust the seasoning and serve sprinkled with parsley.

Nutritional info per serving: Calories 566, Fat 35.3g, Net Carbs 6.7g, Protein 41.5g

Pork Sausage with Sauerkraut

Prep + Cook Time: 60 minutes | Serves: 2-4

Ingredients

2 tbsp olive oil
1 pound pork sausages, sliced
2 cups sauerkraut, rinsed and drained
Salt and black pepper, to taste
½ cup ham, chopped
1 cup chicken broth
1 tbsp tomato paste

1 onion, chopped
2 garlic cloves, minced
1 tbsp butter
½ cup Parmesan cheese, grated
½ tsp cumin
½ tsp nutmeg

Directions

Heat a pot with the butter and olive oil over medium heat, add in the onion and garlic, and cook for 3 minutes. Place in the pork sausages and ham, and cook until slightly browned, about 4-5 minutes.

Place in the sauerkraut and chicken broth and cook for 30 minutes. Stir in tomato paste, black pepper, and salt. Top with Parmesan cheese and bake for 20 minutes at 350 F.

Nutritional info per serving: Calories 455, Fat 25g, Net Carbs 3.6g, Protein 35g

Lettuce Wraps with Ground Pork & Dill Pickles

Prep + Cook Time: 20 minutes | Serves: 2-4

Ingredients

2 tbsp avocado oil
1 pound ground pork
1 tbsp ginger paste
Salt and black pepper to taste
1 tsp ghee

1 head Iceberg lettuce
½ onion, sliced
1 red bell pepper, seeded and chopped
2 dill pickles, finely chopped

Directions

Heat avocado oil in a pan over medium heat and put the in pork with ginger paste, salt, and black pepper. Cook for 10-15 minutes over medium heat while breaking any lumps until the pork is no longer pink.

Pat the lettuce dry with a paper towel and in each leaf, spoon two to three tablespoons of the pork mixture, top with onion slices, bell pepper, and dill pickles.

Nutritional info per serving: Calories 322, Fat 25.3g, Net Carbs 1.5g, Protein 21g

One-Pot Sausage with Spinach & Zucchini

Prep + Cook Time: 20 minutes | Serves: 2-4

Ingredients

2 tbsp olive oil
½ onion, sliced
1 pound pork sausage, sliced
1 small zucchini, chopped
½ cup cherry tomatoes, halved
1 green bell pepper, chopped

Salt and black pepper, to taste
1 pound spinach, chopped
1 garlic clove, minced
½ green chili pepper, chopped
½ cup water
1 tbsp basil, chopped

Directions

Cook the sausages in warm olive oil over medium heat for 10 minutes. Stir in the onion, garlic, zucchini and bell pepper, and fry for 3-4 minutes. Place in the spinach, salt, water, black pepper, chili pepper, and cook for 5 minutes. Sprinkle with basil to serve.

Nutritional info per serving: Calories 487, Fat 28.3g, Net Carbs 9.3g, Protein 46.5g

Oven Roasted Chorizo Sausage with Vegetables

Prep + Cook Time: 25 minutes | Serves: 2-4

Ingredients

2 tbsp olive oil
1 pound chorizo sausage, chopped
1 onion, sliced
3 sun-dried tomatoes, sliced
Salt and black pepper, to taste
1 small eggplant, chopped

½ cup Swiss cheese, grated
1 yellow bell peppers, seeded and chopped
1 orange bell peppers, seeded and chopped
A pinch of red pepper flakes
2 tbsp fresh parsley, chopped

Directions

Preheat oven to 360° F.

Heat olive oil in a pan over medium heat, add in the sun-dried tomatoes, bell peppers, eggplant, and onion, and cook for 5 minutes. Season with black pepper, pepper flakes, and salt and mix well.

Cook for 1 minute, and remove from heat. Stir in chorizo and cook for 3-4 minutes.

Pour the mixture in a baking dish, scatter with the Swiss cheese and bake in the oven for 10 minutes until the cheese melts. Serve topped with fresh parsley.

Nutritional info per serving: Calories 551, Fat 43.4g, Net Carbs 6.8g, Protein 32.3g

Zucchini & Mushroom Smoked Sausage Bake

Prep + Cook Time: 35 minutes | Serves: 2-4

Ingredients

1 zucchini, chopped
1 pound smoked sausages, sliced
Salt and black pepper, to taste
1 pound mushrooms, sliced

1 red onion, chopped
1 tsp sweet paprika
2 tbsp olive oil
1 tbsp fresh rosemary, chopped

Directions

Preheat oven to 350 F.

In a pan over medium heat, warm oil and sauté the sausages with onion, zucchini, and mushrooms for 5 minutes until tender. Season with paprika, salt and black pepper. Pour in 1 cup of water and toss well to ensure everything is coated. Bake in the oven for 20-25 minutes.

To serve, divide the sausages between plates and scatter over the arugula.

Nutritional info per serving: Calories 395, Fat 28g, Net Carbs 9.3g, Protein 25.2g

Cowboy Stew of Bacon, Cheese & Cauliflower

Prep + Cook Time: 40 minutes | Serves: 2-4

Ingredients

2 tbsp olive oil
½ cup mozzarella cheese, grated
1 cup chicken broth
1 garlic clove, minced
1 shallot, chopped
Salt and black pepper, to taste

¼ cup heavy cream
1 pound bacon, chopped
1 head cauliflower, cut into florets
1 small carrot, chopped
1 tsp dried thyme
1 tbsp parsley, chopped

Directions

In a pot, heat the olive oil and sauté garlic and shallot for 3 minutes until soft. Add in the bacon and fry for 4-5 minutes. Then, pour in broth, carrot, and cauliflower and simmer for 10 minutes.

Stir in heavy cream and cheese and cook for 5 minutes. Season with thyme, salt and pepper, and sprinkle with parsley to serve.

Nutritional info per serving: Calories 713, Fat 61.2g, Net Carbs 4.4g, Protein 32.4g

Okra & Sausage Hot Pot

Prep + Cook Time: 35 minutes | Serves: 2-4

Ingredients

1 pound pork sausage, sliced
1 cup mushrooms, sliced
1 onion, chopped
1 tsp cayenne pepper
Salt and black pepper, to taste
1 tbsp fresh parsley, chopped
2 tbsp canola oil

½ cup beef stock
1 garlic clove, minced
2 cups tomatoes, chopped
1 pound okra, trimmed and sliced
1 tbsp coconut aminos
½ tbsp hot sauce

Directions

Heat the oil and sauté the onion, garlic and mushrooms for 5 minutes until tender. Add in the hot sauce, beef stock, tomatoes, coconut aminos, cayenne pepper, okra, sausage and tomato sauce, bring to a simmer and cook for 15 minutes.

Adjust the seasoning with salt and pepper. Sprinkle with fresh parsley to serve.

Nutritional info per serving: Calories 311, Fat 17.5g, Net Carbs 8.1g, Protein 24.6g

Red Wine & Pork Stew

Prep + Cook Time: 1 hour 25 minutes | Serves: 2-4

Ingredients

2 tbsp olive oil
1 pound pork stew meat, cubed
Salt and black pepper, to taste
1 red pepper, minced
1 garlic clove, minced
1 onion, chopped
½ cup beef stock

¼ cup red wine
1 carrot, chopped
1 small cabbage head, shredded
2 tbsp chives, chopped
½ cup sour cream
1 tbsp oregano, chopped

Directions

Sear the pork in warm olive oil over medium heat until brown. Add garlic, onion, red pepper, chives and carrot; sauté for 5 minutes. Pour in the cabbage, beef stock and red wine, and bring to a boil.

Reduce the heat and cook for 1 hour while covered. Add in the sour cream as you stir for 1 minute, adjust the seasonings and serve sprinkled with oregano.

Nutritional info per serving: Calories 367, Fat 15g, Net Carbs 7.6g, Protein 38g

Roasted Chorizo with Mixed Greens

Prep + Cook Time: 30 minutes | Serves: 2-4

Ingredients:

3 tbsp olive oil
1 lb chorizo, sliced
1 lb asparagus, trimmed and halved
2 green bell peppers, deseeded and diced
1 cup green beans, trimmed

2 red onions, cut into wedges
1 head medium broccoli, cut into florets
Salt and black pepper to taste
1 tbsp maple syrup, sugar-free
1 lemon, juiced

Directions:

Preheat oven to 390 F.

On a baking tray, add the chorizo, asparagus, bell peppers, green beans, onions, and broccoli; season with salt and black pepper, and drizzle with olive oil and maple syrup. Rub the seasoning onto the ingredients.

Bake for 15 minutes or until the vegetables soften and become golden at the edges. Remove from the oven, drizzle with lemon juice, and serve warm.

Nutritional info per serving: Calories 696, Fat 54.3, Net Carbs 9.9g, Protein 32g

POULTRY

Rosemary Chicken with Avocado Sauce

Prep + Cook Time: 22 minutes | Serves: 2

Ingredients

Sauce

¼ cup mayonnaise
1 avocado, pitted

1 tbsp lemon juice
Salt to taste

Chicken

2 tbsp olive oil
2 chicken breasts
Salt and black pepper to taste

½ cup rosemary, chopped
¼ cup warm water

Directions

Mash the avocado with a fork, in a bowl, and add in mayonnaise and lemon juice.

Warm olive oil in a large skillet, season the chicken with salt and black pepper and fry for 4 minutes on each side to golden brown. Remove the chicken to a plate.

Pour the warm water in the same skillet and add the rosemary. Bring to simmer for 3 minutes and add the chicken. Cover and cook on low heat for 5 minutes until the liquid has reduced and chicken is fragrant.

Dish chicken into serving plates and spoon the avocado sauce over.

Nutritional info per serving: Calories 406, Fat 34.1g, Net Carbs 3.9g, Protein 22.3g

Zucchini & Bell Pepper Chicken Gratin

Prep + Cook Time: 45 minutes | Serves: 2

Ingredients

1 red bell pepper, sliced
1 zucchini, chopped
Salt and black pepper, to taste
1 tsp garlic powder
1 tbsp olive oil

2 chicken breasts, skinless, boneless, sliced
1 tomato, chopped
½ tsp dried oregano
½ tsp dried basil
½ cup mozzarella cheese, shredded

Directions

Coat the chicken with salt, black pepper and garlic powder. Warm olive oil in a skillet over medium heat and add in the chicken slices. Cook until golden and remove to a baking dish.

To the same pan, add the zucchini, tomato, bell pepper, basil, oregano, and salt, cook for 2 minutes, and spread over the chicken. Bake in the oven at 360 F for 20 minutes.

Sprinkle the mozzarella over the chicken, return to the oven, and bake for 5 minutes until the cheese is melted and bubbling.

Nutritional info per serving: Calories 467, Fat 23.5g, Net Carbs 6.2g, Protein 45.7g

Spiralized Cucumber with Stuffed Chicken Breasts

Prep + Cook Time: 60 minutes | Serves: 2

Ingredients

Chicken

2 tbsp butter
2 chicken breasts
1 cup baby spinach
1 carrot, shredded

1 tomato, chopped
¼ cup goat cheese
Salt and black pepper, to taste
1 tsp dried oregano

Salad

2 cucumbers, spiralized
2 tbsp olive oil

1 tbsp rice vinegar

Directions

Preheat oven to 390 F and grease a baking dish with cooking spray. Place a pan over medium heat. Melt half of the butter and sauté spinach, carrot, and tomato until tender, for about 5 minutes. Season with salt and pepper. Transfer to a medium bowl and let cool for 10 minutes.

Add in the goat cheese and oregano, stir and set to one side. Cut the chicken breasts lengthwise and stuff with the cheese mixture and set into the baking dish. On top, put the remaining butter and bake until cooked through for 20-30 minutes.

Arrange the cucumbers on a serving platter, season with salt, black pepper, olive oil, and vinegar. Top with the chicken and pour over the sauce.

Nutritional info per serving: Calories: 621, Fat: 46.5g, Net Carbs: 7.5g, Protein: 40.7g

Mediterranean Stuffed Chicken Breasts

Prep + Cook Time: 30 minutes | Serves: 2

Ingredients

1 tbsp olive oil
1 cup spinach, chopped
2 chicken breasts
Salt and black pepper, to taste
½ cup cream cheese, softened

½ cup goat cheese, crumbled
1 garlic clove, minced
½ cup white wine
1 tbsp rosemary, chopped

Directions

Wilt the spinach in a saucepan with a half cup of water. Drain and mix in a bowl with the goat cheese, cream cheese, salt, garlic, black pepper and spinach. Cut a pocket in each chicken breast and stuff with the spinach mixture.

Preheat oven to 400 F and grease a baking tray with cooking spray.

Set a pan over medium heat and warm oil, add the stuffed chicken, and cook each side for 5 minutes. Then, put in the baking tray and drizzle with white wine and 2 tablespoons of water.

Bake in the oven for 20 minutes until no more pink. When ready, slice in half and serve sprinkled with rosemary.

Nutritional info per serving: Calories 305, Fat 12g, Net Carbs 4g, Protein 23g

Chicken Breasts with Creamy Kale Sauce

Prep + Cook Time: 15 minutes | Serves: 2

Ingredients

2 chicken breasts, skinless
2 tbsp heavy cream
4 tbsp butter

Salt and black pepper, to taste
1 cup kale
1 tsp fresh sage

Directions

Set the pan over medium heat and warm half of the butter. Place in the heavy cream and cook for 2 minutes. Add in kale and cook for 2-3 more minutes until wilted.

In another pan, melt the remaining butter and add in the chicken breasts. Cook for 4 minutes, flip, and cook for 3 more minutes.

Transfer to a flat surface, let cool for a few minutes, and slice. Arrange the chicken on a platter and drizzle over the sauce. Sprinkle with sage to serve.

Nutritional info per serving: Calories 533, Fat 43.2g, Net Carbs 3.2g, Protein 33.5g

Chicken & Cheese Filled Avocados

Prep + Cook Time: 10 minutes | Serves: 2

Ingredients

2 avocados
¼ cup mayonnaise
1 tsp dried thyme
2 tbsp cream cheese
1 ½ cups chicken, cooked and shredded
Salt and black pepper, to taste

¼ tsp cayenne pepper
½ tsp onion powder
½ tsp garlic powder
1 tsp paprika
Salt and black pepper, to taste
2 tbsp lemon juice

Directions

Halve the avocados and scoop the insides.

Place the flesh in a bowl and add in the chicken; stir in the remaining ingredients.

Fill the avocado cups with chicken mixture and serve.

Nutritional info per serving: Calories 518, Fat 41.6, Net Carbs 5.3g, Protein 23.2g

Green Bean & Broccoli Chicken Stir-Fry

Prep + Cook Time: 30 minutes | Serves: 2

Ingredients

2 chicken breasts, skinless, boneless, cut into strips
2 tbsp olive oil
1 tsp red pepper flakes
1 tsp onion powder
1 tbsp fresh ginger, grated
¼ cup tamari sauce
½ tsp garlic powder

½ cup water
½ cup xylitol
2 oz green beans, chopped
½ tsp xanthan gum
½ cup green onions, chopped
½ head broccoli, cut into florets

Directions

In a pot, steam green beans in salted water for 2-3 minutes; set aside.

Set a pan over medium heat and warm oil, cook in the chicken and ginger for 4 minutes. Stir in the water, onion powder, pepper flakes, garlic powder, tamari sauce, xanthan gum, and xylitol, and cook for 15 minutes. Add in the green onions, green beans and broccoli, and cook for 6 minutes.

Nutritional info per serving: Calories 411, Fat 24.5g, Net Carbs 6.2g, Protein 28.3g

Pan-Fried Chicken with Olive & Anchovy Tapenade
Prep + Cook Time: 30 minutes | Serves: 2

Ingredients

1 chicken breast, cut into 4 pieces
2 tbsp olive oil

Tapenade

2 tbsp olive oil
1 cup black olives, pitted
1 oz anchovy fillets, rinsed
1 garlic clove, crushed

1 garlic clove, minced
1 tsp basil, chopped

Salt and ground black pepper, to taste
¼ cup fresh basil, chopped
1 tbsp lemon juice

Directions

Heat a pan over medium heat and add olive oil, stir in the garlic, and cook for 2 minutes. Place in the chicken pieces and cook each side for 4 minutes. Remove to a serving plate.

Chop the black olives and anchovy and put in a food processor. Add in olive oil, basil, lemon juice, salt, and black pepper, and blend well. Spoon the tapenade over the chicken to serve.

Nutritional info per serving: Calories 522, Fat 37.3g, Net Carbs 5.3g, Protein 43.5g

Crispy Chicken Nuggets
Prep + Cook Time: 25 minutes | Serves: 2

Ingredients

2 tbsp ranch dressing
½ cup almond flour
1 egg
2 tbsp garlic powder

2 chicken breasts, cubed
Salt and black pepper, to taste
1 tbsp butter, melted

Directions

Preheat oven to 400 F and grease a baking dish with the butter.

In a bowl, combine salt, garlic powder, flour, and black pepper, and stir.

In a separate bowl, beat the egg. Add the chicken cubes to the egg mixture, then in the flour mixture. Cook in the oven for 18-20 minutes, turning halfway through, until golden and crispy.

Remove to paper towels, drain the excess grease and serve with ranch dressing.

Nutritional info per serving: Calories 473, Fat 31g, Net Carbs 7.6g, Protein 43g

Paprika Chicken & Pancetta in a Skillet

Prep + Cook Time: 40 minutes | Serves: 2

Ingredients

1 tbsp olive oil
5 pancetta strips, chopped
1/3 cup Dijon mustard
Salt and black pepper, to taste
1 onion, chopped

1 cup chicken stock
2 chicken breasts, skinless and boneless
¼ tsp sweet paprika
2 tbsp oregano, chopped

Directions

In a bowl, combine the paprika, black pepper, salt, and mustard. Sprinkle this mixture the chicken breasts and massage.

Heat a skillet over medium heat, stir in the pancetta, cook until it browns, for about 3-4 minutes, and remove to a plate.

To the pancetta fat, add olive oil and cook the chicken breasts for 2 minutes per side. Place in the stock, black pepper, pancetta, salt, and onion. Sprinkle with oregano and serve.

Nutritional info per serving: Calories 323, Fat 21g, Net Carbs 4.8g, Protein 24.5g

Hot Chicken Meatballs

Prep + Cook Time: 25 minutes | Serves: 2

Ingredients

1 pound ground chicken
Salt and black pepper, to taste
2 tbsp yellow mustard
½ cup almond flour

¼ cup mozzarella cheese, grated
¼ cup hot sauce
1 egg

Directions

Preheat oven to 400 F and line a baking tray with parchment paper.

In a bowl, combine the chicken, black pepper, mustard, flour, mozzarella cheese, salt, and egg. Form meatballs and arrange them on the baking tray. Cook for 16 minutes, then pour over the hot sauce and bake for 5 more minutes.

Nutritional info per serving: Calories 487, Fat 35g, Net Carbs 4.3g, Protein 31.5g

Cheesy Pinwheels with Chicken

Prep + Cook Time: 30 minutes | Serves: 2

Ingredients

2 tbsp ghee
1 garlic, minced
1/3 pound chicken breasts, cubed
1 tsp creole seasoning
1/3 red onion, chopped
1 tomato, chopped
½ cup chicken stock

¼ cup whipping cream
½ cup mozzarella cheese, grated
¼ cup fresh cilantro, chopped
Salt and black pepper, to taste
4 ounces cream cheese
5 eggs
A pinch of garlic powder

Directions

Season the chicken with creole seasoning. Heat a pan over medium heat and warm 1 tbsp ghee. Add chicken and cook each side for 2 minutes; remove to a plate.

Melt the rest of the ghee and stir in garlic and tomato; cook for 4 minutes. Return the chicken to the pan and pour in stock; cook for 15 minutes. Place in whipping cream, red onion, salt, mozzarella cheese, and black pepper; cook for 2 minutes.

In a blender, combine the cream cheese with garlic powder, salt, eggs, and black pepper, and pulse well. Place the mixture into a lined baking sheet, and then bake for 10 minutes in the oven at 320 F. Allow the cheese sheet to cool down, place on a cutting board, roll, and slice into medium slices.

Arrange the slices on a serving plate and top with chicken mixture. Sprinkle with cilantro to serve.

Nutritional info per serving: Calories 463, Fat 36.4g, Net Carbs 6.3g, Protein 35.2g

Peanut-Crusted Chicken

Prep + Cook Time: 30 minutes | Serves: 2

Ingredients

1 egg
Salt and black pepper, to taste
3 tbsp canola oil

1 ½ cups peanuts, ground
2 chicken breast halves, boneless and skinless
Lemon slices for garnish

Directions

Whisk egg in one bowl and pour the peanuts in another one. Season the chicken, dip in the egg and then in peanuts. Warm oil in a pan over medium heat and brown the chicken for 2 minutes per side.

Remove the chicken pieces to a baking sheet, set in the oven, and bake for 10 minutes at 360 F. Serve topped with lemon slices.

Nutritional info per serving: Calories 634, Fat 51g, Net Carbs 4.7g, Protein 43.6g

Turnip Greens & Artichoke Chicken

Prep + Cook Time: 45 minutes | Serves: 2

Ingredients

4 ounces cream cheese
2 chicken breasts
4 oz canned artichoke hearts, chopped
1 cup turnip greens
¼ cup Pecorino cheese, grated

½ tbsp onion powder
½ tbsp garlic powder
Salt and black pepper, to taste
2 ounces Monterrey Jack cheese, shredded

Directions

Line a baking dish with parchment paper and place in the chicken breasts. Season with black pepper and salt. Set in the oven at 350 F and bake for 35 minutes.

In a bowl, combine the artichokes with onion powder, Pecorino cheese, salt, turnip greens, cream cheese, garlic powder, and black pepper. Remove the chicken from the oven, cut each piece in half, divide artichokes mixture on top, spread with Monterrey cheese and bake for 5 more minutes.

Nutritional info per serving: Calories 443, Fat 24.5g, Net Carbs 4.2g, Protein 35.4g

Winter Chicken with Vegetables

Prep + Cook Time: 35 minutes | Serves: 2

Ingredients

2 tbsp olive oil
2 cups whipping cream
1 pound chicken breasts, chopped
1 onion, chopped
1 carrot, chopped
2 cups chicken stock

Salt and black pepper, to taste
1 bay leaf
1 turnip, chopped
1 parsnip, chopped
1 cup green beans, chopped
2 tsp fresh thyme, chopped

Directions

Heat a pan over medium heat and warm the olive oil. Sauté the onion for 3 minutes, pour in the stock, carrot, turnip, parsnip, chicken, and bay leaf. Bring to a boil, and simmer for 20 minutes.

Add in the asparagus and cook for 7 minutes. Discard the bay leaf, stir in the whipping cream, adjust the seasoning and scatter with fresh thyme to serve.

Nutritional info per serving: Calories 483, Fat 32.5g, Net Carbs 6.9g, Protein 33g

Gingered Grilled Chicken

Prep + Cook Time: 35 minutes + marinade time | Serves: 2

Ingredients

1 pound chicken drumsticks
¼ tbsp coconut aminos
¼ tbsp apple cider vinegar
A pinch of red pepper flakes
Salt and black pepper, to taste

½ tsp ground ginger
2 tbsp butter, melted
1 garlic clove, minced
¼ tsp lime zest
¼ cup warm water

Directions

In a large bowl, combine the butter with water, salt, ginger, vinegar, garlic, pepper, lime zest, aminos, and pepper flakes. Mix well.

Add in the chicken and toss to coat. Refrigerate for 1 hour.

Preheat a grill to high heat. Set the chicken pieces skin side down on the preheated grill and cook for 10 minutes, turn, brush with some marinade, and cook for 10 minutes.

Nutritional info per serving: Calories 507, Fat 34.6g, Net Carbs 4.6g, Protein 43g

Pancetta & Cheese Stuffed Chicken

Prep + Cook Time: 40 minutes | Serves: 2

Ingredients

4 slices pancetta
2 tbsp olive oil
2 chicken breasts
1 garlic clove, minced
1 shallot, finely chopped

2 tbsp dried oregano
4 oz mascarpone cheese
1 lemon, zested
Salt and black pepper to taste

Directions

Heat the oil in a small skillet and sauté the garlic and shallots for 3 minutes. Stir in salt, black pepper, and lemon zest. Transfer to a bowl and let it cool. Stir in the mascarpone cheese and oregano.

Score a pocket in each chicken's breast, fill the holes with the cheese mixture and cover with the cut-out chicken. Wrap each breast with two pancetta slices and secure the ends with a toothpick.

Lay the chicken on a greased baking sheet and cook in the oven for 20 minutes at 380 F.

Nutritional info per serving: Calories 643, Fat 44.5g, Net Carbs 6.2g, Protein 52.8g

Awesome Chicken Kabobs with Celery Root Chips

Prep + Cook Time: 60 minutes | Serves: 2

Ingredients

4 tbsp olive oil
2 chicken breasts
Salt and black pepper to taste
1 tsp dried oregano

1 tsp chili powder
¼ cup chicken broth
1 lb celery root, sliced

Directions

Preheat oven to 400 F and grease a baking sheet with cooking spray.

In a large bowl, mix half of the olive oil, oregano, chili powder, salt, black pepper, and the chicken; set in the fridge for 10 minutes.

Arrange the celery slices on the baking tray in an even layer, drizzle with the remaining olive oil and sprinkle with salt and black pepper. Bake for 10 minutes.

Take the chicken from the refrigerator and thread onto skewers. Place over the celery, pour in the chicken broth, then set in the oven for 30 minutes.

Nutritional info per serving: Calories: 365, Fat: 23g, Net Carbs: 4.6g, Protein: 35g

Marinated Fried Chicken

Prep + Cook Time: 20 minutes | Serves: 2

Ingredients

3 tbsp olive oil
2 chicken breasts, cut into strips
½ cup pork rinds, crushed

8 ounces jarred pickle juice
1 egg

Directions

Cover the chicken with pickle juice, in a bowl, and refrigerate for 12 hours while covered.

Whisk the egg in one bowl, and place the pork rinds in a separate one. Dip the chicken pieces in the egg, then in pork rinds. Ensure they are well coated.

Set a pan over medium heat and warm oil, fry the chicken for 3 minutes on each side, remove to paper towels, drain the excess grease and serve.

Nutritional info per serving: Calories 393, Fat 15.6g, Net Carbs 3.1g, Protein 21.8g

Chili Chicken Kebab with Garlic Dressing

Prep + Cook Time: 17 minutes + time refrigeration | Serves: 2-4

Ingredients

Skewers

2 tbsp olive oil
3 tbsp soy sauce, sugar-free
1 tbsp ginger paste

2 tbsp swerve brown sugar
Chili pepper to taste
2 chicken breasts, cut into cubes

Dressing

½ cup tahini
1 tbsp parsley, chopped
1 garlic clove, minced

Salt and black pepper to taste
¼ cup warm water

Directions

To make the marinade, in a small bowl, whisk the soy sauce, ginger paste, brown sugar, chili pepper, and olive oil. Put the chicken in a zipper bag, pour the marinade over, seal and shake for an even coat. Marinate in the fridge for 2 hours.

Preheat a grill to high heat. Thread the chicken on skewers and cook for 10 minutes in total with three to four turnings to be golden brown. Transfer to a plate.

Mix the tahini, garlic, salt, parsley, and warm water in a bowl. Serve the chicken skewers topped with the tahini dressing.

Nutritional info per serving: Calories 410, Fat 32g, Net Carbs 4.8g, Protein 23.5g

Baked Chicken Legs with Basil-Tomato Sauce

Prep + Cook Time: 1 hour 35 minutes | Serves: 2-4

Ingredients

2 tbsp olive oil
1 pound chicken legs
2 green onions, chopped
1 parsnip, chopped
1 carrot, chopped
2 green bell peppers, seeded, cut into chunks

2 garlic cloves, minced
¼ cup coconut flour
1 cup chicken broth
1 (28 oz) can sugar-free tomato sauce
2 tbsp Italian seasoning
Salt and black pepper to taste

Directions

Season the legs with salt and black pepper. Heat the oil in a large skillet over medium heat and fry the chicken until brown on both sides for 10 minutes. Remove to a baking dish.

In the same pan, sauté the onion, parsnip, bell peppers, carrot, and garlic for 10 minutes with continuous stirring. In a bowl, evenly combine the broth, coconut flour, tomato paste, and Italian seasoning together, and pour it over the vegetables in the pan. Stir and cook to thicken for 4 minutes.

Pour the mixture over the chicken in the baking dish, and bake in the oven for around 1 hour at 390 F. Remove from the oven and serve warm.

Nutritional info per serving: Calories 345, Fat 18.2g, Net Carbs 9.5g, Protein 25.3g

Grilled Fennel with Chicken Wrapped in Bacon

Prep + Cook Time: 48 minutes | Serves: 2-4

Ingredients

2 tbsp olive oil
2 chicken breasts
Salt and black pepper to taste
½ pound bacon, sliced

½ lb fennel bulb, sliced
2 tbsp lemon juice
2 tbsp cheddar cheese, shredded
1 tbsp rosemary, chopped

Directions

Preheat your grill on high heat.

Brush the fennel slices with olive oil and season with salt. Grill for 4-6 minutes, frequently turning until slightly golden. Remove to a plate and drizzle with lemon juice. Pour over cheddar cheese so that it melts a little on contact with the hot fennel and forms a cheesy dressing.

Preheat oven to 390 F.

Season chicken breasts with salt and black pepper, and wrap 2 bacon slices around each chicken breast. Arrange on a baking sheet that is lined with parchment paper, drizzle with oil and bake for 25-30 minutes until bacon is brown and crispy.

Serve with grilled fennel sprinkled with rosemary.

Nutritional info per serving: Calories 487, Fat 39.5g, Net Carbs 5.2g, Protein 27.3g

Traditional Indian Dish Chicken with Mushrooms

Prep + Cook Time: 45 minutes | Serves: 2-4

Ingredients

2 tbsp butter
1 lb chicken breasts, sliced lengthwise
1 tbsp olive oil
Salt and black pepper, to taste

1 cup mushrooms
1 ¼ cups heavy whipping cream
1 tbsp cilantro, chopped

Garam masala

1 tsp ground cumin
2 tsp ground coriander
1 tsp ground cardamom
1 tsp turmeric

1 tsp ginger
1 tsp paprika
1 tsp cayenne, ground
1 pinch ground nutmeg

Directions

To make the garam masala, in a bowl, mix all garam masala spices. Coat the chicken with half of the masala mixture. Heat the olive oil and butter in a frying pan over medium heat, and brown the chicken for 3-5 minutes per side. Transfer to a baking dish.

To the remaining masala, add heavy cream and mushrooms. Season with salt and black pepper and pour over the chicken. Bake in the oven for 20 minutes until the mixture starts to bubble.

Garnish with chopped cilantro to serve.

Nutritional info per serving: Calories: 553, Fat: 49.5g, Net Carbs: 4.8g, Protein: 32.5g

Chili & Lemon Marinated Chicken Wings

Prep + Cook Time: 25 minutes | Serves: 2-4

Ingredients

3 tbsp olive oil
1 tsp coriander seeds
1 tsp xylitol
1 pound wings
Juice from 1 lemon
½ cup fresh parsley, chopped

2 garlic cloves, minced
1 red chili pepper, chopped
Salt and black pepper, to taste
Lemon wedges, for serving
½ tsp cilantro

Directions

Using a bowl, stir together lemon juice, xylitol, garlic, salt, red chili pepper, cilantro, olive oil, and black pepper. Place in the chicken wings and toss well to coat. Refrigerate for 2 hours.

Preheat grill over high heat. Add the chicken wings; and grill each side for 6 minutes. Serve the chicken wings with lemon wedges.

Nutritional info per serving: Calories 223, Fat 12g, Net Carbs 5.1g, Protein 16.8g

Braised Chicken with Tomato & Garlic

Prep + Cook Time: 45 minutes | Serves: 2-4

Ingredients

2 tbsp butter
1 lb chicken thighs
Salt and black pepper to taste
3 cloves garlic, minced

2 cups tomatoes, chopped
1 eggplant, chopped
2 tbsp basil leaves, chopped

Directions

Heat a saucepan over medium heat and add in butter to melt. Season the chicken with salt and black pepper, and fry for 4 minutes on each side until golden brown. Remove to a plate.

Sauté the garlic for 2 minutes, pour in the tomatoes, and cook for 8 minutes. Add in the eggplant and cook for 4 minutes. Season the sauce with salt and black pepper, stir and add the chicken. Coat with sauce and simmer for 3 minutes.

Serve the chicken with the sauce and sprinkle with fresh basil leaves.

Nutritional info per serving: Calories 453, Fat 36.8g, Net Carbs 3.3g, Protein 24.7g

Cipollini & Bell Pepper Chicken Souvlaki

Prep + Cook Time: 17 minutes + marinade time | Serves: 2-4

Ingredients

2 chicken breasts, cubed
2 tbsp olive oil
2 cloves garlic, minced
1 red bell pepper, cut into chunks
8 oz small cipollini

½ cup lemon juice
Salt and black pepper to taste
1 tsp rosemary leaves to garnish
2 to 4 lemon wedges to garnish

Directions

Thread the chicken, bell pepper, and cipollini onto skewers and set aside. In a bowl, mix half of the oil, garlic, salt, black pepper, and lemon juice, and add the chicken skewers. Cover the bowl and let the chicken marinate for at least 2 hours in the refrigerator.

Preheat a grill to high heat and grill the skewers for 6 minutes on each side. Remove and serve garnished with rosemary leaves and lemons wedges.

Nutritional info per serving: Calories 363, Fat 14.2g, Net Carbs 4.2g, Protein 32.5g

Creamed Smoked Paprika Chicken

Prep + Cook Time: 50 minutes | Serves: 2-4

Ingredients

2 tbsp ghee
1 pound chicken thighs
Salt and black pepper, to taste
1 tsp onion powder

¼ cup heavy cream
2 tbsp smoked paprika
2 tbsp parsley, chopped

Directions

In a bowl, combine the paprika with onion powder, black pepper and salt. Season chicken pieces with this mixture and lay on a lined baking sheet; bake for 40 minutes in the oven at 400 F. Transfer to a serving plate.

Add the cooking juices to a skillet over medium heat, and mix with the heavy cream and ghee. Cook for 5-6 minutes until the sauce has thickened. Pour the sauce over the chicken and sprinkle with parsley.

Nutritional info per serving: Calories 346, Fat 28.5g, Net Carbs 2.3g, Protein 21g

Thyme Chicken in Foil with Mushrooms & Turnip

Prep + Cook Time: 48 minutes | Serves: 2-4

Ingredients

2 tbsp olive oil
4 tbsp butter
1 pound chicken breasts, skinless, scored
4 tbsp white wine
3 cups mixed mushrooms, teared up
1 turnip, sliced

2 cups water
2 cloves garlic, minced
4 sprigs thyme, chopped
3 lemons, juiced
Salt and black pepper to taste
2 tbsp Dijon mustard

Directions

Preheat the oven to 450 F. Arrange the turnips on a baking sheet, drizzle with a little oil, and bake for 15 minutes; then set aside.

In a bowl, evenly mix the chicken, roasted turnips, mushrooms, garlic, thyme, lemon juice, salt, pepper, and mustard. Share the chicken mixture into large sheets of aluminum foil, top with the white wine, olive oil, and a tablespoon of butter on each. Seal the edges to form packets.

Put on a baking tray and bake the chicken in the middle of the oven for 25 minutes.

Nutritional info per serving: Calories 364, Fat 16.5g, Net Carbs 4.8g, Protein 25g

Coconut Chicken with Creamy Asparagus Sauce

Prep + Cook Time: 20 minutes | Serves: 2-4

Ingredients

2 tbsp butter
1 pound chicken thighs
2 tbsp coconut oil
2 tbsp coconut flour

2 cups asparagus, chopped
1 tsp oregano
1 cup heavy cream
1 cup chicken broth

Directions

Heat a skillet over medium heat and add the coconut oil to melt. Brown the chicken on all sides, about 6-8 minutes. Set aside.

Melt the butter and whisk in the flour over medium heat. Whisk in the heavy cream and chicken broth and bring to a boil. Stir in oregano. Add the asparagus to the skillet and cook for 10 minutes until tender. Transfer to a food processor and pulse until smooth. Season with salt and black pepper.

Return to the skillet and add the chicken; cook for an additional 5 minutes and serve.

Nutritional info per serving: Calories 451, Fat: 36.7g, Net Carbs: 3.2g, Protein: 18.5g

Juicy Chicken with Broccoli & Pine Nuts

Prep + Cook Time: 30 minutes | Serves: 2-4

Ingredients

2 tbsp olive oil
2 chicken breasts, cut into strips
2 tbsp Worcestershire sauce
2 tsp balsamic vinegar
2 tsp xanthan gum
1 lemon, juiced

1 cup pine nuts
2 cups broccoli florets
1 onion, thinly sliced
Salt and black pepper to taste
1 tbsp cilantro, chopped

Directions

In a dry pan over medium heat, toast the pine nuts for 2 minutes until golden-brown; set aside. To the pan, add olive oil and sauté the onion for 4 minutes until soft and browned; remove to the nuts.

In a bowl, mix the Worcestershire sauce, balsamic vinegar, lemon juice, and xanthan gum; set aside. Add the chicken to the pan and cook for 4 minutes. Add in the broccoli, salt, and black pepper.

Stir-fry and pour in the lemon mixture in. Cook the sauce for 4 minutes and pour in the pine nuts and onion. Stir once more and cook for 1 minute. Serve the chicken stir-fry with cilantro.

Nutritional info per serving: Calories 286, Fat 10.1g, Net Carbs 3.4g, Protein 17.3g

Tarragon Chicken with Roasted Balsamic Turnips

Prep + Cook Time: 50 minutes | Serves: 2-4

Ingredients

1 pound chicken thighs
2 lb turnips, cut into wedges
2 tbsp olive oil

1 tbsp balsamic vinegar
1 tbsp tarragon
Salt and black pepper, to taste

Directions

Preheat oven to 400 F and grease a baking dish with olive oil. Cook turnips in boiling water for 10 minutes, drain, and set aside. Add the chicken and turnips to the baking dish.

Sprinkle with tarragon, black pepper, and salt. Roast for 35 minutes. Remove the baking dish, drizzle the turnip wedges with balsamic vinegar and return to the oven for another 5 minutes.

Nutritional info per serving: Calories: 383, Fat: 26g, Net Carbs: 9.5g, Protein: 21.3g

Tomato & Cheese Chicken Chili

Prep + Cook Time: 30 minutes | Serves: 2-4

Ingredients

1 tbsp butter
1 tbsp olive oil
1 pound chicken breasts, skinless, boneless, cubed
½ onion, chopped
2 cups chicken broth
2 cups tomatoes, chopped
2 oz tomato puree

1 tbsp chili powder
1 tbsp cumin
1 garlic clove, minced
1 habanero pepper, minced
½ cup mozzarella cheese, shredded
Salt and black pepper to taste

Directions

Season the chicken with salt and black pepper. Set a large pan over medium heat and add the chicken; cover with water and bring to a boil. Cook until no longer pink, for 10 minutes.

Transfer the chicken to a flat surface to shred with forks. In a pot, pour in the butter and olive oil and set over medium heat. Sauté onion and garlic until transparent for 5 minutes.

Stir in the chicken, tomatoes, cumin, habanero pepper, tomato puree, broth, and chili powder. Adjust the seasoning and let the mixture boil.

Reduce heat to simmer for about 10 minutes. Top with shredded cheese to serve.

Nutritional info per serving: Calories: 322, Fat: 16.6g, Net Carbs: 6.2g, Protein: 29g

Baked Chicken with Butternut Squash & Olives

Prep + Cook Time: 60 minutes | Serves: 2-4

Ingredients

1 pound chicken thighs
1 onion, sliced
1 pound butternut squash, cut into lunes
½ cup black olives, pitted
2 tbsp olive oil

¼ cup goat cheese, crumbled
3 garlic cloves, sliced
1 tbsp dried oregano
Salt and black pepper, to taste

Directions

Preheat oven to 400 F and place the chicken with the skin down in a baking dish. Arrange garlic, onion, and butternut squash around the chicken then drizzle with oil and season to taste.

Roast in the oven for 40 minutes. Sprinkle with olives and goat cheese to serve.

Nutritional info per serving: Calories: 405, Fat: 14.7g, Net Carbs: 5.3g, Protein: 28.5g

Tumeric Chicken Wings with Ginger Sauce

Prep + Cook Time: 25 minutes + marinated time | Serves: 2-4

Ingredients

2 tbsp olive oil
1 pound chicken wings, cut in half
1 tbsp turmeric
1 tbsp cumin
3 tbsp fresh ginger, grated
Salt and black pepper, to taste

Juice of ½ lime
1 cup thyme leaves
¾ cup cilantro, chopped
1 tbsp water
1 jalapeño pepper

Directions

In a bowl, stir together 1 tbsp ginger, cumin, salt, half of the olive oil, black pepper, turmeric, and cilantro. Place in the chicken wings pieces, toss to coat, and refrigerate for 20 minutes.

Heat the grill to high heat. Remove the wings from the marinade, drain and grill for 20 minutes, turning from time to time, then set aside.

Using a blender, combine thyme, remaining ginger, salt, jalapeno pepper, black pepper, lime juice, the remaining olive oil, and water, and blend well. Serve the chicken wings topped with the sauce.

Nutritional info per serving: Calories 253, Fat 16.1g, Net Carbs 4.1g, Protein 21.7g

Italian Chicken Meatballs

Prep + Cook Time: 15 minutes | Serves: 2-4

Ingredients

½ cup passata tomato sauce
1 pound ground chicken
2 tbsp sun-dried tomatoes, chopped
2 tbsp basil, chopped
½ tsp garlic powder

1 egg
Salt and black pepper to taste
¼ cup almond flour
2 tbsp olive oil
½ cup Parmesan cheese, shredded

Directions

To make meatballs, place everything except the oil and basil in a bowl. Mix with your hands until combined. Form meatballs out of the mixture.

Heat the olive oil in a skillet over medium heat. Cook the meatballs for 3 minutes per each side. To finish, pour over the tomato sauce and cook for 3-4 minutes. Serve with sprinkled basil.

Nutritional info per serving: Calories 323, Fat: 25.2g, Net Carbs: 4.1g, Protein: 21.5g

Baked Cheesy Chicken Tenders

Prep + Cook Time: 40 minutes | Serves: 2-4

Ingredients

3 tbsp olive oil
2 eggs, whisked
3 cups coarsely crushed cheddar cheese
½ cup pork rinds, crushed

1 lb chicken tenders
Salt to taste
Lemon wedges for garnish

Directions

Preheat oven to 370 F and line a baking sheet with parchment paper. Combine the eggs with the butter in a bowl, and mix the cheese and pork rinds in another bowl.

Season chicken with salt, dip in egg mixture, and coat generously in cheddar mixture. Place on the baking sheet, cover with aluminium foil and bake for 25 minutes. Remove foil and bake further for 12 minutes to golden brown. Serve chicken with lemon wedges.

Nutritional info per serving: Calories 512, Fat 43g, Net Carbs 2.2g, Protein 33.5g

Chicken Wings with Lemon & Capers

Prep + Cook Time: 30 minutes | Serves: 2-4

Ingredients

2 tbsp butter
1 cup chicken broth
1 tsp garlic powder
1 tsp lemon zest
3 tbsp lemon juice
½ tsp cilantro, chopped

1 tbsp soy sauce
¼ tsp xanthan gum
3 tbsp xylitol
1 pound chicken wings
Salt and black pepper, to taste
¼ cup capers

Directions

Heat a saucepan over medium heat and add lemon juice and zest, soy sauce, cilantro, chicken broth, xylitol, and garlic powder. Bring to a boil, cover, lower the heat, and let simmer for 10 minutes. Stir in the butter, capers, and xanthan gum. Set aside.

Season the wings with salt and black pepper. Preheat grill to high heat and cook the chicken wings for 5 minutes per side. Serve topped with the sauce.

Nutritional info per serving: Calories 343, Fat: 24.6g, Net Carbs: 3.6g, Protein: 19.5g

Creamy Mushroom & White Wine Chicken

Prep + Cook Time: 36 minutes | Serves: 2-4

Ingredients

1 tbsp butter
1 tbsp olive oil
1 pound chicken breasts, cut into chunks
Salt and black pepper to taste
1 packet white onion soup mix

2 cups chicken broth
¼ cup white wine
15 baby bella mushrooms, sliced
1 cup heavy cream
2 tbsp parsley, chopped

Directions

Add butter and olive oil in a saucepan and heat over medium heat. Season the chicken with salt and black pepper, and brown on all sides for 6 minutes in total. Put in a plate.

In a bowl, stir the onion soup mix with chicken broth and white wine, and add to the saucepan.

Simmer for 3 minutes and add the mushrooms and chicken. Cover and simmer for another 20 minutes. Stir in heavy cream and cook on low heat for 3 minutes. Garnish with parsley to serve.

Nutritional info per serving: Calories 432, Fat 35.3g, Net Carbs 3.2g, Protein 24.2g

Dijon Chicken with Rosemary

Prep + Cook Time: 30 minutes | Serves: 2-4

Ingredients

1 tbsp olive oil
½ cup chicken stock
½ cup onion, chopped
1 pound chicken thighs
¼ cup heavy cream

2 tbsp Dijon mustard
1 tsp rosemary, chopped
1 garlic clove, minced
Salt and black pepper to taste

Directions

Heat a pan over medium heat and add the olive oil. Season the chicken with salt and black pepper, and cook in the heated oil for about 4 minutes per side. Set aside.

Sauté the onion and garlic in the same pan for 3 minutes, add the stock, and simmer for 5 minutes. Stir in mustard and heavy cream. Pour the sauce over the chicken and serve sprinkled with rosemary.

Nutritional info per serving: Calories 515, Fat: 39.5g, Net Carbs: 5.2g, Protein: 32.5g

One-Pan Citrus Chicken with Spinach & Pine Nuts

Prep + Cook Time: 25 minutes + marinated time | Serves: 2-4

Ingredients

2 tbsp olive oil
1 pound chicken thighs
Salt and black pepper to serve
2 tbsp lemon juice
1 tsp lemon zest

1 tbsp oregano, chopped
1 garlic clove, minced
1 cup spinach
2 tbsp pine nuts

Directions

In a bowl, combine all ingredients, except for the olive oil, spinach and pine nuts. Place in the fridge for one hour. Heat a skillet over medium heat and warm olive oil.

Remove the chicken from the marinade, drain, and add to the pan. Cook until crispy, for about 7 minutes per side. Pour in the marinade and the spinach and cook for 4-5 minutes until the spinach wilts. Serve sprinkled with pine nuts.

Nutritional info per serving: Calories 465, Fat: 32.3g, Net Carbs: 3.3g, Protein: 29g

Sage Chicken with Kale & Mushrooms

Prep + Cook Time: 40 minutes | Serves: 2-4

Ingredients

1 pound chicken thighs
2 cups mushrooms, sliced
1 cup kale, chopped
2 tbsp butter
1 tbsp olive oil
Salt and black pepper, to taste

½ tsp onion powder
½ tsp garlic powder
½ cup water
1 tsp Dijon mustard
1 tbsp fresh sage, chopped

Directions

Heat a pan over medium heat and warm half of the butter and olive oil. Coat the chicken with onion powder, pepper, garlic powder and salt. Cook in the pan on each side for 3 minutes and set aside.

Stir in the remaining butter and mushrooms and cook for 5 minutes. Place in water and mustard, take the chicken pieces back to the pan, and cook for 15 minutes. Stir in the kale and cook for 5 minutes. Serve sprinkled with sage.

Nutritional info per serving: Calories 422, Fat 24.5g, Net Carbs 4.1g, Protein 27g

Mediterranean Chicken

Prep + Cook Time: 30 minutes | Serves: 2-4

Ingredients

2 tbsp olive oil
1 onion, chopped
4 chicken breasts, skinless and boneless
4 garlic cloves, minced
Salt and black pepper, to taste
½ cup kalamata olives, pitted and chopped

1 tbsp capers
1 tbsp oregano
¼ cup white wine
1 cup tomatoes, chopped
½ tsp red chili flakes

Directions

Brush the chicken with half of the olive oil and sprinkle with black pepper and salt. Heat a pan over high heat and cook the chicken for 2 minutes, flip to the other side, and cook for 2 more minutes.

Transfer to a baking dish, add in the white wine and 2 tbsp of water. Bake in the oven at 380 F for 10-15 minutes. Remove to a serving plate.

In the same pan, warm the remaining oil over medium heat. Place in the onion, olives, capers, garlic, oregano, and chili flakes, and cook for 1 minute. Stir in the tomatoes, black pepper and salt, and cook for 2 minutes. Sprinkle the sauce over the chicken breasts and serve.

Nutritional info per serving: Calories 365, Fat 22g, Net Carbs 3.1g, Protein 22.5g

Feta & Bacon Chicken

Prep + Cook Time: 30 minutes | Serves: 2-4

Ingredients

4 oz bacon, chopped
1 pound chicken breasts
3 green onions, chopped

2 tbsp coconut oil
4 oz feta cheese, crumbled
1 tbsp parsley

Directions

Place a pan over medium heat and coat with cooking spray. Add in the bacon and cook until crispy. Remove to paper towels, drain the grease and crumble.

To the same pan, add in the oil and cook the chicken breasts for 4-5 minutes, then flip to the other side; cook for an additional 4-5 minutes. Add the chicken breasts to a baking dish. Place the green onions, set in the oven, turn on the broiler, and cook for 5 minutes at high temperature. Remove to serving plates and serve topped with bacon, feta cheese, and parsley.

Nutritional info per serving: Calories 459, Fat 35g, Net Carbs 3.1g, Protein 31.5g

Chorizo Sausage & Chicken Bake

Prep + Cook Time: 50 minutes | Serves: 2-4

Ingredients

½ cup mushrooms, chopped
1 pound chorizo sausages, chopped
2 tbsp olive oil
4 cherry peppers, chopped
1 red bell pepper, chopped
1 red onion, sliced
2 garlic cloves, minced
2 cups tomatoes, chopped

1 pound chicken thighs
Salt and black pepper, to taste
½ cup chicken stock
1 tsp turmeric
2 tsp dried oregano
2 tbsp capers
1 tbsp parsley, chopped

Directions

Cook chorizo sausage in half of the olive oil over medium heat, for 5-6 minutes until browned; remove to a bowl. Heat the rest of the oil, place in the chicken thighs, and season to taste.

Cook each side for 3 minutes and set aside. In the same pan, add the onion, garlic, bell pepper, cherry peppers, and mushrooms, and cook for 4 minutes.

Pour in the stock, turmeric, salt, tomatoes, pepper, vinegar, capers, and oregano.

Stir in the chorizo sausages and chicken, place everything to the oven at 400 F, and bake for 30 minutes. Garnish with chopped parsley to serve.

Nutritional info per serving: Calories 422, Fat 32.5g, Net Carbs 3.8g, Protein 23.5g

Creamy Chicken with Pancetta, Mushrooms & Spinach

Prep + Cook Time: 50 minutes | Serves: 2-4

Ingredients

1 pound chicken thighs
Salt and black pepper, to taste
1 onion, chopped
1 tbsp coconut oil
4 pancetta strips, chopped
2 garlic cloves, minced

1 cup white mushrooms, halved
1 cup spinach
2 cups white wine
1 cup whipping cream
2 tbsp parsley, chopped

Directions

Cook the pancetta in a pan over medium heat until crispy, for about 4-5 minutes; remove to paper towels. To the pancetta fat, add the coconut oil and chicken, sprinkle with black pepper and salt and cook until brown. Remove to paper towels too.

In the same pan, sauté the onion and garlic for 4 minutes.

Then, mix in the mushrooms and cook for another 5 minutes. Return the pancetta and browned chicken to the pan.

Stir in the wine and bring to a boil, reduce the heat, and simmer for 20 minutes. Pour in the whipping cream and spinach and warm without boiling. Scatter over the parsley and serve.

Nutritional info per serving: Calories 353, Fat 17.5g, Net Carbs 5.2g, Protein 22.3g

Chicken Pie with Bacon

Prep + Cook Time: 55 minutes | Serves: 2-4

Ingredients

3 tbsp butter
1 onion, chopped
4 oz bacon, sliced
1 carrot, chopped
3 garlic cloves, minced
Salt and black pepper, to taste

¾ cup crème fraîche
½ cup chicken stock
1 pound chicken breasts, cubed
2 tbsp yellow mustard
¾ cup cheddar cheese, shredded

Dough

1 egg
¾ cup almond flour
3 tbsp cream cheese
1 ½ cups mozzarella cheese, shredded

1 tsp onion powder
1 tsp garlic powder
Salt and black pepper, to taste

Directions

Sauté the onion, garlic, black pepper, bacon, and carrot in melted butter for 5 minutes. Add in the chicken and cook for 3 minutes. Stir in the crème fraîche, salt, mustard, black pepper, and stock, and cook for 7 minutes. Add in the cheddar cheese and set aside.

In a bowl, combine the mozzarella cheese with the cream cheese, and heat in a microwave for 1 minute. Stir in the garlic powder, salt, flour, black pepper, onion powder, and egg. Knead the dough well, split into 4 pieces, and flatten each into a circle.

Set the chicken mixture into 4 ramekins, top each with a dough circle, and cook in the oven at 370 F for 25 minutes.

Nutritional info per serving: Calories 563, Fat 44.6g, Net Carbs 7.7g, Protein 36g

Slow-Cooked Chicken Stew with Vegetables

Prep + Cook Time: 4 hours 15 minutes | Serves: 2-4

Ingredients

2 garlic cloves, minced
1 cup mushrooms, chopped
¼ tsp celery seeds, ground
1 carrot, chopped
1 cup chicken stock
1 cup sour cream

1 cup leeks, chopped
1 pound chicken breasts
1 tsp dried thyme
2 tbsp fresh parsley, chopped
Salt and black pepper, to taste
4 zucchinis, spiralized

Directions

Season the chicken with salt, black pepper, and thyme and place into your slow cooker. Stir in leeks, sour cream, celery seeds, garlic, mushrooms, and stock. Cook on high for 4 hours.

Heat a saucepan with salted water over medium heat and bring to a boil. Stir in the zucchini pasta, cook for 1 minute, and drain. Transfer to a serving plate, top with the chicken mixture, and sprinkle with parsley to serve.

Nutritional info per serving: Calories 312, Fat 17.5g, Net Carbs 8.4g, Protein 25.8g

Cabbage & Broccoli Chicken Casserole

Prep + Cook Time: 55 minutes | Serves: 2-4

Ingredients

1 tbsp coconut oil, melted
2 cups mozzarella cheese, grated
½ head cabbage, shredded
½ head broccoli, cut into florets
1 pound chicken breasts, cooked and cubed

1 cup mayonnaise
1/3 cup chicken stock
Salt and black pepper, to taste
Juice of 1 lemon
1 tbsp cilantro, chopped

Directions

Coat a baking dish with coconut oil and set chicken pieces to the bottom. Spread green cabbage and broccoli, followed by half of the cheese.

In a bowl, combine the mayonnaise with black pepper, stock, lemon juice, and salt. Pour this mixture over the chicken, spread the rest of the cheese, cover with aluminum foil, and bake for 30 minutes in the oven at 350 F. Open the aluminum foil and cook for 20 more minutes. Sprinkle with cilantro to serve.

Nutritional info per serving: Calories 623, Fat 42g, Net Carbs 7.4g, Protein 51.5g

Chicken Wings with Lemon & Jalapeno Peppers

Prep + Cook Time: 65 minutes | Serves: 2-4

Ingredients

2 pounds chicken wings
Salt and black pepper, to taste
1 lemon, zested and juiced
3 tbsp coconut aminos

3 tbsp xylitol
¼ cup chives, chopped
½ tsp xanthan gum
5 dried jalapeño peppers, chopped

Directions

Preheat oven to 380 F and line a baking sheet with parchment paper. Season the chicken with salt and black pepper and spread on the baking dish. Bake for 35 minutes, and remove to a serving plate.

Put a small pan over medium heat, add in the lemon juice, coconut aminos, lemon zest, xylitol, xanthan gum, and jalapeño peppers. Bring the mixture to a boil and cook for 2 minutes. Pour the sauce over the chicken, sprinkle with chives and serve.

Nutritional info per serving: Calories 422, Fat 26.3g, Net Carbs 3.4g, Protein 25.5g

Greek-Style Baked Chicken

Prep + Cook Time: 30 minutes | Serves: 2-4

Ingredients

2 tbsp olive oil
1 pound chicken breast halves
2 garlic cloves, minced
Salt and black pepper, to taste
1 cup chicken stock

3 tbsp xylitol
½ cup white wine
2 tomatoes, sliced
4 oz feta cheese, sliced
2 tbsp dill, chopped

Directions

Put a pan over medium heat and warm oil, add the chicken, season with black pepper and salt, and cook until brown. Stir in the xylitol, garlic, stock, and white wine, and cook for 10 minutes.

Remove to a lined baking sheet and arrange tomato and feta slices on top. Bake in the oven for 15 minutes at 380 F. Sprinkle with chopped dill to serve.

Nutritional info per serving: Calories 322, Fat 15.4g, Net Carbs 3.4g, Protein 26g

Cheese & Mayo Topped Chicken Bake

Prep + Cook Time: 45 minutes | Serves: 2-4

Ingredients

2 tbsp butter, melted
1 pound chicken breast, halved
Salt and black pepper, to taste
¼ cup green chilies, chopped
2 oz bacon, chopped
1 cup cottage cheese

½ cup mayonnaise
½ cup Grana Padano cheese, grated
1 cup cheddar cheese, grated
¼ cup pork skins, crushed
½ cup Parmesan cheese, shredded
2 tbsp basil, chopped

Directions

Preheat oven to 420 F and grease a baking dish with cooking spray. Coat the chicken with salt and black pepper and place in the baking dish to bake for 30 minutes.

Cook the bacon in a pan over medium heat for 5 minutes until crispy. Remove to a bowl and let cool for few minutes. Stir in cottage cheese, ½ cup Grana Padano cheese, mayonnaise, chilies, and cheddar cheese, and spread over the chicken. Brush with melted butter and sprinkle with the pork skins and Parmesan cheese. Cook in the oven for 5-10 minutes. Sprinkle with basil to serve.

Nutritional info per serving: Calories 383, Fat 21g, Net Carbs 4.9g, Protein 23.5g

Chicken & Sausage Gumbo

Prep + Cook Time: 40 minutes | Serves: 2-4

Ingredients

1 sausage, sliced
2 chicken breasts, cubed
1 stick celery, chopped
1 bay leaf
1 bell pepper, chopped
1 onion, chopped
1 cup tomatoes, chopped
4 cups chicken broth

2 tbsp garlic powder
2 tbsp dry mustard
1 tbsp chili powder
Salt and black pepper, to taste
2 tbsp cajun seasoning
3 tbsp olive oil
1 tbsp sage, chopped

Directions

Heat olive oil in a saucepan over medium heat. Add the sausages and chicken and cook for 5 minutes. Add the remaining ingredients, except for the sage, and bring to a boil.

Reduce the heat and simmer for 25 minutes. Serve in bowls sprinkled with sage.

Nutritional info per serving: Calories 433, Fat 26.4g, Net Carbs 8.7g, Protein 35.6g

Mouth-Watering Chicken Stuffed Mushrooms

Prep + Cook Time: 40 minutes | Serves: 2-4

Ingredients

2 tbsp ghee
2 (7-oz) packets riced cauliflower
Salt and black pepper, to taste
1 onion, chopped
1 garlic clove, minced

1 pound ground chicken
1 tsp oregano
8 portobello mushroom caps
½ cup chicken broth

Directions

Preheat oven to 360 F and lay the mushroom caps in a greased baking dish; set aside.

Warm ghee in a pan over medium heat, and stir-fry the onion and garlic for 3 minutes. Add in the cauli rice and ground chicken, and cook for 3 more minutes. Season with oregano, salt and pepper.

Stuff the caps with the mixture, pour the chicken broth and bake in the oven for 30 minutes.

Nutritional info per serving: Calories 261, Fat 16g, Net Carbs 6g, Protein 14g

Eggplant & Carrot Chicken Gratin

Prep + Cook Time: 55 minutes | Serves: 2-4

Ingredients

2 tbsp butter
1 tbsp olive oil
1 eggplant, chopped
2 carrots, chopped

2 tbsp Swiss cheese, grated
Salt and black pepper, to taste
2 garlic cloves, minced
1 pound chicken thighs

Directions

Season the chicken with salt and pepper. Put a pan over medium heat and warm 1 tbsp butter with olive oil. Place in the chicken thighs and cook each side for 3 minutes; lay them in a baking dish.

In the same pan, melt the rest of the butter and cook the garlic, eggplant, carrots, black pepper, and salt, for 10 minutes. Top the chicken with this mixture and spread the cheese all over. Bake in the oven at 350 F, for 30 minutes.

Nutritional info per serving: Calories 405, Fat 31g, Net Carbs 6.6g, Protein 23g

Sauced Chicken Legs with Vegetables

Prep + Cook Time: 60 minutes | Serves: 2-4

Ingredients

2 tbsp olive oil
1 parsnip, chopped
2 celery stalks, chopped
2 cups chicken stock
1 onion, chopped
¼ cup red wine
1 pound chicken legs

1 cup tomatoes, chopped
1 cup spinach
¼ tsp dried thyme
Salt and black pepper, to taste
1 tbsp parsley, chopped

Directions

Put a pot over medium heat and heat the olive oil. Add garlic, parsnip, celery, and onion; season with salt and pepper and sauté for 5-6 minutes until tender. Stir in the chicken and cook for 5 minutes.

Pour in the stock, tomatoes, and thyme, and cook for 30 minutes. Sprinkle with parsley to serve.

Nutritional info per serving: Calories 264, Fat 14,5g, Net Carbs 7.1g, Protein 22,5g

Butternut Squash with Chicken & Cottage Cheese

Prep + Cook Time: 1 hour 15 minutes | Serves: 2-4

Ingredients

2 tbsp olive oil
1 pound chicken breasts, halved
¼ tsp garlic powder

1 small butternut squash, sliced
Salt and black pepper, to taste
1 cup cottage cheese, shredded

Directions

Preheat oven to 400 F.

In a food processor, add the butternut squash and pulse until it resembles rice. Transfer to a kitchen towel to soak the excess liquid. Season the chicken breasts with black pepper, garlic powder, and salt and drizzle with some olive oil. Transfer to a baking dish and bake for 30 minutes.

Heat the remaining olive oil in a pan over medium heat and add the squash rice. Season and cook for 2 minutes, stirring frequently. Stir in half cup of water and continue cooking until the liquid evaporates. Remove to a plate and mix with the cottage cheese. Top with chicken to serve.

Nutritional info per serving: Calories 312, Fat 21g, Net Carbs 2.4g, Protein 28g

Carrot & Mushroom Chicken Skillet

Prep + Cook Time: 35 minutes | Serves: 2-4

Ingredients

1 cup carrots, shredded
1 cup mushrooms, sliced
½ tsp onion powder
½ tsp garlic powder
1 tbsp butter

1 tbsp olive oil
½ tsp Dijon mustard
1 tbsp rosemary, chopped
1 pound chicken thighs
Salt and black pepper, to taste

Directions

In a small bowl, mix together salt, black pepper, garlic, and onion powder. Rub the chicken with the spice mixture.

Warm the butter with olive oil in a skillet, and cook the chicken until browned, about 8-10 minutes; set aside. Add mushrooms and carrots to the same fat and cook for about 5 minutes. Season to taste with salt and black pepper.

Stir in mustard and ¼ cup of water. Return the chicken to the skillet and reduce the heat. Cover and let simmer for 15 minutes. Scatter rosemary all over to serve.

Nutritional info per serving: Calories 452, Fat: 36.5g, Net Carbs: 3.2g, Protein: 29g

Satay Chicken with Sauteed Cabbage

Prep + Cook Time: 50 minutes + marinade time | Serves: 2-4

Ingredients

Cabbage:

1/3 small head white cabbage, cored and shredded
2 tbsp olive oil

Salt to taste

Chicken:

1/3 tbsp soy sauce, sugar-free
1/3 tbsp fish sauce, sugar-free
1/3 tbsp lime juice
1/3 tsp cilantro, chopped
1 tsp minced garlic
1/3 tsp minced ginger

1 tbsp olive oil
1/3 tbsp rice wine vinegar
1/3 tsp cayenne pepper
1/3 tsp erythritol
1 pound chicken thighs

Sauce:

¼ cup peanut butter, at room temperature
1/3 tsp minced garlic
1/3 tbsp lime juice
1 tbsp water

1/3 tsp ginger, minced
1/3 tsp cayenne pepper
1 tbsp rice wine vinegar
1/3 tbsp chilli sauce

Directions

Combine all chicken ingredients in a large Ziploc bag. Seal the bag and shake to combine. Refrigerate for 1 hour. Heat 2 tbsp of olive oil in a saucepan over medium heat and add the cabbage, 2 tbsp of water and pinch of salt. Cook until wilted and remove to a plate. Whisk the peanut butter with the remaining sauce ingredients in a bowl. Set aside.

Preheat grill to high heat and grease with cooking spray. Remove the chicken from the marinade.

Put the chicken on the grill, skin side up and grill for 6 minutes, then flip and cook for 4-5 more minutes. Drizzle the chicken with sauce and serve with sauteed cabbage.

Nutritional info per serving: Calories 503, Fat: 37.4g, Net Carbs: 4.2g, Protein: 34.6g

Bacon Rolled Chicken Breasts

Prep + Cook Time: 45 minutes | Serves: 2-4

Ingredients

1 green onion, chopped
1 cup gorgonzola cheese
1 pound chicken breasts, halved

4 oz bacon, sliced
2 tomatoes, chopped
Salt and black pepper, to taste

Directions

Preheat oven to 380 F.

In a bowl, stir together the gorgonzola cheese, green onion, tomatoes, black pepper, and salt. Pound with a rolling pin to flatten the chicken breasts, season and lay the cheese mixture on top.

Roll them up, and wrap each in a bacon slice. Place the wrapped chicken breasts in a greased baking dish, and roast in the oven for 30 minutes.

Nutritional info per serving: Calories 587, Fat 44.3g, Net Carbs 4.5g, Protein 35.4g

Baked Chicken Wings with Paprika-Mayo Dip

Prep + Cook Time: 25 minutes | Serves: 2-4

Ingredients

1 pound chicken wings
Salt and black pepper to taste
2 tbsp olive oil
1 tbsp paprika

1 tsp garlic powder
½ cup mayonnaise
1 tbsp lemon juice
Salt to taste

Directions

Preheat oven to 400 F. Season the wings with salt and black pepper and drizzle with olive oil. Lay them on a lined baking sheet. Bake for 20 minutes until golden brown.

In a bowl, mix the mayo with garlic powder and lemon juice. Season with salt and serve with the wings.

Nutritional info per serving: Calories 315, Fat 21.4g, Net Carbs 2.4g, Protein 27.5g

Oven-Style Salami & Cheddar Chicken

Prep + Cook Time: 40 minutes | Serves: 2-4

Ingredients

1 tbsp olive oil
1 ½ cups canned tomato sauce
1 pound chicken breast, halved
Salt and black pepper, to taste

1 tsp dried oregano
4 oz cheddar cheese, sliced
1 tsp garlic powder
2 oz salami, sliced

Directions

Preheat oven to 380 F. In a bowl, combine oregano, garlic, salt, and pepper and rub the chicken.

Heat a pan with the olive oil over medium heat, add in the chicken, cook each side for 2 minutes; remove to a baking dish. Top with the cheddar cheese,spread the sauce, then cover with salami and bake for 30 minutes.

Nutritional info per serving: Calories 417, Fat 25.3g, Net Carbs 5.2g, Protein 29g

Teriyaki Chicken Wings with Spring Onions

Prep + Cook Time: 40 minutes | Serves: 2-4

Ingredients

2 tbsp sesame oil
1 pound chicken wings
4 tbsp teriyaki sauce
Salt to taste

Chili sauce to taste
Lemon juice from 1 lemon
2 spring onions, sliced

Directions

Preheat oven to 390 F. In a bowl, mix the teriyaki sauce, olive oil, salt, chili sauce, and lemon juice. Add in the wings and toss to coat. Place the chicken in a roasting dish lined with parchment paper and roast for 35 minutes, turning once halfway. Garnish with spring onions to serve.

Nutritional info per serving: Calories 177, Fat 11g, Net Carbs 4.3g, Protein 21g

Chili Chicken with Grilled Bell Peppers

Prep + Cook Time: 5 minutes + marinade time | Serves: 2-4

Ingredients

1 pound chicken breasts, halved
2 cloves garlic, minced
2 tbsp oregano, chopped
2 tbsp lemon juice
1/3 cup olive oil

¼ cup erythritol
Kosher salt and black pepper to taste
1/3 cup chili sauce
2 red bell peppers, cut into strips
2 spring onion, cut diagonally

Directions

In a bowl, mix the garlic, oregano, lemon juice, olive oil, chili sauce, erythritol, salt, and black pepper. Add the chicken and place in the fridge for at least 1 hour.

Preheat a grill to 350 F. Add the chicken and bell pepper strips and grill for 10 minutes. Flip and continue cooking for 5-10 more minutes until the chicken and pepper strips are cooked through. Garnish with spring onion to serve.

Nutritional info per serving: Calories 403, Fat 29g, Net Carbs 6.4g, Protein 24.5g

Chili Chicken with Dill Sauce

Prep + Cook Time: 35 minutes | Serves: 2-4

Ingredients

2 tbsp butter
1 tbsp olive oil
1 onion, chopped
½ tsp chili powder

1 pound chicken breasts, skinless and boneless
Salt and black pepper, to taste
1 cup sour cream
2 tbsp fresh dill, chopped

Directions

Heat a pan with the olive oil and half of the butter over medium heat. Add in the chicken, season with chili powder, black pepper and salt, and fry for 2-3 per side until golden. Transfer to a baking dish and cook in the oven for 15 minutes at 390 F, until no longer pink.

To the pan, add the remaining butter and onion and cook for 2 minutes. Pour in the sour cream, warm through without boil. Slice the chicken and serve on a platter with dill sauce spooned over.

Nutritional info per serving: Calories 381, Fat 27.9g, Net Carbs 6.5g, Protein 25.8g

Cauliflower & Fennel Chicken Cake

Prep + Cook Time: 58 minutes | Serves: 2-4

Ingredients

1 ½ cups leftover chicken, cubed
1 ½ cups spinach
1 cauliflower head, cut into florets
1 fennel bulb, chopped
1 egg, lightly beaten
1 cup sharp cheddar cheese, grated

½ cup pork rinds, crushed
¼ cup unsweetened almond milk
2 tbsp olive oil
1 garlic clove, minced
Salt and black pepper to taste

Directions

Preheat the oven to 360 F and grease a baking dish with cooking spray. Steam the cauli florets for 8 minutes in salted water over medium heat. Drain and set aside.

Also, combine the cheddar cheese and pork rinds in a large bowl and mix in the chicken. Set aside.

Next, heat the olive oil in a large skillet and cook the garlic, fennel, and spinach for about 5 minutes. Season with salt and pepper. Pour in the chicken bowl, add the cauliflower, egg and almond milk.

Transfer everything to the baking dish and cook for 30 minutes. Remove the chicken from the oven, let rest for 5 minutes, and serve.

Nutritional info per serving: Calories 395, Fat 26.4g, Net Carbs 4.2g, Protein 21.6g

Ham & Cheese Stuffed Chicken with Pomodoro Sauce

Prep + Cook Time: 35 minutes | Serves: 2-4

Ingredients

2 tbsp olive oil
¼ cup ham, chopped
1 cup spinach

2 tbsp mozzarella cheese, shredded
1/3 cup tomato basil sauce
1 pound whole chicken breasts

Directions

Preheat oven to 400 F and brush a baking dish with half of the olive oil. Combine the cottage cheese, shredded mozzarella cheese, ham and spinach in a bowl and mix well.

Cut pockets into the sides of the chicken breasts. Stuff with the prepared mixture. Brush the top with olive oil. Place on the baking dish and roast in the oven for 25 minutes.

Pour the tomato-basil sauce over and return to the oven. Cook for an additional 5 minutes.

Nutritional info per serving: Calories 343, Fat: 26.7g, Net Carbs: 4.7g, Protein: 35.6g

Grilled Chicken with Broccoli & Carrots

Prep + Cook Time: 17 minutes | Serves: 2-4

Ingredients

2 tbsp olive oil
1 tbsp smoked paprika
Salt and black pepper to taste
1 tsp garlic powder

2 pounds chicken breasts
1 small head broccoli, cut into florets
2 baby carrots, sliced

Directions

Put broccoli florets and carrots into the steamer basket over the boiling water. Steam for about 8 minutes or until crisp-tender. Set aside to cool, then sprinkle with salt and olive oil.

Grease grill grate with cooking spray and preheat to 400 F.

Combine paprika, salt, black pepper, and garlic powder in a bowl. Brush chicken with olive oil and sprinkle spice mixture over and massage with hands. Grill chicken for 7 minutes per side until well-cooked, and plate. Serve warm with steamed vegetables.

Nutritional info per serving: Calories 466, Fat 29g, Net Carbs 1.9g, Protein 49g

Ham & Emmental Baked Chicken

Prep + Cook Time: 50 minutes | Serves: 2-4

Ingredients

1 pound chicken breasts, halved
Salt and black pepper, to taste
¼ cup mayonnaise
1 tbsp Dijon mustard
¼ tsp xylitol
¼ cup pork rinds, crushed

¼ cup mozzarella cheese, grated
¼ tsp garlic powder
¼ tsp onion powder
Salt and black pepper
4 oz ham, sliced
2 oz Emmental cheese, sliced

Directions

Season the chicken with garlic and onion powders, salt and pepper. Preheat oven to 350 F.

In a bowl, mix mustard, mayonnaise, and xylitol. Take about ¼ of this mixture and spread over the chicken. Preserve the rest. Take half of the pork rinds, half of the mozzarella cheese, and place to the bottom of a greased baking dish. Add the chicken to the top.

Cover the chicken with the remaining mozzarella and pork rinds. Bake in the oven for about 40 minutes until the chicken is cooked completely. Take out from the oven and top with Emmental cheese and ham. Place back in the oven and cook until golden brown.

Nutritional info per serving: Calories: 443, Fat: 32.5g, Net Carbs: 5.1g, Protein: 31g

Green Bean Chicken Curry

Prep + Cook Time: 30 minutes | Serves: 2-4

Ingredients

1 tbsp coconut oil
1 pound chicken breasts
1 cup chicken stock
1 ¼ cups green beans, chopped
1 tbsp lime juice

¼ cup coconut cream
1 tsp curry powder
1 tsp red pepper flakes
1 green onion, chopped
Salt and black pepper, to taste

Directions

In a pan over medium heat, warm coconut oil. Place in the chicken and cook each side for 2 minutes; then set aside. Add green onion and green beans to the pan and cook for 4 minutes. Stir in the black pepper, stock, red pepper flakes, salt, curry powder, coconut cream, and lime juice. Take the chicken back to the pan, and cook for 15 minutes.

Nutritional info per serving: Calories 477, Fat 32.5g, Net Carbs 4.1g, Protein 48g

Creamy Chicken with Tomatoes

Prep + Cook Time: 20 minutes | Serves: 2-4

Ingredients

2 tbsp butter
1 pound chicken thighs
Salt and black pepper to taste
1 cup cherry tomatoes, halved

1 tsp oregano
1 ½ cups chicken broth
½ cup heavy cream
¼ cup Parmesan cheese, shredded

Directions

Rub the chicken with salt, black pepper and oregano. Melt the butter in a saucepan over medium heat and cook the chicken for 5 minutes on each side to brown.

Pour the chicken broth in the pan and cook covered for 8 minutes. Stir in the heavy cream and Parmesan cheese, and simmer for 4 minutes.

Nutritional info per serving: Calories 407, Fat 32g, Net Carbs 6.2g, Protein 21.5g

Baked Zucchini with Chicken and Cheese

Prep + Cook Time: 45 minutes | Serves: 2-4

Ingredients

1 pound chicken breasts, cubed
1 tbsp butter
1 tbsp olive oil
1 red bell pepper, chopped
1 shallot, sliced
2 zucchinis, cubed
1 garlic clove, minced

1 tsp thyme
Salt and black pepper to taste
½ cup cream cheese, softened
¼ cup mayonnaise
1 tbsp Worcestershire sauce (sugar-free)
1 cup mozzarella cheese, shredded

Directions

Set oven to 370 F and grease and line a baking dish. Heat the butter and olive oil in a pan over medium heat and add in the chicken.

Cook until lightly browned, for about 5 minutes. Place in shallot, zucchini cubes, black pepper, garlic, bell pepper, salt, and thyme. Cook until tender and set aside.

In a bowl, mix cream cheese, mayonnaise, and Worcestershire sauce. Stir in meat and sauteed vegetables. Place the mixture into the prepared baking dish and bake for 20 minutes. Then, sprinkle with the mozzarella cheese and bake until browned for 10 more minutes.

Nutritional info per serving: Calories: 488, Fat: 38.3g, Net Carbs: 5.2g, Protein: 23.3g

Chicken Breasts with Lemon

Prep + Cook Time: 30 minutes | Serves: 2-4

Ingredients

2 tbsp olive oil
1 pound skinless chicken breasts
1 turnip, cut into wedges
Salt and black pepper, to taste
1 tsp coriander seeds

1 red onion, sliced
Juice from 1 lemon
Zest from 1 lemon
Lemon rinds from 1 lemon

Directions

Preheat oven to 370 F. Put the chicken in a baking dish, and season with black pepper and salt.

Sprinkle with lemon juice and coriander seeds. Toss well to coat, place in turnip, red onion, lemon rinds and lemon zest. Drizzle with olive oil and bake for 25 minutes. Discard the lemon rinds and serve sprinkled with cooking sauce.

Nutritional info per serving: Calories 288, Fat 11g, Net Carbs 4.3g, Protein 23g

Tasty Chicken Bites

Prep + Cook Time: 1 hour and 20 minutes | Serves: 2-4

Ingredients

1 pound chicken breasts
1 tsp sesame oil
1 tbsp olive oil
1 cup mushrooms, quartered

1 tbsp allspice
1 tbsp granulated sweetener
1 tbsp soy sauce, sugar-free
1 tsp sesame seeds

Directions

Cut the chicken into 1-inch cubes. Combine sesame oil, olive oil, allspice, sweetener, and soy sauce in a bowl. Add the chicken and mushrooms, and let marinate for 1 hour in the fridge.

Preheat the grill. Thread the chicken and mushrooms onto wooden skewers and grill for 3 minutes per side. Transfer to a serving plate, scatter with sesame seeds and serve.

Nutritional info per serving: Calories 273, Fat: 17.5g, Net Carbs: 3.5g, Protein: 23g

Feta & Mozzarella Chicken

Prep + Cook Time: 45 minutes | Serves: 2-4

Ingredients

1 pound chicken breasts, skinless and boneless
½ tsp mixed spice seasoning
Salt and black pepper to season
1 cup baby spinach

2 tsp olive oil
4 oz feta cheese, crumbled
½ cup mozzarella cheese, shredded

Directions

Rub the chicken with spice mix, salt and black pepper. Put in a casserole dish and layer spinach over the chicken. Mix the oil with feta and mozzarella cheeses, black pepper, and stir in 4 tbsp water.

Pour the mixture over the chicken and cover the casserole with aluminium foil. Bake in the oven for 20 minutes at 370 F, remove foil and continue cooking for 15 minutes until a nice golden brown color is formed on top.

Nutritional info per serving: Calories 343, Fat 27g, Net Carbs 5.2g, Protein 23g

Herby Chicken Dippers with Homemade Ketchup

Prep + Cook Time: 50 minutes | Serves: 2-4

Ingredients

1 lb chicken breasts, skinless and boneless
Salt and black pepper, to taste
1 egg
½ cup almond flour
¼ cup Parmesan cheese, grated
½ tsp garlic powder
1 tsp dried parsley
½ tsp thyme

3 tbsp olive oil
2 oz mozzarella cheese, shredded
14 oz canned tomatoes, chopped
1 tbsp tomato paste
½ tbsp xylitol
1 tbsp balsamic vinegar
1 cup tomato sauce
1 tbsp basil, chopped

Directions

In a saucepan over medium heat, combine tomatoes, tomato paste, xylitol, and balsamic vinegar and bring to a boil. Cook for 5-6 minutes, stirring frequently until thickened. Taste and adjust the seasoning. Top with thyme and set aside.

Cut the breasts into strips. In a bowl, combine the almond flour with parsley, Parmesan cheese, pepper, thyme, garlic powder, and salt. In a separate bowl, whisk the egg with black pepper and salt. Dip the chicken in the egg, and then in almond flour mixture.

Heat a pan over medium heat and warm 2 tbsp of olive oil and fry the chicken, until golden, for about 3-4 minutes. Remove to paper towels to soak the excess oil. Serve warm with the ketchup.

Nutritional info per serving: Calories 336, Fat 21g, Net Carbs 7.7g, Protein 25.4g

Chicken "Four Cheeses" with Pancetta & Bell Pepper

Prep + Cook Time: 40 minutes | Serves: 2-4

Ingredients

1 pound chicken breasts
¼ cup mozzarella cheese, cubed
¼ cup mascarpone cheese
¼ cup cheddar cheese, cubed

¼ cup provolone cheese, cubed
1 green bell pepper, sliced
Salt and black pepper, to taste
2 oz pancetta, sliced

Directions

Fry pancetta in a pan over medium heat until crispy, for 5 minutes. Set aside to cool, then crush it.

In a bowl, mix together bell pepper and crushed pancetta. Stir in mascarpone, cheddar cheese, provolone cheese, and mozzarella cheeses.

Cut slits into chicken breasts, season with black pepper and salt, and stuff with the cheese mixture. Set on a lined baking sheet, place in the oven at 400 F, and bake for 45 minutes.

Nutritional info per serving: Calories 355, Fat 22.6g, Net Carbs 2.2g, Protein 33.5g

Turkey & Vegetable Casserole

Prep + Cook Time: 20 minutes | Serves: 2

Ingredients

1 tbsp coconut oil
1 turkey breast, sliced
2 zucchinis, sliced
1 onion, chopped
1 carrot, chopped

1 cup mushrooms, sliced
1 green bell pepper, seeded and chopped
1 garlic clove, minced
Salt and black pepper, to taste
2 tbsp parsley, chopped

Directions

Heat a pan over medium heat and add coconut oil, stir in the onion, garlic, and cook for 3 minutes. Place in the zucchinis, bell pepper, mushrooms, black pepper, salt and carrot and cook for 10 minutes.

Set another pan over medium heat, add in turkey slices and cook each side for 3 minutes. Pour the mixture into the vegetable pan. Cook for 3 minutes, and serve sprinkled with parsley.

Nutritional info per serving: Calories 464, Fat 23.5g, Net Carbs 8.6g, Protein 53g

Stewed Turkey with Greens

Prep + Cook Time: 30 minutes | Serves: 2

Ingredients

1 onion, chopped
2 tbsp olive oil
2 cups leftover turkey meat, chopped
1 cup snow peas
2 cups chicken stock
Salt and black pepper, to taste
1 fresh Jalapeño pepper, chopped

1 garlic clove, minced
½ cup broccoli rabe, chopped
½ tsp ground coriander
1 tsp cumin
¼ cup sour cream
1 tbsp cilantro, chopped

Directions

Heat olive oil in a pan over medium heat. Cook the onion and garlic for 3 minutes until soft. Stir in the snow peas and chicken stock, and cook for 10 minutes.

Place in the turkey, ground coriander, salt, broccoli rabe, Jalapeño pepper, cumin, and black pepper, and cook for 10 minutes. Stir in the sour cream, top with chopped cilantro and serve.

Nutritional info per serving: Calories 443, Fat 28g, Net Carbs 8.2g, Protein 36.4g

Broccoli & Kale Turkey Pie

Prep + Cook Time: 40 minutes | Serves: 2-4

Ingredients

1 tbsp olive oil
½ cup kale, chopped
2 cups chicken stock
1 cup turkey meat, cooked and chopped
Salt and black pepper, to taste
1 tsp fresh rosemary, chopped

½ cup broccoli, chopped
½ cup mozzarella cheese, shredded
¼ tsp paprika
¼ tsp garlic powder
¼ tsp xanthan gum

Crust:

¼ cup butter
¼ tsp xanthan gum
2 cups almond flour

A pinch of salt
1 egg
¼ cup cheddar cheese

Directions

In a pot over medium heat, add in olive oil and turkey, and cook for 5 minutes. Stir in stock, mozzarella cheese, garlic powder, rosemary, black pepper, paprika, broccoli, kale, and salt.

In a bowl, combine ½ cup stock from the pot with ¼ teaspoon xanthan gum, and transfer everything to the pot; set aside. In a separate bowl, stir together salt, ¼ teaspoon xanthan gum, and flour.

Stir in the butter, cheddar cheese, and egg, until a pie crust dough forms. Form into a ball and refrigerate.

Spray a baking dish with cooking spray and sprinkle the filling for the pie on the bottom. Set the dough on a working surface, roll into a circle, and top the filling with the dough. Ensure well pressed and sealed edges, set in the oven at 350 F, and bake for 35 minutes. Allow the pie to cool, and serve.

Nutritional info per serving: Calories 325, Fat 23g, Net Carbs 5.6g, Protein 21g

Herb Turkey Burgers with Sauteed Brussels Sprouts

Prep + Cook Time: 30 minutes | Serves: 2-4

Ingredients

Burgers

1 pound ground turkey
1 egg
1 onion, chopped
2 tbsp pork rinds, crushed

Salt and black pepper to taste
1 tsp dried mixed herbs
2 tbsp butter

Brussels sprouts

1 ½ lb Brussels sprouts, halved
2 tbsp olive oil

Salt and black pepper to taste

Directions

In a pan over medium heat, add the olive oil. Cook the Brussels sprouts until tender, for about 10 minutes. Season with salt and black pepper and set aside.

Combine the burger ingredients in a mixing bowl and create patties from the mixture.

To the same pan, add the butter, and fry the patties until cooked completely, about 8-10 minutes in total.

Nutritional info per serving: Calories: 422, Fat: 24.6g, Net Carbs: 6.1g, Protein: 28.6g

Hot Turkey Patties with Cucumber & Radish Salad

Prep + Cook Time: 30 minutes | Serves: 2-4

Ingredients

2 tbsp olive oil
2 spring onions, thinly sliced
1 pound ground turkey
1 egg

2 garlic cloves, minced
1 tbsp dried oregano
1 tsp Cayenne powder
Salt and black pepper to taste

Cucumber salad

1 tbsp apple cider vinegar
1 tbsp chopped dill
2 cucumbers, sliced

5 radishes, sliced
½ red onion, sliced
2 tbsp extra virgin olive oil

Directions

In a medium bowl, place ground turkey, green onions, egg, garlic, oregano, Cayenne powder, salt, and black pepper and mix to combine. Make patties out of the mixture.

Warm olive oil in a skillet over medium heat and cook the patties for 3 minutes per side. Remove to a plate.

To a bowl, add cucumber, radishes, red onion, olive oil, apple cider vinegar, salt, and dill and toss to coat. Plate along with the turkey patties.

Nutritional info per serving: Calories 432, Fat: 32.5g, Net Carbs: 6.4g, Protein: 25.5g

Leftover Turkey & Veggie Casserole

Prep + Cook Time: 55 minutes | Serves: 2-4

Ingredients

2 cups zucchini cubes
1 onion chopped
1 cup green cabbage, shredded
2 cups leftover roast turkey, shredded
¼ cup chicken stock
½ cup tomato sauce
¼ tsp cumin
¼ cup Parmesan cheese, grated
Salt and black pepper, to taste
1 garlic clove, minced

Directions

Preheat oven to 350 F.

Heat a pan over medium heat. Cook the onion, garlic, zucchini cubes, and cabbage for 7-8 minutes until tender. Stir in the broth, tomato sauce, cumin, black pepper and salt, and simmer for 15 minutes.

Add the turkey and transfer to a baking dish; bake for 35 minutes. Scatter the Parmesan cheese over and bake for 5-10 more minutes until golden on top.

Nutritional info per serving: Calories 273, Fat 14.5g, Net Carbs 8.5g, Protein 23g

Broccoli & Carrot Turkey Bake

Prep + Cook Time: 35 minutes | Serves: 2-4

Ingredients

2 tbsp olive oil
1 lb turkey breasts, cooked
1 carrot, shredded
1 head broccoli, cut into florets
½ cup almond milk
½ cup heavy cream
1 cup cheddar cheese, grated
4 tbsp pork rinds, crushed
Salt and black pepper, to taste
½ tsp paprika
1 tsp oregano

Directions

Preheat oven to 375 F and grease a baking tray with cooking spray. Steam the broccoli and carrot in salted water over medium heat for 5 minutes. Use two forks to shred the turkey.

Place the turkey into a large bowl together with almond milk, olive oil, broccoli, paprika, oregano, salt, and black pepper, and stir to combine. Transfer the mixture to the baking tray. Sprinkle heavy cream over the dish and coat with grated cheese. Cover with the pork rinds.

Place in the oven and cook until bubbling for 20-25 minutes. Ladle to a serving plate and enjoy!

Nutritional info per serving: Calories: 485, Fat: 33.5g, Net Carbs: 4.1g, Protein: 39.5g

Tumeric Turkey Chili with Swiss Chard

Prep + Cook Time: 30 minutes | Serves: 2-4

Ingredients

1 pound turkey breasts, cubed
1 cup Swiss chard, chopped
1 cup canned diced tomatoes
2 tbsp coconut oil
2 tbsp coconut cream
2 garlic cloves, minced
1 onion, chopped
1 tbsp ground coriander
2 tbsp fresh ginger, grated
1 tbsp turmeric
Salt and black pepper, to taste
1 tbsp chili powder
2 tbsp cilantro, chopped

Directions

Sauté turkey, onion, ginger, and garlic for 5 minutes in coconut oil over medium heat. Stir in the tomatoes, black pepper, turmeric, coriander, salt and chili powder.

Place in the coconut cream and cook for 10 minutes. Transfer to an immersion blender alongside Swiss chard; blend well. Simmer for 15 minutes. Serve in bowls sprinkled with cilantro.

Nutritional info per serving: Calories 342, Fat 18.5g, Net Carbs 5.1g, Protein 22g

Italian Turkey Ragu Sauce with Zucchini Pasta

Prep + Cook Time: 30 minutes | Serves: 2-4

Ingredients

1 cup mushrooms, sliced
2 tsp olive oil
1 pound ground turkey
1 cup tomato sauce, sugar-free
1 onion, chopped

1 parsnip, chopped
16 oz zucchini noodles
1 tbsp Italian seasoning
2 tbsp Parmesan cheese, grated

Directions

Heat a skillet over medium heat and add the olive oil. Cook the zucchini noodles for 2-3 minutes, stirring continuously. Season with salt and black pepper and set aside. Add turkey to the skillet and cook until browned, about 7-8 minutes. Transfer to a plate.

Add onion and cook until translucent, about 3 minutes. Add parsnip and mushrooms, and cook for 7 more minutes. Return the turkey to the skillet. Stir in the tomato sauce and Italian seasoning. Cover the pan, lower the heat, and simmer for 15 minutes. Spread the sauce over the zucchini noodles and top with Parmesan cheese to serve.

Nutritional info per serving: Calories 312, Fat: 14.5g, Net Carbs: 9.6g, Protein: 28g

FISH & SEAFOOD

Crispy Salmon with Broccoli & Red Bell Pepper

Prep + Cook Time: 30 minutes | Serves: 2

Ingredients

2 salmon fillets
Salt and black pepper to taste
2 tbsp mayonnaise
2 tbsp fennel seeds, crushed

½ head broccoli, cut in florets
1 red bell pepper, sliced
1 tbsp olive oil
2 lemon wedges

Directions

Brush the salmon with mayonnaise and season with salt and black pepper. Coat with fennel seeds, place in a lined baking dish and bake for 15 minutes at 370 F.

Steam the broccoli and carrot for 3-4 minutes, or until tender, in a pot over medium heat.

Heat the olive oil in a saucepan and sauté the red bell pepper for 5 minutes. Stir in the broccoli and turn off the heat. Let the pan sit on the warm burner for 2-3 minutes. Serve with baked salmon garnished with lemon wedges.

Nutritional info per serving: Calories 563, Fat: 37g, Net Carbs: 6g, Protein: 54g

Baked Cod with Parmesan and Almonds

Prep + Cook Time: 40 minutes | Serves: 2

Ingredients

2 cod fillets
1 cup Brussels sprouts
1 tbsp butter, melted
Salt and black pepper to taste

1 cup crème fraiche
2 tbsp Parmesan cheese, grated
2 tbsp shaved almonds

Directions

Toss the fish fillets and Brussels sprouts in butter and season with salt and black pepper to taste. Spread in a greased baking dish.

Mix the crème fraiche with Parmesan cheese, pour and smear the cream on the fish. Bake in the oven for 25 minutes at 400 F until golden brown on top, take the dish out, sprinkle with the almonds and bake for another 5 minutes. Best served hot.

Nutritional info per serving: Calories 560, Fat 44.7g, Net Carbs 5.4g, Protein 25.3g

Sardines with Green Pasta & Sun-Dried Tomatoes

Prep + Cook Time: 20 minutes | Serves: 2

Ingredients

2 tbsp olive oil
4 cups zoodles (spiralled zucchini)
½ pound whole fresh sardines, gutted and cleaned

½ cup sun-dried tomatoes, drained and chopped
1 tbsp dill
1 garlic clove, minced

Directions

Preheat the oven to 350 F and line a baking sheet with parchment paper.

Arrange the sardines on the dish, drizzle with olive oil, sprinkle with salt and black pepper. Bake in the oven for 10 minutes until the skin is crispy.

Warm oil in a skillet over medium heat and stir-fry the zucchini, garlic and tomatoes for 5 minutes. Adjust the seasoning. Transfer the sardines to a plate and serve with the veggie pasta.

Nutritional info per serving: Calories 431, Fat: 28.3g, Net Carbs: 5.6g, Protein: 32.5g

Greek Sea Bass with Olive Sauce

Prep + Cook Time: 15 minutes | Serves: 2

Ingredients

2 sea bass fillets
2 tbsp olive oil
1 garlic clove, minced
A pinch of chili pepper

1 tbsp green olives, pitted and sliced
1 lemon, juiced
Salt to taste

Directions

Preheat a grill.

In a small bowl mix together half of the olive oil, chili pepper, garlic, and salt and rub onto the sea bass fillets. Grill the fish on both sides for 5-6 minutes until brown.

In a skillet over medium heat, warm the remaining olive oil and stir in the lemon juice, olives, and some salt; cook for 3-4 minutes. Plate the fillets and pour the lemon sauce over to serve.

Nutritional info per serving: Calories 267, Fat: 15.6g, Net Carbs: 1.6g, Protein: 24g

Grilled Salmon with Mustard Sauce

Prep + Cook Time: 15 minutes | Serves: 2

Ingredients

2 salmon fillets
¾ tsp fresh thyme
1 tbsp butter

¾ tsp tarragon
Salt and black pepper to taste

Sauce

¼ cup Dijon mustard
2 tbsp white wine

½ tsp tarragon
¼ cup heavy cream

Directions

Season the salmon with thyme, tarragon, salt, and black pepper. Melt the butter in a pan over medium heat. Add salmon and cook for about 4-5 minutes on both sides until the salmon is cooked through. Remove to a warm dish and cover.

To the same pan, add the sauce ingredients over low heat and simmer until the sauce is slightly thickened, stirring continually. Cook for 60 seconds to infuse the flavors and adjust the seasoning. Serve the salmon, topped with the sauce.

Nutritional info per serving: Calories 537, Fat: 26.4g, Net Carbs: 1.5g, Protein: 67g

Tilapia Cabbage Tortillas with Cauliflower Rice

Prep + Cook Time: 20 minutes | Serves: 2

Ingredients

1 tsp avocado oil
1 cup cauli rice
2 tilapia fillets, cut into cubes
¼ tsp taco seasoning

Sea salt and hot paprika to taste
2 whole cabbage leaves
2 tbsp guacamole
1 tbsp cilantro, chopped

Directions

Microwave the cauli rice in microwave safe bowl for 4 minutes. Fluff with a fork and set aside.

Warm avocado oil in a skillet over medium heat, rub the tilapia with the taco seasoning, salt, and hot paprika, and fry until brown on all sides, for about 8 minutes in total.

Divide the fish among the cabbage leaves, top with cauli rice, guacamole and cilantro.

Nutritional info per serving: Calories 170, Fat 6.4g, Net Carbs 1.4g, Protein 24.5g

Fish Tacos with Slaw, Lemon and Cilantro

Prep + Cook Time: 20 minutes | Serves: 2

Ingredients

1 tbsp olive oil
1 tsp chili powder

2 halibut fillets, skinless, sliced
2 low carb tortillas

Slaw

2 tbsp red cabbage, shredded
1 tbsp lemon juice
Salt to taste

½ tbsp extra-virgin olive oil
½ carrot, shredded
1 tbsp cilantro, chopped

Directions

Combine red cabbage with salt in a bowl; massage cabbage to tenderize. Add in the remaining slaw ingredient, toss to coat and set aside.

Rub the halibut with olive oil, chili powder and paprika. Heat a grill pan over medium heat. Add halibut and cook until lightly charred and cooked through, about 3 minutes per side.

Divide between the tortillas. Combine all slaw ingredients in a bowl. Split the slaw among the tortillas.

Nutritional info per serving: Calories 385, Fat: 26g, Net Carbs: 6.5g, Protein: 23.8g

Mediterranean Tilapia Bake

Prep + Cook Time: 30 minutes | Serves: 2

Ingredients

2 tilapia fillets
2 garlic cloves, minced
1 tsp basil, chopped
1 cup canned tomatoes
¼ tbsp chilli powder

2 tbsp white wine
1 tbsp olive oil
½ red onion, chopped
2 tbsp parsley
10 black olives, pitted and halved

Directions

Preheat oven to 350 F.

Heat the olive oil in a skillet over medium heat and cook the onion and garlic for about 3 minutes. Stir in tomatoes, olives, chilli powder, and white wine and bring the mixture to a boil. Reduce the heat and simmer for 5 minutes. Put the tilapia in a baking dish, pour over the sauce and bake in the oven for 10-15 minutes. Serve garnished with basil.

Nutritional info per serving: Calories 282, Fat: 15g, Net Carbs: 6g, Protein: 23g

Speedy Salmon in Creamy Parsley Sauce

Prep + Cook Time: 25 minutes | Serves: 2

Ingredients

2 salmon fillets
½ cup heavy cream
1 tbsp mayonnaise
½ tbsp parsley, chopped

½ lemon, zested and juiced
Salt and black pepper to season
1 tbsp Parmesan cheese, grated

Directions

In a bowl, mix the heavy cream, parsley, mayonnaise, lemon zest, lemon juice, salt and pepper, and set aside.

Season the fish with salt and black pepper, drizzle lemon juice on both sides of the fish and arrange them in a parchment paper–lined baking sheet. Spread the parsley mixture and sprinkle with Parmesan cheese. Bake in the oven for 15 minutes at 400 F. Great served with steamed broccoli.

Nutritional info per serving: Calories 554, Fat 30.4g, Net Carbs 2.2g, Protein 56.2g

Grilled Tuna Steaks with Shirataki Pad Thai

Prep + Cook Time: 30 minutes | Serves: 2

Ingredients

½ pack (7-oz) shirataki noodles
2 cups water
1 red bell pepper, seeded and sliced
2 tbsp soy sauce, sugar-free
1 tbsp ginger-garlic paste
1 tsp chili powder

1 tbsp water
2 tuna steaks
Salt and black pepper to taste
1 tbsp olive oil
1 tbsp parsley, chopped

Directions

In a colander, rinse the shirataki noodles with running cold water. Bring a pot of salted water to a boil; blanch the noodles for 2 minutes. Drain and set aside.

Preheat a grill on medium-high. Season the tuna with salt and black pepper, brush with olive oil, and grill covered. Cook for 3 minutes on each side.

In a bowl, whisk together soy sauce, ginger-garlic paste, olive oil, chili powder, and water. Add bell pepper, and dry noodles and toss to coat. Assemble the noodles and tuna in serving plate and garnish with parsley.

Nutritional info per serving: Calories 287, Fat 16.2g, Net Carbs 6.8g, Protein 23.4g

Omelet Wraps with Tuna

Prep + Cook Time: 15 minutes | Serves: 2

Ingredients

1 avocado, sliced
1 tbsp chopped chives
1/3 cup canned tuna, drained
2 spring onions, sliced

4 eggs, beaten
4 tbsp mascarpone cheese
1 tbsp butter
Salt and black pepper, to taste

Directions

In a small bowl, combine the chives and mascarpone cheese; set aside. Melt the butter in a pan over medium heat. Add the eggs to the pan and cook for about 3 minutes. Flip the omelet over and continue cooking for another 2 minutes until golden. Season with salt and black pepper.

Remove the omelet to a plate and spread the chive mixture over. Arrange the tuna, avocado, and onion slices. Wrap the omelet and serve immediately.

Nutritional info per serving: Calories 481, Fat: 37.9g, Net Carbs: 6.2g, Protein: 26.9g

Baked Trout and Asparagus Foil Packets

Prep + Cook Time: 20 minutes | Serves: 2

Ingredients

½ pound asparagus spears
1 tbsp garlic puree
½ pound deboned trout, butterflied
Salt and black pepper to taste
3 tbsp olive oil

2 sprigs rosemary
2 sprigs thyme
2 tbsp butter
½ medium red onion, sliced
2 lemon slices

Directions

Preheat the oven to 400 F. Rub the trout with garlic puree, salt and black pepper.

Prepare two aluminum foil squares. Place the fish on each square. Divide the asparagus and onion between the squares, top with a pinch of salt and pepper, a sprig of rosemary and thyme, and 1 tbsp of butter. Also, lay the lemon slices on the fish. Wrap and close the fish packets securely, and place them on a baking sheet. Bake in the oven for 15 minutes, and remove once ready.

Nutritional info per serving: Calories 498, Fat 39.3g, Net Carbs 4.8g, Protein 27g

Baked Haddock with Cheesy Hazelnut Topping

Prep + Cook Time: 50 minutes | Serves: 2-4

Ingredients

1 tbsp butter
1 shallot, sliced
1 pound haddock fillet
2 eggs, hard-boiled, chopped
½ cup water
3 tbsp hazelnut flour

2 cups sour cream
1 tbsp parsley, chopped
½ cup pork rinds, crushed
1 cup mozzarella cheese, grated
Salt and black pepper to taste

Directions

Melt the butter in a saucepan over medium heat and sauté the shallots for about 3 minutes. Reduce the heat to low and stir the hazelnut flour into it to form a roux. Cook the roux to be golden brown and stir in the sour cream until the mixture is smooth. Season with salt and pepper, and stir in the parsley.

Spread the haddock fillet in a greased baking dish, sprinkle the eggs on top, and spoon the sauce over. In a bowl, mix the pork rinds with the mozzarella cheese, and sprinkle it over the sauce. Bake in the oven for 20 minutes at 370 F until the top is golden and the sauce and cheese are bubbly.

Nutritional info per serving: Calories 788, Fat 57g, Net Carbs 8.5g, Protein 65g

Chilli Cod with Chive Sauce

Prep + Cook Time: 20 minutes | Serves: 2

Ingredients

1 tsp chilli powder
2 cod fillets
Salt and black pepper to taste
1 tbsp olive oil

1 garlic clove, minced
1/3 cup lemon juice
2 tbsp vegetable stock
2 tbsp chives, chopped

Directions

Preheat oven to 400 F and grease a baking dish with cooking spray. Rub the cod fillets with chili powder, salt, and black pepper and lay in the baking dish.

Bake for 10-15 minutes until fish fillets are easily removed with a fork.

In a skillet over low heat, warm the olive oil and sauté the garlic for 3 minutes. Add the lemon juice, vegetable stock, and chives. Season with salt, black pepper, and cook for 3 minutes until the stock slightly reduces. Divide fish into 2 plates, top with sauce, and serve.

Nutritional info per serving: Calories 448, Fat 35.3g, Net Carbs 6.3g, Protein 20g

Grilled Salmon with Radish Salad

Prep + Cook Time: 22 minutes | Serves: 2-4

Ingredients

1 lb skinned salmon, cut into 4 steaks each
1 cup radishes, sliced
Salt and black pepper to taste
8 green olives, pitted and chopped
1 cup arugula
2 large tomatoes, diced

3 tbsp red wine vinegar
2 green onions, sliced
3 tbsp olive oil
2 slices day-old zero carb bread, cubed
¼ cup parsley, chopped

Directions

In a bowl, mix the radishes, olives, black pepper, arugula, tomatoes, wine vinegar, green onion, olive oil, bread, and parsley. Let sit for the flavors to incorporate.

Season the salmon steaks with salt and pepper; grill them on both sides for 8 minutes in total. Serve the salmon steaks warm on a bed of the radish salad.

Nutritional info per serving: Calories 338, Fat 21.7g, Net Carbs 3.1g, Protein 28.5g

Coconut Fried Shrimp with Cilantro Sauce

Prep + Cook Time: 15 minutes | Serves: 2

Ingredients

2 tsp coconut flour
2 tbsp grated Pecorino cheese
1 egg, beaten in a bowl
¼ tsp curry powder

½ pound shrimp, shelled
3 tbsp coconut oil
Salt to taste

Sauce

2 tbsp ghee
2 tbsp cilantro leaves, chopped
½ onion, diced

½ cup coconut cream
½ ounce Paneer cheese, grated

Directions

Combine coconut flour, Pecorino cheese, curry powder, and salt in a bowl.

Melt the coconut oil in a skillet over medium heat. Dip the shrimp in the egg first, and then coat with the dry mixture. Fry until golden and crispy, about 5 minutes.

In another skillet, melt the ghee. Add onion and cook for 3 minutes. Add curry and cilantro and cook for 30 seconds. Stir in coconut cream and Paneer cheese and cook until thickened. Add the shrimp and coat well. Serve warm.

Nutritional info per serving: Calories 741, Fat: 64g, Net Carbs: 4.3g, Protein: 34.4g

Catalan Shrimp with Garlic

Prep + Cook Time: 22 minutes | Serves: 2-4

Ingredients

¼ cup olive oil, divided
1 pound shrimp, peeled and deveined
Salt to taste

¼ tsp cayenne pepper
3 garlic cloves, sliced
2 tbsp chopped parsley

Directions

Warm olive oil in a large skillet over medium heat. Reduce the heat and add the garlic; cook for 6-8 minutes, but make sure it doesn't brown or burn. Add the shrimp, season with salt and cayenne pepper, stir for one minute and turn off the heat. Let the shrimp finish cooking with the heat of the hot oil for about 8-10 minutes. Serve garnished with parsley.

Nutritional info per serving: Calories 441, Fat 29g, Net Carbs 1.2g, Protein 43g

Pan-Seared Scallops with Sausage & Mozzarella

Prep + Cook Time: 15 minutes | Serves: 2-4

Ingredients

2 tbsp butter
12 fresh scallops, rinsed and pat dry
8 ounces sausage, chopped
1 red bell pepper, seeds removed, sliced

1 red onion, finely chopped
1 cup Grana Padano cheese, grated
Salt and black pepper to taste

Directions

Melt half of the butter in a skillet over medium heat, and cook the onion and bell pepper for 5 minutes until tender. Add the sausage and stir-fry for another 5 minutes. Remove and set aside.

Pat dry the scallops with paper towels, and season with salt and pepper. Add the remaining butter to the skillet and sear the scallops for 2 minutes on each side to have a golden brown color. Add the sausage mixture back, and warm through. Transfer to serving platter and top with Grana Padano cheese.

Nutritional info per serving: Calories 834, Fat 62g, Net Carbs 9,5g, Protein 56g

Round Zucchini Stuffed with Shrimp and Tomato

Prep + Cook Time: 35 minutes | Serves: 2

Ingredients

1 pound zucchinis, tops removed and reserved
1 lb small shrimp, peeled, deveined
¼ onion, chopped
1 tsp olive oil

1 small tomato, chopped
Salt and black pepper to taste
1 tbsp basil leaves, chopped

Directions

Scoop out the seeds of the zucchinis with a spoon and set aside.

Warm olive oil in a skillet and sauté the onion and tomato for 3 minutes. Add the shrimp, zucchini flesh, basil leaves, salt, and pepper and cook for another 5 minutes.

Fill the zucchini shells with the mixture. Cover with the zucchini tops and place them on a greased baking sheet to cook for 15 to 20 minutes at 390 F. The shrimp should no longer be pink by this time. Remove the zucchinis and serve with tomato and mozzarella salad.

Nutritional info per serving: Calories 252, Fat 6.4g, Net Carbs 8.9g, Protein 37.6g

Mustardy Crab Cakes

Prep + Cook Time: 15 minutes | Serves: 2-4

Ingredients

1 tbsp coconut oil
1 pound lump crab meat
1 tsp Dijon mustard
1 egg

¼ cup mayonnaise
1 tbsp coconut flour
1 tbsp cilantro, chopped

Directions

In a bowl, add crab meat, mustard, mayonnaise, coconut flour, egg, cilantro, salt, and black pepper; mix well to combine. Make patties out of the mixture.

Melt the coconut oil in a skillet over medium heat. Add the crab patties and cook for about 2-3 minutes per side. Remove with a perforated spoon and drain on kitchen paper.

Nutritional info per serving: Calories 315, Fat: 24.5g, Net Carbs: 1.6g, Protein: 15.3g

Chimichurri Tiger Shrimp

Prep + Cook Time: 55 minutes | Serves: 2-4

Ingredients

1 pound tiger shrimp, peeled and deveined
2 tbsp olive oil
1 garlic clove, minced

Chimichurri

Salt and black pepper to taste
¼ cup extra-virgin olive oil
2 garlic cloves, minced
1 lime, juiced

Juice of 1 lime
Salt and black pepper to taste

¼ cup red wine vinegar
2 cups parsley, minced
¼ tsp red pepper flakes

Directions

Combine the shrimp, olive oil, garlic, and lime juice, in a bowl, and let marinate in the fridge for 30 minutes.

To make the chimichurri dressing, blitz the chimichurri ingredients in a blender until smooth; set aside. Preheat your grill to medium. Add shrimp and cook about 2 minutes per side.

Serve shrimp drizzled with the chimichurri dressing.

Nutritional info per serving: Calories 523, Fat: 30.3g, Net Carbs: 7.2g, Protein: 49g

Mussel Coconut Curry

Prep + Cook Time: 25 minutes | Serves: 2-4

Ingredients

2 tbsp cup coconut oil
2 green onions, chopped
1 lb mussels, cleaned, de-bearded
1 shallot, chopped
1 garlic clove, minced

½ cup coconut milk
½ cup white wine
1 tsp red curry powder
2 tbsp parsley, chopped

Directions

Cook the shallots and garlic in the wine over low heat. Stir in the coconut milk and red curry powder and cook for 3 minutes.

Add the mussels and steam for 7 minutes or until their shells are opened. Then, use a slotted spoon to remove to a bowl leaving the sauce in the pan. Discard any closed mussels at this point.

Stir the coconut oil into the sauce, turn the heat off, and stir in the parsley and green onions. Serve the sauce immediately with a butternut squash mash.

Nutritional info per serving: Calories 356, Fat 20.6g, Net Carbs 0.3g, Protein 21.1g

SNACKS & SIDE DISHES

Party Spiced Cheese Chips

Prep + Cook Time: 18 minutes | Serves: 2

Ingredients

2 cups Monterrey Jack cheese, grated
Salt to taste
½ tsp garlic powder

½ tsp cayenne pepper
½ tsp dried rosemary

Directions

Mix grated cheese with spices. Create 2 tablespoons of cheese mixture into small mounds on a lined baking sheet. Bake for about 15 minutes at 420 F; then allow to cool to harden the chips.

Nutritional info per serving: Calories: 438; Fat 36.8g, Net Carbs 1.8g, Protein 27g

Asparagus & Chorizo Traybake

Prep + Cook Time: 30 minutes | Serves: 2

Ingredients

2 tbsp olive oil
A bunch of asparagus, ends trimmed and chopped
4 oz Spanish chorizo, sliced

Salt and black pepper to taste
¼ cup chopped parsley

Directions

Preheat your oven to 325 F and grease a baking dish with olive oil.

Add in the asparagus and season with salt and black pepper. Stir in the chorizo slices. Bake for 15 minutes until the chorizo is crispy. Arrange on a serving platter and serve sprinkled with parsley.

Nutritional info per serving: Calories 411, Fat: 36.5g, Net Carbs: 3.2g, Protein: 14.5g

Mortadella & Bacon Balls

Prep + Cook Time: 45 minutes | Serves: 2

Ingredients

4 ounces Mortadella sausage
4 bacon slices, cooked and crumbled
2 tbsp almonds, chopped

½ tsp Dijon mustard
3 ounces cream cheese

Directions

Combine the mortadella and almonds in the bowl of your food processor. Pulse until smooth. Whisk the cream cheese and mustard in another bowl. Make balls out of the mortadella mixture.

Make a thin cream cheese layer over. Coat with bacon, arrange on a plate and chill before serving.

Nutritional info per serving: Calories 547, Fat: 51g, Net Carbs: 3.4g, Protein: 21.5g

Speedy Italian Appetizer Balls

Prep + Cook Time: 5 minutes | Serves: 2

Ingredients

2 oz bresaola, chopped
2 oz ricotta cheese, crumbled
2 tbsp mayonnaise

6 green olives, pitted and chopped
½ tbsp fresh basil, finely chopped

Directions

In a bowl, mix mayonnaise, bresaola and ricotta cheese. Place in fresh basil and green olives. Form balls from the mixture and refrigerate. Serve chilled.

Nutritional info per serving: Calories 175; Fat: 13.7g, Net Carbs: 1.1g, Protein: 11g

Hard–Boiled Eggs Stuffed with Ricotta Cheese

Prep + Cook Time: 30 minutes | Serves: 2

Ingredients

4 eggs
1 tbsp green tabasco
2 tbsp Greek yogurt

2 tbsp ricotta cheese
Salt to taste

Directions

Cover the eggs with salted water and bring to a boil over medium heat for 10 minutes. Place the eggs in an ice bath and let cool for 10 minutes. Peel and slice in half lengthwise. Scoop out the yolks to a bowl; mash with a fork.

Whisk together the tabasco, Greek yogurt, ricotta cheese, mashed yolks, and salt, in a bowl. Spoon this mixture into egg white. Arrange on a serving plate to serve.

Nutritional info per serving: Calories 173, Fat: 12.5g, Net Carbs: 1.5g, Protein: 13.6g

Delicious Egg Cups with Cheese & Spinach

Prep + Cook Time: 20 minutes | Serves: 2

Ingredients

4 eggs
1 tbsp fresh parsley, chopped
¼ cup cheddar cheese, shredded

¼ cup spinach, chopped
Salt and black pepper to taste

Directions

Grease muffin cups with cooking spray. In a bowl, whisk the eggs and add in the rest of the ingredients. Season with salt and black pepper. Fill ¾ parts of each muffin cup with the egg mixture.

Bake in the oven for 15 minutes at 390 F. Serve warm!

Nutritional info per serving: Calories: 232; Fat 14.3g, Net Carbs 1.5g, Protein 16.2g

Jalapeno Turkey Tomato Bites

Prep + Cook Time: 5 minutes | Serves: 2

Ingredients

2 tomatoes, sliced with a 3-inch thickness
1 cup turkey ham, chopped
¼ jalapeño pepper, seeded and minced
1 tbsp parsley

1/3 tbsp Dijon mustard
¼ cup mayonnaise
Salt and black pepper to taste

Directions

Combine turkey ham, jalapeño pepper, mustard, mayonnaise, salt, and black pepper, in a bowl.

Arrange tomato slices in a single layer on a serving platter. Divide the turkey mixture between the tomato slices, garnish with parsley and serve.

Nutritional info per serving: Calories 245, Fat 15.3g, Net Carbs 6.3g, Protein 21g

Quail Eggs & Prosciutto Wraps

Prep + Cook Time: 15 minutes | Serves: 2

Ingredients

3 thin prosciutto slices
9 basil leaves

9 quail eggs

Directions

Cover the quail eggs with salted water and bring to a boil over medium heat for 2-3 minutes. Place the eggs in an ice bath and let cool for 10 minutes, then peel them.

Cut the prosciutto slices into three strips. Place basil leaves at the end of each strip. Top with a quail egg. Wrap in prosciutto, secure with toothpicks and serve.

Nutritional info per serving: Calories 243, Fat: 21g, Net Carbs: 0.5g, Protein: 12.5g

Tomato & Cheese in Lettuce Packets

Prep + Cook Time: 10 minutes | Serves: 2

Ingredients

¼ pound Gruyere cheese, grated
¼ pound feta cheese, crumbled
½ tsp oregano

1 tomato, chopped
½ cup buttermilk
½ head lettuce

Directions

In a bowl, mix feta and Gruyere cheese, oregano, tomato, and buttermilk.

Separate the lettuce leaves and put them on a serving platter. Divide the mixture between them, roll up, folding in the ends to secure and serve.

Nutritional info per serving: Calories 433; Fat: 32.5g, Net Carbs: 6.6g, Protein: 27.5g

Basil Mozzarella & Salami Omelet

Prep + Cook Time: 15 minutes | Serves: 2

Ingredients

1 tbsp butter
4 eggs
6 basil, chopped
½ cup mozzarella cheese

2 tbsp water
4 slices salami
2 tomatoes, sliced
Salt and black pepper, to taste

Directions

In a bowl, whisk the eggs with a fork. Add in the water, salt, and black pepper.

Melt the butter in a skillet and cook the eggs for 30 seconds. Spread the salami slices over. Arrange the sliced tomato and mozzarella over the salami. Cook for about 3 minutes. Cover the skillet and continue cooking for 3 more minutes until omelet is completely set.

When ready, remove the pan from heat; run a spatula around the edges of the omelet and flip it onto a warm plate, folded side down. Serve garnished with basil leaves.

Nutritional info per serving: Calories 443, Fat: 34g, Net Carbs: 2.8g, Protein: 29.3g

Zucchini & Avocado Eggs with Pork Sausage

Prep + Cook Time: 20 minutes | Serves: 2

Ingredients

½ red onion, sliced
1 tsp canola oil
4 oz pork sausage, sliced
1 cup zucchinis, chopped

1 avocado, pitted, peeled, chopped
3 eggs
Salt and black pepper to season

Directions

Warm canola oil in a pan over medium heat and sauté the onion for 3 minutes. Add the smoked sausage and cook for 3-4 minutes more, flipping once. Introduce the zucchinis, season lightly with salt, stir and cook for 5 minutes. Mix in the avocado and turn the heat off.

Create 3 holes in the mixture, crack the eggs into each hole, sprinkle with salt and black pepper, and slide the pan into the preheated oven and bake for 6 minutes until the egg whites are set or firm but with the yolks still runny.

Nutritional info per serving: Calories 402, Fat 31g, Net Carbs 3.4g, Protein 25g

Jalapeno Vegetable Frittata Cups

Prep + Cook Time: 25 minutes | Serves: 2

Ingredients

1 tbsp olive oil
2 green onions, chopped
1 garlic clove, minced
½ jalapeño pepper, chopped
½ carrot, chopped

1 zucchini, shredded
2 tbsp mozzarella cheese, shredded
4 eggs, whisked
Salt and black pepper, to taste
½ tsp dried oregano

Directions

Sauté green onions and garlic in warm olive oil over medium heat for 3 minutes. Stir in carrot, zucchini, and jalapeño pepper, and cook for 4 more minutes.

Remove the mixture to a lightly greased baking pan with a nonstick cooking spray. Top with mozzarella cheese. Cover with the whisked eggs; season with oregano, black pepper, and salt. Bake in the oven for about 20 minutes at 360 F.

Nutritional info per serving: Calories 335; Fat: 28g, Net Carbs: 4.7g, Protein: 14g

Crabmeat Egg Scramble with White Sauce

Prep + Cook Time: 15 minutes | Serves: 2

Ingredients

1 tbsp olive oil
4 eggs

Sauce:

¾ cup crème fraiche
½ cup chives, chopped

4 oz crabmeat
Salt and black pepper to taste

½ tsp garlic powder
Salt to taste

Directions

Whisk the eggs with a fork in a bowl, and season with salt and black pepper.

Set a sauté pan over medium heat and warm olive oil. Add in the eggs and scramble them.

Stir in crabmeat and cook until cooked thoroughly. In a mixing dish, combine crème fraiche and garlic powder. Season with salt and sprinkle with chives. Serve the eggs with the white sauce.

Nutritional info per serving: Calories 405; Fat: 32.5g, Net Carbs: 4.3g, Protein: 23.2g

Mexican-Style Squash Omelet with Chorizo & Cheese

Prep + Cook Time: 10 minutes | Serves: 2

Ingredients

4 eggs, beaten
8 oz chorizo sausages, chopped
½ cup cotija cheese, crumbled
8 ounces roasted squash, mashed

2 tbsp olive oil
Salt and black pepper, to taste
Cilantro to garnish

Directions

Season the eggs with salt and pepper and stir in the cotija cheese and squash.

Heat half of olive oil in a pan over medium heat. Add chorizo sausage and cook until browned on all sides, turning occasionally. Drizzle the remaining olive oil and pour the egg mixture over.

Cook for about 2 minutes per side until the eggs are thoroughly cooked and lightly browned. Remove the pan and run a spatula around the edges of the omelet; slide it onto a warm platter. Fold in half, and serve sprinkled with fresh cilantro.

Nutritional info per serving: Calories 683, Fat 52g, Net Carbs 8.5g, Protein 38.3g

Oven Baked Frittata with Ham and Cheese

Prep + Cook Time: 25 minutes | Serves: 2

Ingredients

4 eggs
4 oz ham
2 tbsp butter, melted
2 tbsp almond milk

Salt and black pepper to taste
1 cup cheddar cheese, shredded
1 green onion, chopped

Directions

Chop the ham into small pieces. Whisk the eggs, butter, almond milk, salt, and pepper. Mix in the ham and pour the mixture into a greased baking dish. Sprinkle with cheddar cheese and green onion, and bake in the oven for 10 minutes at 390 F or until the eggs are thoroughly cooked.

Slice the frittata into wedges and serve warm.

Nutritional info per serving: Calories 331, Fat 26g, Net Carbs 2.2g, Protein 14.5g

Basil Omelet with Cheddar Cheese & Asparagus

Prep + Cook Time: 15 minutes | Serves: 2

Ingredients

2 tbsp olive oil
4 eggs
Salt and black pepper, to taste

½ cup asparagus, chopped
½ cup cheddar cheese
2 tbsp fresh basil, chopped

Directions

Whisk the eggs with a fork, season with salt and black pepper, in a bowl.

Set a pan over medium heat and warm the oil. Sauté the asparagus for 4-5 minutes until tender. Add in the eggs and ensure they are evenly spread. Top with the cheese. When ready, slice the omelet into two halves. Decorate with fresh basil and serve.

Nutritional info per serving: Calories 387; Fat: 33.6g, Net Carbs: 1.5g, Protein: 20.7g

Tuna Pickle Boats

Prep + Cook Time: 40 minutes | Serves: 2

Ingredients

1 (5-oz) can tuna, drained
2 large dill pickles
¼ tsp lemon juice

2 tsp mayonnaise
¼ tbsp onion flakes
1 tsp dill. chopped

Directions

Cut the pickles in half lengthwise. With a spoon, scoop out the seeds to create boats; set aside.

Combine the mayonnaise, tuna, onion flakes, and lemon juice in a bowl. Fill each boat with tuna mixture. Sprinkle with dill and place in the fridge for 30 minutes before serving.

Nutritional info per serving: Calories 213, Fat: 5.6g, Net Carbs: 3.2g, Protein: 31.5g

Prosciutto-Wrapped Serrano Poppers

Prep + Cook Time: 30 minutes | Serves: 2

Ingredients

6 serrano peppers
2 tbsp shredded colby cheese
3 oz cream cheese, softened

1 tsp dried thyme
2 tbsp pork rinds, crushed
6 slices prosciutto, halved

Directions

Preheat oven to 400 F and line a baking sheet with parchment paper; set aside. Slice the serrano peppers in half, and remove the membrane and seeds. Combine cheeses and thyme and stuff into the pepper halves. Sprinkle with pork rinds. Wrap each pepper with a prosciutto strip and secure with toothpicks. Bake in the oven for 25 minutes until prosciutto is crispy and peppers are soft. Arrange on a serving plate to serve warm.

Nutritional info per serving: Calories 311, Fat 22g, Net Carbs 4.7g, Protein 16.5g

Creamy Aioli Salsa

Prep + Cook Time: 10 minutes | Serves: 2-4

Ingredients

1 egg yolk, at room temperature
½ lemon, juiced
1 clove garlic, mashed
½ tsp mustard powder

Salt and white pepper to taste
½ cup extra virgin olive oil
2 tbsp parsley, chopped

Directions

Using a blender, place in salt, lemon juice, garlic, and egg yolk; pulse well to get a smooth and creamy mixture. Set blender to slow speed. Slowly sprinkle in olive oil and combine to ensure the oil incorporates well. Stir in parsley and black pepper. Refrigerate the mixture until ready.

Nutritional info per serving: Calories 146; Fat: 13.2g, Net Carbs: 0.3g, Protein: 0.3g

Bell Pepper Frittata with Greek Cheese & Dill

Prep + Cook Time: 40 minutes | Serves: 2

Ingredients

½ cup green bell pepper, chopped
½ cup feta cheese, crumbled
1 tomato, sliced
4 eggs

1 tbsp olive oil
2 scallions, diced
1 tsp dill, chopped
Salt and black pepper, to taste

Directions

Preheat oven to 360 F. In a bowl, whisk the eggs along with the pepper and salt, until combined. Stir in the bell pepper, feta cheese, and scallions. Pour the mixture into a greased casserole, top with the tomato slices and bake for 25 minutes until the frittata is set in the middle. Sprinkle with dill.

Nutritional info per serving: Calories 311, Fat: 25g, Net Carbs: 3.6g, Protein: 16g

Bacon & Egg Radish Hash

Prep + Cook Time: 25 minutes | Serves: 2

Ingredients

8 radishes, sliced
4 bacon slices
2 eggs

1 tbsp olive oil
1 shallot, chopped
1 tbsp Cajun seasoning

Directions

Fry the bacon in a skillet over medium heat until crispy, for about 5 minutes; set aside.

Warm the olive oil and cook the shallot until soft, for about 3-4 minutes, stirring occasionally. Add the radishes, and cook for 10 more minutes until brown and tender, but not mushy. Transfer to a plate and season with Cajun seasoning.

Crack the eggs into the same skillet and fry over medium heat. Top the radishes mixture with the bacon slices and a fried eggs. Serve hot.

Nutritional info per serving: Calories 352, Fat: 31.8g, Net Carbs: 2.6g, Protein: 12.4g

Hard-Boiled Eggs Wrapped in Sausage Meat

Prep + Cook Time: 25 minutes | Serves: 2-4

Ingredients

4 eggs, hard-boiled
1 egg
½ cup pork rinds, crushed
1 pound pork sausages, skinless
2 tbsp grana padano cheese, grated

1 garlic clove, minced
½ tsp onion powder
½ tsp cayenne pepper
1 tsp fresh parsley, chopped
Salt and black pepper to taste

Directions

Preheat oven to 370 F.

In a mixing dish, mix the ingredients, except for the egg and pork rinds. Take a handful of the sausage mixture and wrap around each of the eggs. With fingers, mold the mixture until sealed.

Whisk the egg with a fork in a bowl.

Dip the sausage eggs in the beaten egg, coat with pork rinds and place in a greased baking dish. Bake for 25 minutes, until golden brown and crisp. Allow cooling before serving.

Nutritional info per serving: Calories 255; Fat 12g, Net Carbs 1.1g, Protein 29g

Gruyere Crackers with Sesame Seeds

Prep + Cook Time: 20 minutes | Serves: 2-4

Ingredients

1/3 cup almond flour
Salt to taste
1 tsp baking powder
5 eggs

1/3 cup butter, melted
1 ¼ cups Gruyère cheese, grated
1 tbsp sesame seeds
1/3 cup natural yogurt

Directions

Mix the flour, salt, baking powder and Gruyère cheese, in a bowl.

In a separate bowl, whisk the eggs, butter, and natural yogurt, and then pour the resulting mixture into the dry ingredients. Stir well until a dough-like consistency has formed.

Fetch a soupspoon of the mixture onto a baking sheet with 2-inch intervals between each batter. Sprinkle with sesame seeds and bake in the oven for 12 minutes at 350 F until golden brown.

Nutritional info per serving: Calories 373, Fat 32.5g, Net Carbs 5.4g, Protein 16.4g

Fried Chicken Strips with Mint Dip

Prep + Cook Time: 40 minutes + cooling time | Serves: 2-4

Ingredients

3 tbsp olive oil
1 pound chicken breasts, thinly sliced
1 ¼ cups mayonnaise
¼ cup coconut flour
2 eggs
Salt and black pepper to taste

1 cup cheddar cheese, grated
4 tbsp mint, chopped
1 cup Greek yogurt
1 tsp garlic powder
1 tbsp chopped parsley
2 green onions, chopped

Directions

First make the dip: in a bowl, mix 1 cup of the mayonnaise, 3 tbsp of mint, yogurt, garlic powder, green onion, and salt. Cover the bowl with plastic wrap and refrigerate for 30 minutes.

Mix the chicken, remaining mayonnaise, coconut flour, eggs, salt, black pepper, cheddar cheese, and remaining mint, in a bowl. Cover the bowl with plastic wrap and refrigerate it for 2 hours.

Place a skillet over medium heat to warm the olive oil. Fetch 2 tablespoons of chicken mixture into the skillet, use the back of a spatula to flatten the top. Cook for 4 minutes, flip, and fry for 4 more.

Remove onto a wire rack and repeat the cooking process until the batter is finished, adding more oil as needed. Garnish the fritters with parsley and serve with mint dip.

Nutritional info per serving: Calories 674, Fat 57g, Net Carbs 6.8g, Protein 32g

Rolls with Serrano Ham & Cottage Cheese

Prep + Cook Time: 40 minutes | Serves: 2-4

Ingredients

8 oz cottage cheese
10 oz serrano ham, sliced

10 canned pepperoncini peppers, sliced and drained

Directions

Lay a large piece of plastic wrap on a flat surface and arrange the serrano ham all over slightly overlapping each other. Spread the cottage cheese on top and cover with the pepperoncini.

Hold two opposite ends of the plastic wrap and roll the serrano ham. Twist both ends to tighten and refrigerate for 2 hours. Unwrap the serrano ham roll and slice into 2-inch pinwheels. Serve.

Nutritional info per serving: Calories 266, Fat 24g, Net Carbs 0g, Protein 13g

Chili Zucchini Sticks with Aioli

Prep + Cook Time: 20 minutes | Serves: 2-4

Ingredients

2 tbsp olive oil
¼ cup pork rinds, crushed
1 tsp chili pepper
¼ cup Parmesan cheese, shredded

Aioli:

½ cup mayonnaise
1 garlic clove, minced

Salt to taste
3 eggs
2 zucchinis, cut into strips

Juice and zest from ½ lemon
Salt to taste

Directions

In a bowl, place the mayonnaise, lemon juice, and garlic, and gently stir until everything is well incorporated. Add the lemon zest, adjust the seasoning and stir again.

Cover and place in the refrigerator until ready to serve.

Preheat oven to 425 F and line a baking sheet with foil. Mix the pork rinds, Parmesan cheese, salt, and chili pepper in a bowl.

Beat the eggs in another bowl.

Coat zucchini strips in eggs, then in the Parmesan mixture and arrange on the baking sheet. Drizzle with olive oil and bake for 15 minutes, turning halfway through the cooking time until crispy.

Serve the zucchini strips with garlic aioli for dipping.

Nutritional info per serving: Calories 312, Fat 28.5g, Net Carbs 4.7g, Protein 12g

Crispy Bacon & Spinach Salad with Turnip & Olives

Prep + Cook Time: 40 minutes | Serves: 2-4

Ingredients

6 turnips, cut into wedges
1 tsp olive oil
1/3 cup black olives, pitted and sliced
1 cup baby spinach
3 radishes, sliced
3 oz bacon, sliced

4 tbsp buttermilk
2 tsp mustard seeds
1 tsp Dijon mustard
1 tbsp red wine vinegar
Salt and black pepper to taste
1 tbsp chives, chopped

Directions

Fry the bacon in a skillet over medium heat until crispy, about 5 minutes. Set aside, then crumble it.

Line a baking sheet with parchment paper, toss the turnips with black pepper, drizzle with the olive oil, and bake in the oven for 25 minutes at 390 F, turning halfway through. Let cool.

Spread the baby spinach at the bottom of a salad platter and top with the radishes, bacon, and turnips. Mix the buttermilk, mustard seeds, Dijon mustard, vinegar, and salt. Pour the dressing over the salad, stir well and scatter with the chives and olives to serve.

Nutritional info per serving: Calories 233, Fat 21.2g, Net Carbs 3.4g, Protein 8.6g

Spicy Squid Salad with Minty Dressing

Prep + Cook Time: 30 minutes | Serves: 2-4

Ingredients

2 tbsp olive oil
1 cup arugula
4 medium squid tubes, cut into rings
½ cup mint leaves
2 medium cucumbers, halved and cut in strips
½ cup cilantro leaves, reserve the stems
½ red onion, finely sliced

Salt and black pepper to taste
1 tsp fish sauce
1 red chili, roughly chopped
1 tsp swerve
1 clove garlic
2 limes, juiced
1 tbsp cilantro, chopped

Directions

In a salad bowl, mix arugula, mint leaves, cucumber strips, coriander leaves, and red onion. Season with salt, pepper and a little drizzle of olive oil; set aside.

Pound the cilantro stems, red chili, and swerve into a paste. Add the fish sauce and lime juice, and mix with the pestle.

Heat a skillet over high heat and warm the remaining olive oil. Sear the squid to lightly brown, about 5 minutes. Pour the squid on the salad and drizzle with the chili dressing. Toss the ingredients with two spoons, garnish with cilantro, and serve the salad.

Nutritional info per serving: Calories 322, Fat 24.2g, Net Carbs 4.4g, Protein 23.5g

Hearty Cobb Salad with Roquefort Cheese Dressing

Prep + Cook Time: 2 hours 40 minutes | Serves: 2-4

Ingredients

½ cup whipping cream
¼ cup buttermilk
½ cup mayonnaise
1 tbsp Worcestershire sauce, sugar-free
½ cup Roquefort cheese, crumbled
Salt and black pepper to taste
1 tbsp chives, chopped
3 eggs, hard-boiled, chopped

1 chicken breast, boneless and skinless
2 strips bacon, cooked and crumbled
1 cup endive, chopped
½ romaine lettuce, chopped
1 cup watercress
1 avocado, pitted and diced
1 large tomato, chopped
½ cup feta cheese, crumbled

Directions

In a bowl, whisk the whipping cream, buttermilk, mayonnaise, and Worcestershire sauce. Stir in the Roquefort cheese, salt, pepper, and chives. Place in the refrigerator to chill for 2 hours.

Preheat the grill pan over high heat. Season the chicken with salt and pepper. Grill for 3 minutes on each side. Remove to a plate to cool for 3 minutes, and cut into bite-size chunks.

Arrange the lettuce leaves, endive and watercress in a salad bowl and add the avocado, tomato, eggs, bacon, and chicken. Sprinkle the feta cheese over the salad and drizzle with the cheese dressing.

Nutritional info per serving: Calories 527, Fat 42.3g, Net Carbs 7.2g, Protein 28.3g

Crisps of Beetroot, Parsnip and Carrot with Garlic Dip

Prep + Cook Time: 40 minutes | Serves: 2-4

Ingredients

¼ tsp mustard
3 tbsp mayonnaise
1 garlic clove, minced

Salt and black pepper to taste
3 tbsp lemon juice

Fries

1 medium parsnip, sliced
1 large carrot, sliced
1 beet, sliced

1 tsp cumin
2 tbsp olive oil
Salt and black pepper to taste

Directions

Make the dip by mixing the mayonnaise with mustard, garlic, salt, black pepper, and lemon juice. Place in the fridge until ready to use.

Spread the parsnip, beet and carrot on a large baking sheet in a single layer. Drizzle with olive oil, sprinkle with salt, and black pepper, and rub the mustard mixture onto the veggies. Bake for 10-15 minutes until golden and crispy. Remove to a plate, garnish the vegetables with cumin and serve with the chilled dip.

Nutritional info per serving: Calories 153, Fat 12g, Net Carbs 5.5g, Protein 1.4g

Radish Chips & Cheese Bites

Prep + Cook Time: 15 minutes | Serves: 2-4

Ingredients

½ cup cheddar cheese, shredded
¼ cup natural yogurt
½ cup pecorino cheese, grated
1 tbsp tomato puree
½ tsp dried rosemary leaves, crushed

¼ tsp dried thyme leaves, crushed
Salt and black pepper, to taste
1 pound radishes, sliced
1 tbsp olive oil

Directions

Preheat oven to 400 F. Coat radishes with salt, pepper and olive oil. Arrange in a single layer on a cookie sheet. Bake for 10 minutes, shaking once or twice.

In a mixing bowl, mix cheddar cheese, tomato puree, black pepper, salt, rosemary, yogurt, and thyme. Place in foil liners-candy cups and serve with the radish chips.

Nutritional info per serving: Calories 167; Fat: 13.2g, Net Carbs: 5.3g, Protein: 9.1g

Baked Parsley Cheese Fingers

Prep + Cook Time: 15 minutes | Serves: 2-4

Ingredients

1 cup pork rinds, crushed
1 egg

1 tbsp dried parsley
1 lb cheddar cheese, cut into sticks

Directions

Preheat oven to 350 F and line a baking sheet with parchment paper. Combine pork rinds and parsley in a bowl to be evenly mixed. Beat the egg in another bowl.

Coat the cheese sticks in the egg and then generously dredge in pork rind mixture. Arrange on the baking sheet. Bake for 4 to 5 minutes, take out after, let cool for 2 minutes, and serve with marinara sauce.

Nutritional info per serving: Calories 213, Fat 19.5g, Net Carbs 1.5g, Protein 8.7g

Kale & Cheese Gnocchi

Prep + Cook Time: 13 minutes | Serves: 2-4

Ingredients

2 tbsp butter
3 cups kale, chopped
1 cup cottage cheese
1 cup Parmesan cheese, grated

¼ tsp nutmeg powder
1 egg
Salt and black pepper
1/3 cup almond flour

Directions

Place cottage cheese, half of the Parmesan cheese, egg, nutmeg powder, salt, kale, almond flour, and black pepper in a bowl; mix well. Make gnocchi balls of the mixture.

Pour 3 cups of water in a pot and bring to a boil on high heat on a stovetop. Place one gnocchi in the water, if it breaks apart; add some more flour to the other gnocchi to firm it up.

Put the remaining gnocchi in the water to poach and rise to the top, about 2 minutes. Remove the gnocchi with a perforated spoon to a serving plate. Melt the butter in a microwave and pour over the gnocchi. Sprinkle with the remaining Parmesan cheese and serve with a green salad.

Nutritional info per serving: Calories 243, Fat 17.3g, Net Carbs 6.8g, Protein 17.2g

Paprika & Dill Devilled Eggs

Prep + Cook Time: 30 minutes | Serves: 2-4

Ingredients

6 large eggs
6 tbsp mayonnaise
Salt and black pepper to taste
1 tsp dill, chopped

1 tsp paprika
½ tsp Worcestershire sauce, sugar-free
¼ tsp Dijon mustard

Directions

Cover the eggs with salted water in a pot and bring to a boil on high heat. Reduce the heat to medium and cook for 10 minutes. Then, remove to cool water. Rinse under running water, then peel and in half lengthways. Remove the yolks into a medium bowl. Use a fork to crush the yolks.

Add the mayonnaise, salt, black pepper, Worcestershire sauce, mustard, and paprika. Mix together until a smooth paste has formed. Spoon the mixture into the piping bag and fill the egg white holes with it. Garnish with chopped dill and serve.

Nutritional info per serving: Calories 213, Fat 16.3g, Net Carbs 2.1g, Protein 11.5g

Cheesy Chips with Avocado Dip

Prep + Cook Time: 10 minutes | Serves: 2-4

Ingredients

1 cup Parmesan cheese, grated
¼ tsp sweet paprika
¼ tsp Italian seasoning
2 soft avocados, pitted and scooped

1 tomato, chopped
1 tsp cilantro, chopped
1 tsp tabasco sauce
Salt to taste

Directions

Preheat oven to 350 F and line a baking sheet with parchment paper.

Mix Parmesan cheese, Italian seasoning, and paprika. Make mounds on the baking sheet creating spaces between each mound. Flatten mounds. Bake for 5 minutes, let cool and remove to a plate.

To make the guacamole, mash avocado, with a fork in a bowl, add in tomato, cilantro, and tabasco sauce and continue to mash until mostly smooth; season with salt. Serve crackers with avocado dip.

Nutritional info per serving: Calories 283, Fat 22.4g, Net Carbs 3.1g, Protein 12.7g

Rosemary Roast Vegetable Traybake

Prep + Cook Time: 32 minutes | Serves: 2-4

Ingredients

3 tbsp olive oil
2 cups green beans, chopped
1 lb cremini mushrooms, quartered
2 carrots, julienned
3 tomatoes, quartered

2 garlic cloves, minced
1 onion, sliced
1 fennel bulb, sliced
1 tbsp rosemary, chopped
Salt and black pepper to season

Directions

Preheat oven to 450 F and grease a baking tray with some olive oil.

In a bowl, mix the green beans, mushrooms, tomatoes, carrots, garlic, onion, fennel, salt, and black pepper. Spread the vegetables on the baking tray. Drizzle with the remaining olive oil. Place in the oven and roast for 20 to 25 minutes until tender and golden brown. Sprinkle with rosemary to serve.

Nutritional info per serving: Calories 187, Fat 12.5g, Net Carbs 9.6g, Protein 5.4g

Root Vegetable Mash with Garlic & Basil

Prep + Cook Time: 30 minutes | Serves: 2-4

Ingredients

½ pound celeriac, chopped
½ pound parsnips, chopped
2 carrots, chopped
2 turnips, chopped
2 oz cream cheese

2 tbsp butter
1/3 cup sour cream
½ tsp garlic powder
2 tsp basil, chopped
Salt and black pepper to taste

Directions

In a pot over high heat, place celeriac, parsnips, carrots and turnips and cover with enough water. Bring to a boil for 5 minutes and then reduce the heat to low to simmer for 15 minutes. Drain the vegetables through a colander.

Transfer to a large bowl and mash until smooth. Add in the cream cheese, butter, sour cream, garlic powder, salt, and black pepper. Sprinkle with basil and serve with pan-grilled salmon.

Nutritional info per serving: Calories 223, Fat 13.5g, Net Carbs 12.3g, Protein 4g

Fried Artichokes with Pesto

Prep + Cook Time: 20 minutes | Serves: 2-4

Ingredients

2 tbsp olive oil
12 fresh baby artichokes
2 tbsp lemon juice

1 tbsp vinegar
4 tbsp pesto
Salt to taste

Directions

Place the artichokes in cold water with vinegar for 10 minutes. Drain and pat dry well with kitchen towels. Cut the artichokes down the middle vertically, and with a teaspoon, scoop out the stringy stifle to uncover the heart. Slice the artichokes vertically into narrow wedges.

Heat olive oil in a skillet over high heat. Fry the artichokes until browned and crispy. Drain excess oil using paper towels. Sprinkle with salt and lemon juice and serve with pesto.

Nutritional info per serving: Calories 235, Fat: 17.4g, Net Carbs: 8.7g, Protein: 8.2g

Cauliflower & Mushroom Arancini

Prep + Cook Time: 20 minutes | Serves: 2-4

Ingredients

1 cup cauli rice
2 tbsp butter, softened
1 garlic clove, minced
1 cup mushrooms, chopped
4 tbsp ground flax seeds
4 tbsp hemp seeds

4 tbsp sunflower seeds
1 tbsp dried basil
1 tsp mustard
1 egg
½ cup Pecorino cheese, grated

Directions

Set a pan over medium heat and warm 1 tablespoon of butter. Add in mushrooms and garlic and sauté until there is no more water in mushrooms. Remove to a bowl and let cool for a few minutes.

Place in Pecorino cheese, cauli rice, hemp seeds, mustard, egg, sunflower seeds, flax seeds, and basil. Create balls from the mixture.

In a pan, warm the remaining butter; fry the balls for 7 minutes. Flip them over with a wide spatula and cook for 6 more minutes.

Nutritional info per serving: Calories 363; Fat: 29.5g, Net Carbs: 7.2g, Protein: 15.3g

Sausage & Vegetable Bake

Prep + Cook Time: 40 minutes | Serves: 2-4

Ingredients

1 cup mushrooms, quartered
1 large butternut squash, cut into chunks
¼ pound smoked sausages, sliced
1 onion, sliced
¼ lb Brussels sprouts

1 tbsp rosemary, chopped
1 tbsp thyme, chopped
4 garlic cloves, peeled only
3 tbsp olive oil
Salt and black pepper to taste

Directions

Preheat the oven to 450 F.

Arrange the butternut squash, onion, mushrooms, garlic cloves, sausages, and Brussels sprouts on a baking tray. Season with salt, pepper, olive oil, and toss them. Roast the vegetables for 15–20 minutes. Sprinkle with the chopped thyme and rosemary to serve.

Nutritional info per serving: Calories 225, Fat 17.3g, Net Carbs 8.2g, Protein 7.3g

Cauliflower and Broccoli Cakes with Cheese

Prep + Cook Time: 20 minutes | Serves: 2-4

Ingredients

½ head broccoli, cut into florets
½ head cauliflower, cut into florets
½ cup Parmesan cheese, shredded
½ onion, chopped
½ cup almond flour
1 egg

½ tsp lemon juice
2 tbsp olive oil
Salt and black pepper to taste
2 tbsp chives, chopped
2 tbsp Greek yogurt

Directions

Steam the cauliflower and broccoli in a pot filled with salted water for 10-12 minutes until tender. Drain and transfer to a bowl. Mash and add in the other ingredients, except for the olive oil.

Season to taste and mix to combine. Place a skillet over medium heat and heat olive oil. Shape fritters out of the mixture. Fry in batches, for about 3 minutes per side. Garnish with Greek yogurt and sprinkle with chives.

Nutritional info per serving: Calories 155, Fat: 15.5g, Net Carbs: 4.2g, Protein: 5.5g

Cauliflower & Cheese Bake with Dilled Mayo

Prep + Cook Time: 27 minutes | Serves: 2-4

Ingredients

1 head cauliflower, cut into florets
2 tbsp butter, melted
Salt and black pepper to taste
1 pinch red pepper flakes
½ cup mayonnaise

¼ tsp Dijon mustard
3 tbsp Pecorino cheese, grated
1 tbsp dill, chopped
1 tsp garlic powder

Directions

Preheat oven to 400 F and grease a baking dish with cooking spray. Mix the mayonnaise, garlic powder, mustard, dill, and salt in a bowl. Place in the fridge until ready to serve.

Combine the cauli florets, butter, salt, black pepper, and red pepper flakes in a bowl until well mixed. Arrange cauliflower florets on the prepared baking dish. Sprinkle with grated Pecorino cheese and bake for 25 minutes until the cheese has melted and golden brown on the top.

Remove, let sit for 3 minutes to cool, and serve with the dilled sauce.

Nutritional info per serving: Calories 233, Fat 19.5g, Net Carbs 4.2g, Protein 6.3g

Caprese Gratin with Zucchini & Bell Pepper

Prep + Cook Time: 40 minutes | Serves: 2-4

Ingredients

2 zucchinis, sliced
1 red bell pepper, seeded and sliced
Salt and black pepper to taste
1 cup ricotta cheese, crumbled
4 oz fresh mozzarella cheese, sliced

2 tomatoes, sliced
2 tbsp butter
¼ tsp xanthan gum
½ cup heavy whipping cream

Directions

Preheat oven to 370 F.

Grease a baking dish with cooking spray and make a layer of zucchinis and bell peppers in the dish overlapping one on another. Season with black pepper, and sprinkle with some ricotta cheese.

Repeat the layering process a second time. Combine the butter, xanthan gum, and whipping cream in a microwave dish for 2 minutes, stir to mix completely, and pour over the vegetables. Top with remaining ricotta cheese.

Bake the gratin for 30 minutes until golden brown on top. Remove from the oven and cover with tomato and fresh mozzarella slices. Bake for 5-10 more minutes. Cut out slices and serve warm.

Nutritional info per serving: Calories 283, Fat 22.3g, Net Carbs 5.6g, Protein 16.5g

Cheddar & Cream Cheese Chicken Casserole

Prep + Cook Time: 30 minutes | Serves: 2-4

Ingredients

2 tbsp olive oil
4 oz cream cheese, at room temperature
1 lb ground chicken

½ cup tomato sauce
½ cup natural yogurt
1 cup cheddar cheese, grated

Directions

Preheat oven to 350 F. Warm the oil in a skillet over medium heat and brown the chicken for a couple of minutes; set aside. Spread cream cheese at the bottom of a greased baking sheet, top with chicken, pour tomato sauce over, add yogurt dressing, and sprinkle with cheddar cheese. Bake for 23 minutes until cheese has melted and golden brown on top.

Nutritional info per serving: Calories 512, Fat 38.6g, Net Carbs 6.9g, Protein 32.3g

Oven Roasted Cauliflower with Parma Ham & Nuts

Prep + Cook Time: 30 minutes | Serves: 2-4

Ingredients

2 tbsp olive oil
1 head cauliflower, cut into 1-inch slices
Salt and black pepper to taste
¼ tsp chili pepper
1 tsp garlic powder

10 slices Parma ham, chopped
¼ cup hazelnuts, chopped
1 tsp capers
1 tsp parsley, chopped

Directions

Preheat oven to 400 F and line a baking sheet with foil. Spread the cauli steaks on the baking sheet and brush with olive oil. Season with black pepper, chili pepper, garlic, and salt.

Roast in the oven for 10 minutes until tender and lightly browned. Remove the sheet and sprinkle the Parma ham and hazelnuts all over the steaks. Bake for another 10 minutes until the ham is crispy and a nutty aroma is perceived.

Take out, sprinkle with capers and parsley. Serve with ground beef stew and braised asparagus.

Nutritional info per serving: Calories 211, Fat 15.3g, Net Carbs 4.7g, Protein 12.5g

Energy Goji Berry Snacks

Prep + Cook Time: 5 minutes | Serves: 2-4

Ingredients

½ cup raw pumpkin seeds
½ cup raw walnuts
¼ tsp cinnamon powder
2 tbsp dried goji berries
½ tsp vanilla extract

1 tbsp unsweetened chocolate chips
1 tbsp coconut oil
½ tbsp golden flax meal
½ tsp xylitol

Directions

Combine the pumpkin seeds and walnuts in the food processor and process until smooth. Add the cinnamon powder, goji berries, vanilla extract, chocolate chips, coconut oil, golden flax meal, and xylitol. Process further until the mixture begins to stick to each other, for about 2 minutes.

Spread out a large piece of plastic wrap on a flat surface and place the dough on it. Wrap the dough and use a rolling pin to spread it out into a thick rectangle. Unwrap the dough after and use an oiled knife to cut the dough into bars.

Nutritional info per serving: Calories 153, Fat 13.2g, Net Carbs 4.5g, Protein 22.g

Bacon & Guacamole Stuffed Eggs

Prep + Cook Time: 15 minutes | Serves: 2-4

Ingredients

8 large eggs
2 bacon slices, cooked and crumbled
4 tbsp guacamole

Salt to taste
¼ tsp chili powder
1 tbsp cilantro, chopped

Directions

Boil eggs in salted water in a pot over high heat, and then reduce the heat to simmer for 10 minutes. Transfer eggs to an ice water bath, let cool completely and peel the shells.

Slice the eggs in half height wise and empty the yolks into a bowl. Smash with a fork and mix in guacamole, bacon, and chili powder until smooth.

Spoon filling into a piping bag with a round nozzle and fill the egg whites to be slightly above the brim. Garnish with cilantro to serve.

Nutritional info per serving: Calories 223, Fat 17.9g, Net Carbs 1.2g, Protein 14.4g

Home-Bake Chili Macaroons

Prep + Cook Time: 20 minutes | Serves: 2-4

Ingredients

1 finger ginger root, peeled and pureed
3 egg whites
½ cup finely shredded coconut
1 tsp stevia

¼ tsp chili powder
½ cup water
Chilli threads to garnish

Directions

Line a baking sheet with parchment paper and set aside. In a heatproof bowl, whisk the ginger, egg whites, shredded coconut, stevia, and chili powder.

In a pot over medium heat, bring to boil the water and place the heatproof bowl on the pot. Continue whisking the mixture until it is glossy, about 4 minutes. Do not let the bowl touch the water or be too hot so that the eggs don't cook.

Spoon the mixture into the piping bag and pipe out 40 to 50 little mounds on the lined baking sheet. Bake the macaroons in the middle part of the oven for 15 minutes at 350 F.

Once they are ready, transfer them to a wire rack, garnish with chilli threads to serve.

Nutritional info per serving: Calories 110, Fat 5.2g, Net Carbs 1.4g, Protein 8.3g

Roasted Brussels Sprouts & Bacon

Prep + Cook Time: 40 minutes | Serves: 2-4

Ingredients

1 tbsp olive oil
1 garlic clove, sliced
6 pearl onions, halved
3 tbsp vinegar

1 tbsp erythritol
Salt and black pepper to taste
1 lb Brussels sprouts, halved
4 oz bacon, chopped

Directions

Preheat oven to 400 F and line a baking sheet with parchment paper.

Mix balsamic, erythritol, olive oil, salt, and black pepper and combine with the Brussels sprouts, garlic, bacon, and pearl onions, in a bowl. Spread the mixture on the baking sheet and roast for 30 minutes until tender on the inside and crispy on the outside. Serve immediately.

Nutritional info per serving: Calories 183, Fat 15.6g, Net Carbs 1.5g, Protein 8.8g

Roasted Green Beans with Garlic & Almond Flakes

Prep + Cook Time: 30 minutes | Serves: 2-4

Ingredients

2 tbsp butter, melted
¼ cup almond flakes
¼ cup pork rind crumbs

2 garlic cloves, sliced
Salt and black pepper to taste
1 lb green beans, thread removed

Directions

Preheat oven to 400 F. Place the green beans and garlic in a baking dish, and season with salt and black pepper. Pour the butter over and toss to coat. Bake for 20 minutes.

In a dry pan over medium heat, toast the almonds until golden. Pour over the green beans to serve.

Nutritional info per serving: Calories 187, Fat 12.3g, Net Carbs 4.5g, Protein 3.5g

Parsley Roasted Radishes with Cheesy Sauce

Prep + Cook Time: 25 minutes | Serves: 2-4

Ingredients

1 pound radishes, greens removed
1 tbsp olive oil
Salt and black pepper to season
1 tbsp parsley, chopped

¼ cup sour cream
¼ cup heavy cream
¼ cup gorgonzola cheese

Directions

Preheat oven to 370 F and line a baking sheet with parchment paper. Toss radishes with olive oil, salt, and black pepper. Spread on the baking sheet and roast for 20 minutes until browned.

Add in sour cream and heavy cream. Stir in gorgonzola cheese and season with salt and black pepper; remove to a bowl. Transfer the radishes to a serving plate. Sprinkle with parsley and serve with the sauce.

Nutritional info per serving: Calories 154, Fat 13g, Net Carbs 4.8g, Protein 3.5g

Steamed Broccoli with Parsley Butter

Prep + Cook Time: 10 minutes | Serves: 2-4

Ingredients

2 tbsp parsley, chopped
1 head broccoli, cut into florets

Salt and black pepper to taste
¼ cup butter

Directions

Put the broccoli in a pot filled with salted water and bring to a boil. Cook for about 3 minutes. Drain and set aside.

Melt the butter in a pan over low heat. Stir in the broccoli, season with salt and black pepper, and remove to a plate. Sprinkle with parsley to serve.

Nutritional info per serving: Calories 105, Fat: 7.5g, Net Carbs: 5.1g, Protein: 4g

Coconut Flour Cheese Crackers

Prep + Cook Time: 25 minutes | Serves: 2-4

Ingredients

1 cup coconut flour
1 cup fontina cheese, grated
Salt and black pepper to taste
¼ tsp garlic powder
¼ tsp onion powder
¼ cup butter, softened
¼ tsp smoked paprika
¼ cup heavy cream

Directions

Preheat the oven to 350 F.

Mix the coconut flour, fontina cheese, salt, pepper, garlic powder, onion powder, and smoked paprika in a bowl. Add in the butter and mix well. Top with the heavy cream and mix again until smooth, add 1 to 2 tablespoon of water, if it is too thick.

Place the dough on a cutting board and cover with plastic wrap. Use a rolling pin to spread out the dough into a light rectangle.

Cut cracker squares out of the dough and arrange them on a baking sheet without overlapping. Bake for 20 minutes until browned. Let cool completely before serving.

Nutritional info per serving: Calories 287, Fat 26.3g, Net Carbs 3.1g, Protein 10.5g

Thyme-Mashed Cauliflower with Bacon & Cheese

Prep + Cook Time: 40 minutes | Serves: 2-4

Ingredients

4 oz bacon, sliced
1 head cauliflower, leaves removed
2 tbsp melted butter
½ cup buttermilk
Salt and black pepper to taste
¼ cup cheddar cheese, grated
2 tbsp thyme, chopped

Directions

Fry bacon in a heated skillet over medium heat for 5 minutes until crispy. Remove to a paper towel-lined plate, allow to cool, and crumble.

Boil cauliflower head in salted water in a pot over high heat for 7 minutes, until tender. Drain and transfer to a bowl. Mash and add in butter, buttermilk, salt, black pepper, and stir well.

Sprinkle with cheddar cheese and place under the broiler for 4 minutes on high, until the cheese melts.

Remove and top with bacon and chopped thyme to serve.

Nutritional info per serving: Calories 321, Fat 26.3g, Net Carbs 5.4g, Protein 13.6g

Spanish Piquillo Peppers with Cheese Stuffing

Prep + Cook Time: 20 minutes | Serves: 2-4

Ingredients

4 canned roasted piquillo peppers
2 tbsp olive oil
1 tbsp parsley, chopped

Filling

4 ounces goat cheese
2 tbsp heavy cream
1 tbsp olive oil

Directions

Preheat the oven to 350 F and grease a baking sheet with some olive oil. Mix all filling ingredients in a bowl. Place in a freezer bag, press down and squeeze, and cut off the bottom.

Drain and deseed the peppers. Squeeze about 2 tbsp of the filling into each pepper.

Arrange them on the baking sheet, drizzle over the remaining olive oil and bake for 10 minutes.

Nutritional info per serving: Calories 274, Fat: 24.3g, Net Carbs: 4.2g, Protein: 11g

Cheese Spinach Balls with Yogurt Sauce

Prep + Cook Time: 30 minutes | Serves: 2-4

Ingredients

2 tbsp Greek yogurt
Salt to taste
1 tbsp walnuts, chopped
1 tbsp extra virgin olive oil
1 tsp dill, chopped
¼ cup ricotta cheese, crumbled
¼ tsp nutmeg
2 tbsp heavy cream
1/3 tsp garlic powder
1/3 tbsp onion powder
1 tbsp butter, melted
1/3 cup Parmesan cheese, grated
1 egg
1/3 cup spinach
1/3 cup almond flour

Directions

In a bowl, combine together Greek yogurt, walnuts, olive oil, dill, and salt, and mix well. Set aside.

Place ricotta cheese, nutmeg, heavy cream, garlic powder, onion powder, Parmesan cheese, egg, spinach, and almond flour, in a food processor. Process until smooth.

Transfer to the freezer for 10 minutes. Make balls out of the mixture and arrange them on a lined baking sheet. Bake at 350 F for about 10-12 minutes. Serve with yogurt sauce for dipping.

Nutritional info per serving: Calories 173, Fat: 14.5g, Net Carbs: 1.8g, Protein: 7.5g

DESSERTS & DRINKS

Raspberry Yogurt Parfait

Prep + Cook Time: 5 minutes | Serves: 2

Ingredients:

1 cup Greek yogurt
1 cup fresh raspberries
½ lemon, zested

3 mint sprigs, leaves extracted and chopped
2 tbsp chia seeds
2 drops liquid stevia

Directions:

In a small bowl, whisk the Greek yogurt with stevia. In medium serving glasses, layer half of the Greek yogurt, raspberries, lemon zest, mint, chia seeds, and drizzle with maple syrup. Repeat with another layer. Serve cold.

Nutritional info per serving: Calories: 183; Fat: 10g; Net Carbs: 8.9g; Protein: 7.8g

Blueberry Ice Balls

Prep + Cook Time: 12 minutes | Serves: 2

Ingredients

½ tsp vanilla extract
2 packets gelatine, without sugar
2 tbsp heavy whipping cream
1 cup water

3 tbsp mashed blueberries
2 cups crushed Ice
1 cup cold water

Directions

Boil the water over medium heat and dissolve the gelatine inside. Transfer to a blender and add the remaining ingredients. Pulse until smooth and make balls. Freeze them for 3 hours.

Nutritional info per serving: Calories 142, Fat: 9g, Net Carbs: 7.8g, Protein: 3.5g

Green Detox Drink

Prep + Cook Time: 5 minutes | Serves: 2

Ingredients:

2 large ripe avocados, halved and pitted
1 small cucumber, peeled and chopped
2 tbsp swerve sugar

¼ cup cold almond milk
½ tsp vanilla extract
1 tbsp cold heavy cream

Directions:

In a blender, add the avocado pulp, cucumber, swerve sugar, almond milk, vanilla extract, and heavy cream. Process until smooth.

Pour the mixture into 2 tall serving glasses, garnish with strawberries, and serve immediately.

Nutritional info per serving: Calories: 423; Fat: 34.2g; Net Carbs: 9.5g; Protein: 8.2g

Homemade Marshmallows Topped with Chocolate

Prep + Cook Time: 30 minutes | Serves: 2-4

Ingredients

2 tbsp unsweetened cocoa powder
½ tsp vanilla extract
½ cup erythritol
1 tbsp xanthan gum mixed in 1 tbsp water

A pinch salt
6 tbsp cool water
2 ½ tsp gelatin powder

Dusting

1 tbsp unsweetened cocoa powder

1 tbsp swerve confectioner's sugar

Directions

Grease a lined with parchment paper loaf pan with cooking spray; set aside. Mix the erythritol, 2 tbsp of water, xanthan gum mixture and salt in a saucepan. Place the pan over high heat and bring to a boil. Insert a thermometer and let the ingredients simmer at 220 F, for 8 minutes.

Add 2 tbsp of water and sprinkle the gelatin on top, in a small bowl. Let sit to dissolve for 5 minutes. While the gelatin dissolves, pour the remaining water in a small bowl and heat in the microwave for 30 seconds. Stir in cocoa powder and mix it into the gelatin.

When the erythritol solution has hit the right temperature, gradually pour it directly into the gelatin mixture, stirring continuously. Beat for 12 minutes to get a light and fluffy consistency.

Then, stir in the vanilla and pour the blend into the loaf pan. Let the marshmallows set for 3 hours in the fridge. Use an oiled knife to cut into cubes and place them on a plate. Mix the remaining cocoa powder and confectioner's sugar together. Sift it over the marshmallows.

Nutritional info per serving: Calories 83, Fat 5.3g, Net Carbs 3.6g, Protein 2.2g

Coconut Panna Cotta with Cream & Caramel

Prep + Cook Time: 10 minutes | Serves: 2-4

Ingredients

4 eggs
1/3 cup erythritol, for caramel
2 cups coconut milk
1 tbsp vanilla extract

1 tbsp lemon zest
½ cup erythritol, for custard
2 cup heavy whipping cream
Mint leaves, to serve

Directions

In a deep pan, heat the erythritol for the caramel. Add two tablespoons of water and bring to a boil. Lower the heat and cook until the caramel turns to a golden brown color.

Divide between 4 metal tins, set aside and let cool. In a bowl, mix the eggs, remaining erythritol, lemon zest, and vanilla. Beat in the coconut milk until well combined.

Pour the custard into each caramel-lined ramekin and place them into a deep baking tin. Fill over the way with the remaining hot water. Bake at 350 F for around 45 minutes.

Carefully, take out the ramekins with tongs and refrigerate for at least 3 hours. Run a knife slowly around the edges to invert onto a dish. Serve with dollops of whipped cream and scattered with mint leaves.

Nutritional info per serving: Calories 268, Fat: 31g, Net Carbs: 2.5g, Protein: 6.5g

Healthy Chia Pudding With Strawberries

Prep + Cook Time: 10 minutes | Serves: 2

Ingredients

1 cup yogurt, full-fat
2 tsp xylitol
2 tbsp chia seeds

1 cup fresh strawberries, sliced
1 tbsp lemon zest
Mint leaves, to serve

Directions

In a bowl, combine the yogurt and xylitol together. Add in the chia seeds and stir. Reserve a couple of strawberries for garnish, and mash the remaining ones with a fork until pureed.

Stir in the yogurt mixture and refrigerate for 45 minutes. Once cooled, divide the mixture between glasses. Top each with the reserved slices of strawberries, mint leaves, and lemon zest.

Nutritional info per serving: Calories 187, Fat: 11g, Net Carbs: 6.3g, Protein: 6.7g

Almond Milk Berry Shake

Prep + Cook Time: 5 minutes | Serves: 2

Ingredients:

½ cup fresh blueberries
½ cup raspberries
½ cup almond milk
¼ cup heavy cream

Maple syrup to taste, sugar-free
1 tbsp sesame seeds
Chopped pistachios for topping
1 tsp chopped mint leaves

Directions:

Combine the blueberries, milk, heavy cream, and syrup in a blender. Process until smooth and pour into serving glasses. Top with the sesame seeds, pistachios, and mint leaves. Serve immediately.

Nutritional info per serving: Calories: 228g; Fat: 21g; Net Carbs: 5.4g; Protein: 7.9g

Easy Citrus Mousse with Almonds

Prep + Cook Time: 5 minutes + chill time | Serves: 2-4

Ingredients

3/4 lb cream cheese, softened
2 cups swerve confectioner's sugar
1 lemon, juiced and zested
1 lime, juice and zested

Salt to taste
1 cup whipped cream + extra for garnish
¼ cup toasted almonds, chopped

Directions

In a bowl and with a hand mixer, whip the cream cheese until light and fluffy. Add in the sugar, lemon and lime juices and salt, and mix well. Fold in the whipped cream to evenly combine.

Spoon the mousse into serving cups and refrigerate to thicken for 1 hour. Swirl with extra whipped cream and garnish with lemon and lime zest. Serve immediately topped with almonds.

Nutritional info per serving: Calories 242, Fat 18g, Net Carbs 3.3g, Protein 6.5g

Chocolate Candies with Blueberries

Prep + Cook Time: 6 minutes + cooling time | Serves: 2-4

Ingredients

2 cups raw cashew nuts
2 tbsp flax seed
1 ½ cups blueberry preserves, sugar-free

3 tbsp xylitol
10 oz unsweetened chocolate chips
3 tbsp olive oil

Directions

Grind the cashew nuts and flax seeds in a blender for 50 seconds until smoothly crushed; add the blueberries and 2 tbsp of xylitol. Process further for 1 minute until well combined.

Form 1-inch balls of the mixture. Line a baking sheet with parchment paper and place the balls on the baking sheet. Freeze for 1 hour or until firmed up.

In a microwave, melt the chocolate chips, oil and the remaining xylitol, for 95 seconds. Toss the truffles to coat in the chocolate mixture, put on the baking sheet, and freeze up for at least 3 hours.

Nutritional info per serving: Calories 253, Fat 17.5g, Net Carbs 4.1g, Protein 10g

Matcha Brownies with Macadamia Nuts

Prep + Cook Time: 28 minutes | Serves: 2-4

Ingredients

1 tbsp tea matcha powder
¼ cup unsalted butter, melted
4 tbsp swerve confectioner's sugar
A pinch of salt

¼ cup coconut flour
½ tsp baking powder
1 egg
½ cup chopped pistachios

Directions

Line a square baking dish with parchment paper and preheat the oven to 350 F. In a bowl, pour the melted butter, add swerve sugar and salt, and whisk to combine. Crack the egg into the bowl.

Beat the mixture until the egg is incorporated. Pour the coconut flour, matcha and baking powder into a fine-mesh sieve and sift them into the egg bowl; stir. Stir in the pistachios and pour the mixture into the baking dish to cook for 18 minutes. Remove and slice into brownie cubes.

Nutritional info per serving: Calories 243, Fat 22g, Net Carbs 4.3g, Protein 7.2g

Lazy Strawberry Mini Cakes

Prep + Cook Time: 45 minutes | Serves: 2-4

Ingredients

4 eggs
2 tsp coconut oil
2 cups strawberries
1 cup coconut milk
1 cup almond flour

¼ cup xylitol
½ tsp vanilla powder
¼ tsp powdered sugar
A pinch of salt

Directions

Place all ingredients, except coconut oil, berries and powdered sugar, in a blender, and blend until smooth. Gently fold in the strawberries. Preheat the oven to 330 F.

Grease a baking dish with the oil. Pour the mixture into the prepared pan and bake for 40 minutes. Sprinkle with powdered sugar and cut into mini cakes.

Nutritional info per serving: Calories 311, Fat: 28.3g, Net Carbs: 6.4g, Protein: 13.7g

Lassi with Lychee, Yogurt and Milk

Prep + Cook Time: 2 hours 28 minutes | Serves: 2-4

Ingredients

2 cups lychee pulp, seeded
2 ½ cups coconut milk
4 tsp xylitol
2 limes, zested and juiced

1 ½ cups plain yogurt
1 lemongrass, white part only, crushed
Toasted coconut shavings for garnish

Directions

Add the lychee pulp, coconut milk, xylitol, lemongrass, and lime zest in a saucepan. Stir and bring to boil on medium heat for 3 minutes, stirring continually. Then reduce the heat and simmer for about a minute. Turn the heat off and let the mixture sit for 15 minutes.

Discard the lemongrass and pour the mixture into a smoothie maker or a blender, add the yogurt and lime juice, and process the ingredients until smooth, for about 60 seconds.

Pour into a jug and refrigerate for 2 hours until cold; stir. Serve garnished with coconut shavings.

Nutritional info per serving: Calories 283, Fat 23.6g, Net Carbs 3.2g, Protein 6g

Blackcurrant Juice with Lime

Prep + Cook Time: 8 minutes | Serves: 2-4

Ingredients

5 unflavored tea bags
2 cups water
½ cup sugar-free blackcurrant extract

1 tbsp erythritol + some more to taste
Ice cubes for serving
Lime slices to garnish, cut on the side

Directions

In a saucepan over medium heat, bring the water to a boil for about 4 minutes; then turn the heat off. Stir in the erythritol to dissolve and steep the tea bags in the water for 3 minutes.

In the meantime, pour the ice cubes into a pitcher and place it in the fridge.

To the saucepan, remove the bags and let the tea cool down. Add in the blackcurrant extract and stir until well combined. Remove the pitcher from the fridge, and pour the mixture over the ice cubes.

Allow to cool for 3 minutes and pour the mixture into tall glasses. Add some more ice cubes, place the lime slices on the rim of the glasses and serve cold.

Nutritional info per serving: Calories 21, Fat 0.4g, Net Carbs 2.8g, Protein 0.5g

Quick Raspberry Vanilla Shake

Prep + Cook Time: 2 minutes | Serves: 2

Ingredients

2 cups raspberries
2 tbsp erythritol
6 raspberries to garnish

½ cup cold unsweetened almond milk
2/3 tsp vanilla extract
½ cup heavy whipping cream

Directions

In a large blender, process the raspberries, milk, vanilla extract, whipping cream, and erythritol for 2 minutes; work in two batches if needed. The shake should be frosty. Pour into glasses, stick in straws, garnish with raspberries and serve.

Nutritional info per serving: Calories 213, Fat 13.4g, Net Carbs 7.7g, Protein 4.5g

Strawberry Chocolate Mousse

Prep + Cook Time: 30 minutes | Serves: 2

Ingredients

3 eggs
½ cup dark chocolate chips
1 cup heavy cream

1 cup fresh strawberries, sliced
1 vanilla extract
1 tbsp xylitol

Directions

In a bowl, melt the chocolate in the microwave for a minute on high and let it cool for 10 minutes.

In another bowl, whip the cream until very soft. Add the eggs, vanilla extract, and xylitol; whisk to combine. Fold in the cooled chocolate.

Divide the mousse between glasses, top with the strawberry slices and chill in the fridge for at least 30 minutes before serving.

Nutritional info per serving: Calories 567, Fat: 45.6g, Net Carbs: 9.6g, Protein: 13.6g

Peanut Butter Ice Cream

Prep + Cook Time: 50 minutes + cooling time | Serves: 2-4

Ingredients

½ cup smooth peanut butter
½ cup erythritol
3 cups half and half

1 tsp vanilla extract
1 pinch of salt
½ cups raspberries

Directions

In a bowl, beat peanut butter and erythritol with a hand mixer until smooth. Gradually whisk in half and half until thoroughly combined. Add in vanilla and salt and mix.

Transfer the mixture to a loaf pan and freeze for 50 minutes until firmed up. Scoop into glasses when ready and serve topped with raspberries.

Nutritional info per serving: Calories 436, Fat 38.5g, Net Carbs 9.5g, Protein 13g

Grandma's Coconut Treats

Prep + Cook Time: 3 hours | Serves: 2-4

Ingredients

1/3 cup ghee
10 saffron threads
1 1/3 cups coconut milk

1 ¾ cups shredded coconut
4 tbsp xylitol
1 tsp cardamom powder

Directions

In a bowl, combine the shredded coconut with a cup of coconut milk. In another bowl, mix together the remaining coconut milk with xylitol and saffron. Let sit for 30 minutes.

In a wok, heat the ghee. Add the coconut mixtures and cook for 5 minutes on low heat, mixing continuously. Stir in the cardamom and cook for another 5 minutes. Spread the mixture onto a small container and freeze for 2 hours. Cut into bars to enjoy.

Nutritional info per serving: Calories 224, Fat: 21.7g, Net Carbs: 2.7g, Protein: 3.3g

Keto Chocolate Fat Bombs

Prep + Cook Time: 3 minutes + cooling time | Serves: 2-4

Ingredients

½ cup almond butter
½ cup almond oil

4 tbsp unsweetened cocoa powder
½ cup xylitol

Directions

In the microwave, melt butter and almond oil for 45 seconds, stirring twice until thoroughly combined. Stir in cocoa powder and xylitol until completely combined.

Transfer to muffin moulds and refrigerate for 4 hours to firm up.

Nutritional info per serving: Calories 445, Fat 43.5g, Net Carbs 3.8g, Protein 8.4g

Hot Chocolate with Almonds & Cinnamon

Prep + Cook Time: 10 minutes | Serves: 2-4

Ingredients

3 cups almond milk
4 tbsp unsweetened cocoa powder
2 tbsp xylitol

3 tbsp almond butter
Finely chopped almonds to garnish
Ground cinnamon to garnish

Directions

Add the almond milk, cocoa powder, and xylitol in a saucepan, and stir until the sweetener dissolves. Set the pan over low to heat through for 6 minutes, without boiling. Swirl the mix occasionally.

Stir in the almond butter until incorporated and turn the heat off. Transfer the hot chocolate to mugs and sprinkle with almonds and cinnamon, before serving it hot.

Nutritional info per serving: Calories 273, Fat 20.8g, Net Carbs 8.3g, Protein 10g

Avocado & Berries Fruit Fool

Prep + Cook Time: 3 minutes + cooling time | Serves: 2-4

Ingredients

½ cup walnuts, toasted
1 avocado, chopped
1 cup cream cheese, softened

1 cup fresh blueberries
1 cup fresh raspberries
1 cup fresh blackberries

Directions

Share half of the cream cheese, half of the mixed berries, half of the walnuts, and half of the avocado in dessert glasses. Repeat the layering process for a second time to finish the ingredients.

Cover the glasses with plastic wrap and refrigerate for 1 hour until quite firm.

Nutritional info per serving: Calories 322, Fat 28.3g, Net Carbs 6.5g, Protein 9g

No-Bake Raw Coconut Balls

Prep + Cook Time: 22 minutes + chill time | Serves: 2-4

Ingredients

¼ tsp coconut extract
2/3 cup melted coconut oil
15-oz can coconut milk

16 drops stevia liquid
1 cup unsweetened coconut flakes

Directions

In a bowl, mix the coconut oil with the milk, coconut extract, and stevia to combine. Stir in the coconut flakes until well distributed. Pour into silicone muffin molds and freeze for 1 hour to harden.

Nutritional info per serving: Calories 211, Fat 19g, Net Carbs 2.2g, Protein 2.9g

Sunday Chocolate Cookies

Prep + Cook Time: 20 minutes | Serves: 2-4

Ingredients

7 oz butter, softened
2 cups swerve brown sugar
3 eggs

2 cups almond flour
2 cups unsweetened dark chocolate chips

Directions

Line a baking sheet with parchment paper and preheat oven to 330 F.

In a bowl with a hand mixer, whisk the butter and swerve sugar for 3 minutes or until light and fluffy. Add the eggs one at a time and scrape the sides as you whisk. Mix in the almond flour at low speed until well combined.

Fold in the chocolate chips. Scoop 3 tablespoons each on the baking sheet, creating spaces between each mound and bake for 13-15 minutes to swell and harden. Remove, cool and serve.

Nutritional info per serving: Calories 293, Fat 24.5g, Net Carbs 7.3g, Protein 6g

Chocolate & Minty Protein Cocktail

Prep + Cook Time: 4 minutes | Serves: 2-4

Ingredients

3 cups almond milk, chilled
3 tsp unsweetened cocoa powder
1 avocado, pitted, peeled, sliced
1 cup coconut milk, chilled

3 mint leaves + extra to garnish
3 tbsp xylitol
1 tbsp vanilla protein powder
Whipping cream for topping

Directions

In a blender, mix the almond milk, cocoa powder, avocado, coconut milk, mint leaves, xylitol, and protein powder, and blend for a minute until smooth.

Transfer to serving glasses, lightly add some whipping cream on top and garnish with mint leaves.

Nutritional info per serving: Calories 287, Fat 15.7g, Net Carbs 6.7g, Protein 12g

Refreshing Strawberry Lemonade with Basil

Prep + Cook Time: 3 minutes | Serves: 2-4

Ingredients

2 cups water
12 strawberries, leaves removed
¼ cup fresh lemon juice
1/3 cup fresh mint, reserve some for garnishing

½ cup erythritol
Crushed Ice
Halved strawberries to garnish
Basil leaves to garnish

Directions

Add some ice into 2 serving glasses and set aside. In a pitcher of a blender, add water, strawberries, lemon juice, mint, and erythritol. Process the ingredients for 30 seconds. The mixture should be pink and the mint finely chopped. Adjust the taste and divide between the ice glasses.

Drop 2 strawberry halves and basil leaves in each glass and serve immediately.

Nutritional info per serving: Calories 36, Fat 0.7g, Net Carbs 5.1g, Protein 1.5g

Creamy Berry Bowl with Pecans

Prep + Cook Time: 8 minutes | Serves: 2-4

Ingredients

4 cups Greek yogurt
Liquid stevia to taste
1 ½ cups mascarpone cheese

1 ½ cups blackberries and raspberries
1 cup toasted pecans

Directions

In a bowl, mix the yogurt, stevia, and mascarpone until thoroughly combined. Divide the mixture into bowls, share the berries and pecans on top of the cream. Serve immediately.

Nutritional info per serving: Calories 398, Fat 37.3g, Net Carbs 4.2g, Protein 16g

Chocolate Mousse with Cherries

Prep + Cook Time: 45 minutes | Serves: 2-4

Ingredients

12 oz unsweetened dark chocolate
8 eggs, separated into yolks and whites
2 tbsp salt

¾ cup swerve sugar
½ cup olive oil
3 tbsp brewed coffee

Cherries

1 cup cherries, pitted and halved
½ stick cinnamon
½ cup swerve sugar

½ cup water
½ lime, juiced

Directions

In a bowl, add the chocolate and melt in the microwave for 95 seconds. In a separate bowl, whisk the yolks with half of the swerve sugar until a pale yellow has formed, then, beat in the salt, olive oil, and coffee. Mix in the melted chocolate until smooth.

In a third bowl, whisk the whites with the hand mixer until a soft peak has formed. Sprinkle the remaining swerve sugar over and gently fold in with a spatula. Fetch a tablespoon of the chocolate mixture and fold in to combine. Pour in the remaining chocolate mixture and whisk to mix. Ladle the mousse into ramekins, cover with plastic wrap, and refrigerate overnight.

The next morning, pour ½ cup of water, ½ cup of swerve, ½ stick cinnamon, and the lime juice in a saucepan and bring to a simmer for 4 minutes, occasionally stirring to ensure the swerve has dissolved and a syrup has formed.

Add the cherries and poach in the sweetened water for 20 minutes until soft. Turn the heat off and discard the cinnamon stick. Spoon a plum each with syrup on the chocolate mousse and serve.

Nutritional info per serving: Calories 288, Fat 23.4g, Net Carbs 8.1g, Protein 10g

Lavender and Raspberry Pie

Prep + Cook Time: 2 hours 25 minutes | Serves: 2-4

Ingredients

1 large low carb pie crust
1 ½ cups heavy cream
2 tbsp erythritol + some for topping

1 tbsp culinary lavender
1 vanilla, seeds extracted
2 cups fresh raspberries

Directions

Place the pie crust with its pan on a baking tray and bake in a preheated to 380 F oven for 30 minutes, until golden brown; remove and let cool.

In a saucepan over medium heat, mix the heavy cream and lavender, and bring to a boil; turn the heat off and let cool. Refrigerate for 1 hour to infuse the cream.

Remove the cream from the fridge and strain through a colander into a bowl to remove the lavender pieces. Mix erythritol and vanilla into the cream, and pour into the cooled crust. Scatter the raspberries on and refrigerate the pie for 45 minutes. Remove and top with erythritol, before slicing.

Nutritional info per serving: Calories 323, Fat 33.6g, Net Carbs 11.3g, Protein 5.2g

Homemade Cakes with Chocolate Frosting

Prep + Cook Time: 25 minutes | Serves: 2-4

Ingredients

½ cup almond flour
¼ cup erythritol
1 tsp baking powder
½ tsp baking soda
1 tsp cinnamon, ground
A pinch of salt

A pinch of ground cloves
½ cup butter, melted
½ cup buttermilk
1 egg
1 tsp pure almond extract

Frosting

1 cup heavy cream

1 cup dark chocolate, flaked

Directions

Grease a donut pan with cooking spray and preheat the oven to 360 F. Mix the cloves, almond flour, baking powder, salt, baking soda, erythritol, and cinnamon in a bowl.

In a separate bowl, combine the almond extract, butter, egg, and buttermilk. Mix the wet mixture into the dry mixture. Evenly ladle the batter into the donut pan. Bake for 17 minutes.

Set a pan over medium heat and warm heavy cream; simmer for 2 minutes. Fold in the chocolate flakes; combine until all the chocolate melts; and let cool. Spread the frosting on top of the cakes.

Nutritional info per serving: Calories 321, Fat: 26.4g, Net Carbs: 8.2g, Protein: 7.3g

Raspberry Coconut Cheesecake

Prep + Cook Time: 50 minutes + cooling time | Serves: 1 piece

Ingredients

Crust

¼ cup xylitol
3 cups desiccated coconut
2 egg whites

1 tsp coconut oil
¼ cup butter, melted

Filling

6 ounces raspberries
3 tbsp lemon juice
2 cups xylitol

1 cup whipped cream
Zest of 1 lemon
3 cups cream cheese

Directions

Grease the bottom and sides of a springform pan with oil and line with parchment paper.

In a bowl, mix all crust ingredients and pour the crust into the pan. Preheat the oven to 330 F.

Bake for 30 minutes; then let cool. Meanwhile, beat the cream cheese with an electric mixer until soft. Add the lemon juice, zest and xylitol.

Fold the whipped cream into the cheese cream mixture. Gently fold in the raspberries and spoon the filling into the baked and cooled crust. Chill for 4 hours.

Nutritional info per serving: Calories 376, Fat: 32.2g, Net Carbs: 6.2g, Protein: 7.5g

Easy Blackberry Popsicles

Prep + Cook Time: 5 minutes + cooling time | Serves: 2-4

Ingredients

2 cups blackberries
½ tbsp lemon juice

1/3 cup erythritol
¼ cup water

Directions

In a blender, pour the blackberries, lemon juice, erythritol, and water and puree on high speed for 2 minutes until smooth. Strain through a sieve into a bowl and discard the solids.

Stir in more water if too thick. Divide the mixture into ice pop molds, insert stick cover, and freeze for 4 hours to 1 week. When ready to serve, dip in warm water and remove the pops.

Nutritional info per serving: Calories 113, Fat 3.3g, Net Carbs 5.8g, Protein 3.4g

No Bake Mousse with Strawberries

Prep + Cook Time: 6 minutes + cooling time | Serves: 2-4

Ingredients

2 cups chilled heavy cream
2 cups fresh strawberries, hulled
4 tbsp xylitol

2 tbsp lime juice
¼ tsp strawberry extract
2 tbsp sugar-free strawberry preserves

Directions

In a bowl, beat the heavy cream with a hand mixer at high speed until a stiff peak forms, for about 1 minute; refrigerate immediately. Puree the strawberries in a blender and pour into a saucepan.

Stir in xylitol and lime juice, and cook on low heat for 3 minutes while stirring continuously. Stir in the strawberry extract evenly, and turn off the heat to cool. Fold in the cream until evenly incorporated, and spoon into ramekins. Refrigerate for 3 hours, garnish with strawberry preserves and serve.

Nutritional info per serving: Calories 353, Fat 32.4g, Net Carbs 4.8g, Protein 5.3g

Cheesy Fat Bombs with Brewed Coffee

Prep + Cook Time: 3 minutes + cooling time | Serves: 2-4

Ingredients

1 cup cottage cheese
¼ cup melted butter
2 tbsp unsweetened cocoa powder

2 tbsp xylitol
3 tbsp brewed coffee, room temperature

Directions

In a bowl, whisk the cottage cheese, butter, cocoa powder, xylitol, and coffee with a hand mixer until creamy and fluffy, for about a minute. Fill into muffin tins and freeze for 4 hours until firm.

Nutritional info per serving: Calories 153, Fat 14.6g, Net Carbs 3.2g, Protein 4.5g

Cinnamon Pumpkin Pie

Prep + Cook Time: 65 minutes | Serves: 2-4

Ingredients

Crust

6 tbsp butter
2 cups almond flour

1 tsp cinnamon
1/3 cup sweetener

Filling

2 cups shredded pumpkin
¼ cup butter
¼ cup erythritol

½ tsp cinnamon
½ tsp lemon juice

Topping

¼ tsp cinnamon

2 tbsp erythritol

Directions

Combine all crust ingredients in a bowl. Press this mixture into the bottom of a greased pan. Bake for 5 minutes in a preheated to 370 F oven.

Meanwhile, in a bowl, combine the pumpkin and lemon juice and let them sit until the crust is ready. Arrange on top of the crust. Combine the rest of the filling ingredients, and brush this mixture over the apples. Bake for about 35 minutes.

Press the apples down with a spatula, return to oven and bake for 20 more minutes. Combine the cinnamon and 2 tbsp erythritol, in a bowl, and sprinkle over the tart.

Nutritional info per serving: Calories 388, Fat: 33.6g, Net Carbs: 7.6g, Protein: 8.5g

Almond Drunk Crumble

Prep + Cook Time: 55 minutes | Serves: 2-4

Ingredients:

1 cup raspberries
½ teaspoon cinnamon
¼ cup erythritol, divided
½ tsp almond extract

½ cup red wine
½ cup salted butter, cubed
1 cup almond flour
2 tbsp ground almonds

Directions:

In a baking dish, add the raspberries, except for 5-6 for garnish, half of the erythritol, almond extract, and stir.

In a bowl, rub the butter with the almond flour, and the remaining erythritol, and almonds until it resembles large breadcrumbs.

Spoon the mixture to cover the raspberries, place in the oven, and bake in the oven for 45 minutes at 375 F until the top looks golden brown.

Remove, let cool for 3 minutes, and serve topped with the reserved raspberries.

Nutritional info per serving: Calories: 213; Fat: 16.4g; Net Carbs: 8.5g; Protein: 1.3g

Vanilla Passion Fruit Galette

Prep + Cook Time: 2 hours 30 minutes | Serves: 2-4

Ingredients

1 cup crushed almond biscuits

½ cup butter, melted

Filling

1 ½ cups mascarpone cheese
¾ cup swerve sugar
1 ½ cups whipping cream

1 tsp vanilla bean paste
4-6 tbsp cold water
1 tbsp gelatin powder

Passionfruit fruit

1 cup passion fruit pulp
¼ cup swerve confectioner's sugar

1 tsp gelatin powder
¼ cup water, room temperature

Directions

In a bowl, mix the crushed biscuits and butter. Spoon into a spring-form pan, and use the back of the spoon to level at the bottom; set aside in the fridge. In another bowl, put the mascarpone cheese, swerve sugar, and vanilla paste, and whisk with a hand mixer until smooth; set aside.

In a third bowl, add 2 tbsp of cold water and sprinkle 1 tbsp of gelatin powder. Let dissolve for 5 minutes. Pour the gelatin liquid and the whipping cream in the cheese mixture and fold gently.

Remove the spring-form pan from the refrigerator and pour over the mixture. Return to the fridge. Then, repeat the dissolving process for the remaining gelatin and once your out of ingredients, pour the confectioner's sugar, and ¼ cup of water into it. Mix and stir in the passion fruit pulp.

Remove the cake again and pour the jelly over it. Swirl the pan to msake the jelly level up. Place the pan back into the fridge to cool for 2 hours. When completely set, remove and unlock the spring-pan. Lift the pan from the cake and slice the dessert.

Nutritional info per serving: Calories 383, Fat 26.4g, Net Carbs 6.8g, Protein 9.3g

Homemade Snickerdoodles with Cinnamon

Prep + Cook Time: 25 minutes | Serves: 2-4

Ingredients

Cookies

2 tbsp walnuts, chopped
2 cups almond flour
½ tsp baking soda

¾ cup xylitol sweetener
½ cup butter, softened
A pinch of salt

Coating

2 tbsp xylitol sweetener

1 tsp cinnamon

Directions

Combine all cookies' ingredients in a bowl. Make balls out of the mixture and flatten them with hands.

Mix the cinnamon and xylitol. Dip the cookies in the cinnamon mixture and arrange them on a lined baking sheet. Bake for 15 minutes, or until crispy in a preheated to 370 F oven.

Nutritional info per serving: Calories 177, Fat: 13.8g, Net Carbs: 3.7g, Protein: 4.5g

Chocolate Barks with Cranberries & Pecans

Prep + Cook Time: 5 minutes | Serves: 2-4

Ingredients

5 oz unsweetened dark chocolate, chopped
¼ cup xylitol
¼ cup dried cranberries, chopped
¼ cup toasted pecans, chopped
¼ tsp salt

Directions

Pour chocolate and xylitol in a bowl, and melt in the microwave for 30 seconds, stirring three times until fully melted. Stir in the cranberries, pecans, and salt, reserving a few cranberries and pecans for garnishing. Line a baking sheet with parchment paper.

Spread the mixture on the sheet and spread out. Sprinkle with remaining cranberries and pecans. Refrigerate for 3 hours to set. Break into bite-size pieces to serve.

Nutritional info per serving: Calories 231, Fat 22.4g, Net Carbs 4.2g, Protein 5.2g

Mochaccino & Chocolate Ice Balls

Prep + Cook Time: 10 minutes + freezing time | Serves: 2-4

Ingredients

½ pound cottage cheese
4 tbsp powdered sweetener
2 ounces strong coffee
2 tbsp cocoa powder, unsweetened
1 ounce cocoa butter, melted
2 ½ ounces dark chocolate, melted

Directions

In a food processor, combine the cheese, sweetener, coffee, and cocoa powder. Form two tablespoons of the mixture into balls and place them on a lined tray. Mix the melted cocoa butter and dark chocolate, and coat the balls with it. Freeze for 3 hours.

Nutritional info per serving: Calories 176, Fat: 14.2g, Net Carbs: 6.5g, Protein: 4g

Dark Chocolate Cheesy Mini-Snacks

Prep + Cook Time: 4 minutes + cooling time | Serves: 2-4

Ingredients

5 oz unsweetened dark chocolate chips
¼ cup half and half
2 cups cream cheese, softened
¼ cup erythritol
½ tsp vanilla extract

Directions

Melt the chocolate with half and a half in a saucepan over low heat for 1 minute. Turn the heat off.

Whisk the cream cheese, erythritol, and vanilla extract in a bowl, with a hand mixer until smooth. Add the chocolate mixture and stir. Transfer to silicone muffin tins and freeze for 5 hours until firm.

Nutritional info per serving: Calories 273, Fat 24.5g, Net Carbs 5.2g, Protein 3.6g

Chocolate Almond Ice Cream Treats

Prep + Cook Time: 20 minutes + cooling time | Serves: 2-4

Ingredients

Ice cream

½ cup heavy whipping cream
½ tsp vanilla extract
½ tsp xanthan gum
¼ cup almond butter
½ cup half and half

1 cup almond milk
¼ tsp stevia powder
½ tbsp vegetable glycerin
2 tbsp erythritol

Chocolate

¾ cup coconut oil
¼ cup cocoa butter pieces, chopped

2 ounces unsweetened chocolate
3 ½ tsp THM super sweet blend

Directions

In a bowl, blend all ice cream ingredients until smooth. Place in an ice cream maker and follow the instructions. Spread the ice cream into a lined pan, and freezer for about 4 hours.

Mix all chocolate ingredients in a microwave-safe bowl and heat until melted. Allow cooling. Remove the ice cream from the freezer and slice into bars. Dip them into the cooled chocolate mixture and return to the freezer for about 10 minutes before serving.

Nutritional info per serving: Calories 306, Fat: 25.2g, Net Carbs: 5.3g, Protein: 6.2g

Mom's Walnut and Pecan Cookies

Prep + Cook Time: 25 minutes | Serves: 2-4

Ingredients

1 egg
1 cup ground pecans
2 tbsp sweetener

¼ tsp baking soda
1 tbsp butter
4 walnuts, halved

Directions

Mix all ingredients, except the walnuts, until well combined. Make balls out of the mixture and press them with your thumb onto a lined cookie sheet.

Top each cookie with a walnut half. Bake for about 12 minutes in a preheated to 340 degrees F oven.

Nutritional info per serving: Calories 163, Fat: 13.5g, Net Carbs: 2.4g, Protein: 3.1g

Lime & Chocolate Energy Balls

Prep + Cook Time: 5 minutes + chilling time | Serves: 2-4

Ingredients:

1/4 tsp salt
1/3 cup heavy cream
1/3 cup unsweetened dark chocolate, chopped
1 tsp lime extract

1 lime, zested
2 tbsp unsweetened cocoa powder
1 tbsp swerve sugar

Directions:

Mix the cocoa powder with swerve sugar in a small bowl and set aside.

Heat the heavy cream in a small pan over low heat until tiny bubbles form around the edges of the pan. Turn the heat off.

Pour the dark chocolate and salt into the pan, swirl the pan to allow the hot cream over the chocolate, and then stir the mixture until smooth. Mix in the lime extract and transfer the mixture to a bowl. Refrigerate for 4 hours and more.

Line a baking tray with parchment papers. Pour the cocoa powder mixture into a shallow dish and the lime zest in a separate one.

Take out the chocolate mixture; form bite-size balls out of the mix and roll all round in the lime zest, then in the cocoa powder to completely coat.

Place the truffles on the baking tray and chill in the fridge for 30 minutes before serving.

Nutritional info per serving: Calories: 134; Fat: 11g; Net Carbs: 5.6g; Protein: 2.1g

Fresh Berry Galette

Prep + Cook Time: 30 minutes + chilling time | Serves: 2-4

Ingredients:

Piecrust

¼ cup almond flour + extra for dusting
3 tbsp coconut flour
½ tsp salt
¼ cup butter, cold and crumbled

3 tbsp erythritol
1 ½ tsp vanilla extract
4 whole eggs

Filling

2 ¼ cup strawberries and blackberries
1 cup erythritol + extra for sprinkling

1 vanilla pod, bean paste extracted
1 egg, beaten

Directions:

In a large bowl, mix the almond flour, coconut flour, and salt.

Add the butter and mix with an electric hand mixer until crumbly. Add the erythritol and vanilla extract until mixed in. Then, pour in the 4 eggs one after another while mixing until formed into a ball. Flatten the dough a clean flat surface, cover in plastic wrap, and refrigerate for 1 hour.

Preheat oven to 350 F and grease a pie pan with cooking spray. Lightly dust a clean flat surface with almond flour, unwrap the dough, and roll out the dough into a large rectangle, ½ - inch thickness and fit into a pie pan. Pour some baking beans onto the pastry and bake in the oven until golden. Remove after, pour pout the baking beans, and allow cooling.

In a bowl, mix the berries, erythritol, and vanilla bean paste. Spoon the mixture into the pie, level with a spoon, and use the pastry strips to create a lattice top over the berries.

Brush with the beaten egg, sprinkle with more erythritol, and bake for 30 minutes or until the fruit is bubbling and the pie golden brown. Remove from the oven, allow cooling, slice, and serve with whipped cream.

Nutritional info per serving: Calories: 313; Fat: 23.5g; Net Carbs: 7.3g; Protein: 10g

Sage Chocolate Cheesecake

Prep + Cook Time: 15 minutes + chilling time | Serves: 2-4

Ingredients:

Crust

1 cup raw almonds
½ cup salted butter, melted

2 tbsp swerve sugar

Cake

4 tbsp unsalted butter, melted
2 gelatine sheets
2 tbsp lime juice
2/3 cup unsweetened dark chocolate, chopped
2 tbsp cocoa powder, for garnishing

1 ½ cups cream cheese
½ cup swerve sugar
1 cup Greek yogurt
1 fresh sage leaf, chopped

Directions:

For the crust:

Preheat oven to 350 F.

In a blender, process the almonds until finely ground. Add the butter and sweetener, and mix until combined.

Press the crust mixture into the bottom of the cake pan until firm.

Bake for 5 minutes. Place in the fridge to chill afterward.

For the cake:

In a small pot, combine the gelatin with the lime juice, and a tablespoon of water. Allow sitting for 5 minutes and then, place the pot over medium heat to dissolve the gelatin. Set aside.

Pour the dark chocolate in a bowl and melt in the microwave for 1 minute, stirring at every 10 seconds interval. Set aside.

In another, beat the cream cheese and swerve sugar using an electric mixer until smooth. Stir in the yogurt and gelatin until evenly combined. After, fold in the melted dark chocolate and then the sage leaf.

Remove the pan from the fridge and pour the cream mixture on top. Tap the side gently to release any trapped air bubbles and transfer to the fridge to chip for 3 hours or more. Dust the cake with cocoa powder and slice to serve.

__Nutritional info per serving__: Calories: 675; Fat: 53g; Net Carbs: 13.4g; Protein: 21g

Hazelnut & Chocolate Cake

Prep + Cook Time: 10 minutes + chilling time | Serves: 2-4

Ingredients:

½ cup olive oil
1 cup almond flour
½ cup unsweetened dark chocolate, melted
1 cup swerve sugar
2 tsp hazelnut extract
½ tsp salt

2 tsp cinnamon powder
½ cup boiling water
3 large eggs
¼ cup ground hazelnuts
1 tbsp unsweetened dark chocolate, shaved

Directions:

Preheat oven to 350 F and lightly grease a springform pan with cooking spray and line with parchment paper.

In a large bowl, combine the olive oil, almond flour, chocolate, swerve sugar, hazelnut extract, salt, cinnamon powder, and boiling water. Crack the eggs one after the other while beating until smooth.

Pour the batter into the springform pan and bake in the oven for 45 minutes or until a toothpick inserted comes out clean.

Take out from the oven; allow cooling in the pan for 10 minutes, then turn over onto a wire rack.

Sprinkle with ground hazelnuts and shaved chocolate, slice, and serve.

Nutritional info per serving: Calories: 505; Fat: 46.5g; Net Carbs: 8.9g; Protein: 6.1g

Minty Lemon Tart

Prep + Cook Time: 50 minutes + chilling time | Serves: 2-4

Ingredients:

Piecrust

¼ cup almond flour + extra for dusting
3 tbsp coconut flour
½ tsp salt
¼ cup butter, cold and crumbled

3 tbsp erythritol
1 ½ tsp vanilla extract
4 whole eggs

Filling

4 tbsp melted butter
3 tsp swerve brown sugar
1 cup fresh blackberries
1 tsp vanilla extract

1 lemon, juiced
1 cup ricotta cheese
3 to 4 fresh mint leaves to garnish
1 egg, lightly beaten

Directions:

In a large bowl, mix the almond flour, coconut flour, and salt.

Add the butter and mix with an electric hand mixer until crumbly. Add the erythritol and vanilla extract until mixed in. Then, pour in the 4 eggs one after another while mixing until formed into a ball.

Flatten the dough a clean flat surface, cover in plastic wrap, and refrigerate for 1 hour.

Preheat the oven to 350 F and grease a pie pan with cooking spray. Lightly dust a clean flat surface with almond flour, unwrap the dough, and roll out the dough into a 1-inch diameter circle.

In a 10-inch shallow baking pan, mix the butter, swerve brown sugar, blackberries, vanilla extract, and lemon juice. Arrange the blackberries uniformly across the pan.

Lay the pastry over the fruit filling and tuck the sides into the pan. Brush with the beaten egg and bake in the oven for 35 to 40 minutes or until the golden and puffed up.

Remove, allow cooling for 5 minutes, and then run a knife around the pan to losing the pastry. Turn the pie over onto a plate, crumble the ricotta cheese on top, and garnish with the mint leaves.

Nutritional info per serving: Calories: 533; Fat: 44.5g; Net Carbs: 8.7g; Protein: 17.3g

Quick Vanilla Tart

Prep + Cook Time: 75 minutes | Serves: 2-4

Ingredients:

Piecrust
¼ cup almond flour + extra for dusting
3 tbsp coconut flour
½ tsp salt

¼ cup butter, cold and crumbled
3 tbsp erythritol
1 ½ tsp vanilla extract
4 whole eggs

Filling
2 whole eggs + 3 egg yolks
½ cup swerve sugar
1 tsp vanilla bean paste
2 tbsp coconut flour

1 ¼ cup almond milk
1 ¼ cup heavy cream
1 ½ tbsp maple syrup, sugar-free
¼ cup chopped almonds

Directions:

Preheat the oven to 350 F and grease a pie pan with cooking spray.

In a large bowl, mix the almond flour, coconut flour, and salt.

Add the butter and mix with an electric hand mixer until crumbly. Add the erythritol and vanilla extract until mixed in. Then, pour in the 4 eggs one after another while mixing until formed into a ball.

Flatten the dough a clean flat surface, cover in plastic wrap, and refrigerate for 1 hour.

After, lightly dust a clean flat surface with almond flour, unwrap the dough, and roll out the dough into a large rectangle, ½ - inch thickness and fit into a pie pan.

Bake in the oven until golden. Remove after and allow cooling.

In a large mixing bowl, whisk the whole 3 eggs, egg yolks, swerve sugar, vanilla bean paste, and coconut flour.

Put the almond milk, heavy cream, and maple syrup into a medium pot and bring to a boil over medium heat. Pour the mixture into the egg mixture and whisk while pouring.

Run the batter through a fine strainer into a bowl and skim off any froth.

Take out the pie pastry from the oven, pour out the baking beans, remove the parchment paper, and transfer the egg batter into the pie. Bake in the oven for 40 to 50 minutes or until the custard sets with a slight wobble in the center. Garnish with the chopped almonds, slice, and serve when cooled.

Nutritional info per serving: Calories: 542; Fat: 41g; Net Carbs: 8.5g; Protein: 16g

Valentine's Day Cookies

Prep + Cook Time: 30 minutes + chilling time | Serves: 2-4

Ingredients:

½ lemon, zested
1 cup unsalted butter, softened
2/3 cup swerve sugar
1 large egg, beaten

2 tsp vanilla extract
2 cups almond flour + extra for dusting
½ cup unsweetened dark chocolate
Chopped pistachios, to garnish

Directions:

Preheat oven to 350 F.

Add the butter and swerve sugar to a bowl; beat with an electric whisk until smooth and creamy. Whisk in the egg until combined.

Mix in the vanilla extract, lemon zest, and almond flour until a smooth dough forms. Wrap the dough in plastic wrap and chill for 10 minutes.

Dust a chopping board with some almond flour. Unwrap the dough and roll out on the chopping board to 2-inch thickness.

Using a heart-shaped cookie cutter, cut out as many biscuits as you can get while rerolling the trimming and making more biscuits.

Arrange the biscuits on the parchment paper-lined baking sheet and bake for 12 to 15 minutes or until crisp at the edges and pale golden.

Remove and transfer to a wire rack to cool completely when ready.

In two separate bowls, melt the chocolate in a microwave while adding some maple syrup a taste.

Dip one side of each biscuit in the dark chocolate and then in the white chocolate. Garnish the dark chocolate's side with the pistachios and allow cooling on the wire rack.

Nutritional info per serving: Calories: 476; Fat: 43.5g; Net Carbs: 5.9g; Protein: 4.5g

Grandma's Zucchini & Nut Cake

Prep + Cook Time: 30 minutes + chilling time | Serves: 2-4

Ingredients:

1 cup butter, softened + extra for greasing	2/3 cup ground almonds
1 cup erythritol	1 lemon, zested and juiced
4 eggs	1 cup finely grated zucchini
2/3 cup coconut flour	1 cup crème fraiche, for serving
2 tsp baking powder	1 tbsp chopped walnuts

Directions:

Grease a springform pan with cooking spray, and line with parchment paper.

In a bowl, beat the butter and erythritol until creamy and pale. Add the eggs one after another while whisking. Sift the coconut flour and baking powder into the mixture and stir along with the ground almonds, lemon zest, juice, and zucchini.

Preheat oven to 375 F.

Spoon the mixture into the springform pan and bake in the oven for 40 minutes or until risen and a toothpick inserted into the cake comes out clean.

Remove the cake from the oven when ready; allow cooling in the pan for 10 minutes, and transfer to a wire rack. Spread the crème fraiche on top of the cake and sprinkle with the walnuts. Slice and serve the cake.

Nutritional info per serving: Calories: 778; Fat: 65.4g; Net Carbs: 9.6g; Protein: 29.2g

Berry Power Balls

Prep + Cook Time: 15 minutes + chilling time | Serves: 2-4

Ingredients:

1 cup strawberries
1 cup raspberries + extra to garnish
1 cup blueberries
1 tsp vanilla extract

16 oz cream cheese, room temperature
4 tbsp peanut butter
2 tbsp maple syrup, sugar-free

Directions:

Line a small pan with parchment paper. Puree the fruits in a blender with the vanilla. Set aside

In a small saucepan, melt the cream cheese and butter over medium heat until completely mixed.

Then, in a medium bowl, combine the fruit, cheese mixture, and maple syrup. Spread out the mixture into the prepared pan. Refrigerate for 40 minutes, cut into squares and serve.

Nutritional info per serving: Calories: 487; Fat: 43g; Net Carbs: 12.3g; Protein: 10g

Dark Chocolate Bars with Hazelnuts

Prep + Cook Time: 5 minutes + cooling time | Serves: 2-4

Ingredients

¼ cup toasted hazelnuts, chopped
¼ cup butter
5 drops stevia

¼ tsp salt
¼ cup unsweetened coconut flakes
2 ounces dark chocolate

Directions

In a microwave-safe bowl, melt together the butter and chocolate, for 85 seconds.

Remove and stir in stevia.

Line a cookie sheet with waxed paper and spread the chocolate evenly. Scatter the hazelnuts on top, then the coconut flakes and sprinkle with salt. Refrigerate for 2 hours and then cut into bars.

Nutritional info per serving: Calories 215, Fat: 16.8g, Net Carbs: 2.8g, Protein: 3.6g

Coconut Lemon Syrup Cake

Prep + Cook Time: 40 minutes | Serves: 2-4

Ingredients:

For the lemon puree:

4 large lemons
¼ cup maple syrup, sugar-free

¼ tsp salt

For the cake:

½ cup unsalted butter, softened
½ cup erythritol
1 tsp vanilla extract
½ cup coconut flour

3 large eggs, lightly beaten
½ cup heavy cream
1 tbsp swerve confectioner's sugar, for dusting

Directions:

Make the lemon puree: peel and juice the lemons. Remove any white strains from the peel and transfer both peels and juice to a small saucepan. Add the erythritol and salt and simmer over low heat for 30 minutes. Pour the mixture into a blender and process until smooth. Pour into a jar and set aside.

Preheat the oven to 350 F, grease a two springform pans and line with parchment paper.

In a bowl, cream the butter, erythritol, and vanilla extract with an electric whisk until light and fluffy. Pour in the eggs gradually while beating until mixed. Carefully fold in the coconut flour and share the mixture into the pans. Bake for 25 minutes or until springy when touched and a toothpick inserted comes out clean. Remove and allow cooling for 5 minutes before turning out onto a wire rack.

In a bowl, whip the double cream until a soft peak forms. Spoon onto the bottom sides of the cake and spread the lemon puree on top. Sandwich both cakes and sift the confectioner's sugar on top.

Nutritional info per serving: Calories: 273; Fat: 23.2g; Net Carbs: 4.9g; Protein: 7.3g

Chocolate-Ginger Fudge

Prep + Cook Time: 30 minutes | Serves: 2-4

Ingredients:

¼ tsp ginger extract
4 large eggs
1 cup swerve sugar

1 cup unsweetened dark chocolate, melted
½ cup butter, melted
1/3 cup coconut flour

Directions:

Preheat the oven to 350 F and line a rectangular baking tray with parchment paper.

In a bowl, cream the eggs with swerve sugar until smooth. Add the melted chocolate, butter, ginger extract and whisk until evenly combined. Carefully fold in the coconut flour to incorporate and pour the mixture into the baking tray. Bake in the oven for 20 minutes or until a toothpick inserted comes out clean. Remove from the oven and allow cooling in the tray. After, cut into squares and serve.

Nutritional info per serving: Calories: 477 ; Fat: 42.3g; Net Carbs: 6.8g; Protein: 13.2g

Cranberry Granola Bars

Prep + Cook Time: 50 minutes | Serves: 2-4

Ingredients

2 tbsp dried cranberries
1 cup hazelnuts and walnuts, chopped
¼ cup flax meal
¼ cup coconut milk
¼ cup poppy seeds
¼ cup pumpkin seeds

4 drops stevia
¼ cup coconut oil, melted
½ tsp vanilla paste
½ tsp ground cloves
½ tsp grated nutmeg
½ tsp lemon zest

Directions

Preheat oven to 280 F and line a baking sheet with parchment paper. In a large mixing bowl, combine all ingredients with ¼ cup of water and stir to coat. Spread the mixture onto the baking sheet. Bake for 45 minutes, stirring at intervals of 15 minutes. Let cool at room temperature. Cut into bars to serve.

Nutritional info per serving: Calories 451; Fat: 43g, Net Carbs: 6.3g, Protein: 10.2g

28-DAY MEAL PLAN

Drink 7 to 9 glasses of water daily

Day	Breakfast	Lunch	Dinner	Dessert/Snacks	Cal
1	Tofu Scrambled with Tomatoes & Mushrooms	Baked Sausage with Roasted Peppers & Fresh Salad	Zucchini & Eggplant Steaks with Salad	Raspberry Coconut Cheesecake	1,798
2	Yummy Blue Cheese & Mushroom Omelet	Feta & Cabbage Stir-Fry	Crispy Bacon & Spinach Salad with Turnip	Minty Lemon Tart	1,717
3	Morning Herbed Eggs	Vegan Sandwich with Tofu & Lettuce Slaw	Chicken Salad with Parmesan	Herbed Cheese Sticks with Yogurt Dip	1,853
4	Strawberry Chia Seed Pudding in Glass Jars	Gorgonzola & Ricotta Stuffed Red Peppers	Curried Shrimp & Green Bean Soup	Chocolate Barks with Cranberries & Pecans (x2)	1,629
5	Rolled Smoked Salmon with Avocado & Cheese	Sausage & Cauliflower Bake	Kale & Cheese Stuffed Zucchini -	Easy Citrus Mousse with Almonds	1,617
6	Jalapeno & Cheese Waffles with Bacon & Avocado	Chilli Cod with Chive Sauce - 448	Zucchini Balls with Bacon & Capers -	Mochaccino & Chocolate Ice Balls	1,793
7	Roasted Stuffed Avocados	Baked Chicken Wrapped in Smoked Bacon	Stewed Vegetables	Keto Chocolate Fat Bombs	1,779
8	Broccoli, Egg & Pancetta Gratin - 464	Hearty Cobb Salad with Roquefort Cheese Dressing - 527	Colorful Peppers Stuffed with Mushrooms & "Rice" - 233	No-Bake Raw Coconut Balls - 211 (x2)	1,646
9	Chia Seed Pudding with Strawberries	Minty Green Chicken Salad	Cheddar & Cream Cheese Chicken Casserole	Energy Goji Berry Snacks	1,802
10	Ham & Cheese Keto Sandwiches	Anchovy Caprese Pizza	Broccoli & Kale Turkey Pie	Dark Chocolate Cheesy Mini-Snacks	1,579
11	Creamy Vanilla Keto Cappuccino	Spiralized Cucumber with Stuffed Chicken Breasts	Pepperoni & Mixed Mushroom White Pizza	Creamy Berry Bowl with Pecans	1,784
12	Chorizo Sausage Egg Cakes	Eggplant Pizza with Tofu	Thyme-Mashed Cauliflower with Bacon & Cheese	Matcha Brownies with Macadamia Nuts	1,733
13	Vegan Chocolate Smoothie	Feta & Baby Spinach Lasagna	Red Wine Lamb with Mint & Sage	Almond Drunk Crumble	1,682
14	Hard-Boiled Eggs with Tuna & Chili Mayo	Chargrilled Halloumi with Avocado & Eggs	Stewed Veal with Vegetables	Sunday Chocolate Cookies	1,652

Day	Breakfast	Lunch	Dinner	Dessert/Snacks	Cal
15	Coconut Shake with Avocado	Habanero Coconut Pie	Caprese Gratin with Zucchini & Bell Pepper	Grandma's Coconut Treats	1,574
16	Sesame & Poppy Seed Bagels	Pork Chops with Creamy Bacon & Mushrooms	Salmon Salad with Lettuce & Avocado	Lavender and Raspberry Pie	1,750
17	Lemon-Ginger Pancakes	Chicken Breasts with Creamy Kale Sauce	Spinach Salad with Goat Cheese & Pine Nuts	Bacon & Egg Radish Hash	1,638
18	Breakfast Serrano Ham Frittata with Fresh Salad	Broccoli & Carrot Turkey Bake	Spicy Vegetarian Burgers with Fried Eggs	Dark Chocolate Cheesy Mini-Snacks	1,578
19	Spinach & Feta Cheese Pancakes	Caramelized Onion over Pork Burgers	Cheese & Mayo Topped Chicken Bake	Fresh Berry Galette	1,618
20	Microwave Bacon Mug Eggs	Crispy Salmon with Broccoli & Red Bell Pepper	Oven-Style Salami & Cheddar Chicken	Coconut Lemon Syrup Cake	1,623
21	Turkey Bacon & Spinach Crepes	Baked Haddock with Cheesy Hazelnut Topping	Slow-Cooked Chicken Stew with Vegetables	Dark Chocolate Bars with Hazelnuts	1,636
22	Chili Omelet with Avocado	Coconut Fried Shrimp with Cilantro Sauce	Butternut Squash Bolognese	Baked Parsnip Chips with Yogurt Dip	1,644
23	Thyme Eggs with Parma Ham	Pan-Seared Scallops with Sausage & Mozzarella	Mediterranean Tilapia Bake	Tasty Tofu & Swiss Chard Dip (x2)	1,709
24	Salty Muffins with Bacon & Blue Cheese	Mexican-Style Squash Omelet with Chorizo & Cheese	Four-Cheese Pizza	Chocolate Nut Granola	1,626
25	Lazy Eggs with Feta Cheese	Basil & Chicken Meatball Bake	Green Pork Bake	Lazy Strawberry Mini Cakes	1,569
26	Almond & Raspberries Cakes	Thick Creamy Broccoli Cheese Soup	Chicken Pizza with Sundried Tomatoes	Quail Eggs & Prosciutto Wraps	1,660
27	Mixed Nuts & Smoothie Breakfast	Bacon & Brussels Sprouts Bake	Spicy Cauliflower Falafel	Roasted Tomatoes with Vegan Cheese Crust	1,749
28	Eggplant Sausage Pie	Mushroom & Zucchini with Spinach Dip	Burritos Wraps with Avocado & Cauliflower	Tumeric Chicken Wings with Ginger Sauce	1,736

Made in the USA
San Bernardino,
CA